RECUSANT YEOMEN

For Catherine, our children, our grandchildren, and our extended family

RECUSANT YEOMEN

IN THE COUNTIES OF YORK AND LANCASTER

The Survival of a Catholic Farming Family

JOHN RICHARD ROBINSON

FRONTIER
2003

First published 2003.
Frontier Publishing
Kirstead, Norfolk NR15 1EG, UK

RECUSANT YEOMEN IN THE COUNTIES
OF YORK AND LANCASTER
The survival of a Catholic farming family

Copyright © John Richard Robinson 2003

A CIP catalogue record for this book is
available from the British Library

This book is sold subject to the condition that it shall not, by way of trade or otherwise, be lent, re-sold, hired out, or circulated in any form of binding or cover other than in which it is published without a similar condition including this condition being imposed on the subsequent purchaser.

ISBN 1 872914 18 7

All rights reserved.

PRINTED IN GREAT BRITAIN
Biddles of Guildford and King's Lynn

Contents

List of Charts		6
List of Illustrations		7
Acknowledgements		9
Foreword by Timothy Radcliffe, OP		10
Introduction		12
I	The Oral Tradition and Childhood Interest	15
II	Nuthill	29
III	Hutton Hall: a Nursery for the 'Second Spring'	56
IV	The French Revolution: a Family Concern at Hutton Hall	71
V	Of Roses White and Red	82
VI	Charnock Richard to Cornamucklagh: a Bridge Across the Sea	91
VII	The End of an Era: Demise of the Stuarts and Deaths at Wycliffe and in Lancashire	94
VIII	Recusants of Lancashire and Loyalty to the King	101
IX	Oral Tradition and The Wrights of Ploughland Hall	110
X	Foster alias Charnock	118
XI	Severed from the Unity of Christendom: a People Confused	128
Epilogue		141
Appendix Robert Robinson of Hutton Hall, 1721-1809: in Search of His Origins		142
Notes and references		163
Selected bibliography		197
Index		210

Charts

1. Descendants of Thomas Robinson and Sarah Wright Ford, of Nuthill, E. Yorkshire (1)   54
2. Descendants of Thomas Robinson and Sarah Wright Ford, of Nuthill, E. Yorkshire (2)   55
3. Descendants of Robert Robinson and Cecily Foster, of Hutton Hall, Hutton Magna, N. Yorkshire   69
4. Descendants of John Robinson of South Park and Elizabeth Troath Caley   70
5. Descendants of John Foster of Charnock Richard and Ellen   81
6. Descendants of Adam Daile and Sarah Richinson of Hutton, N. Yorkshire   90
7. Descendants of Richard Holden of Chaigley Hall and Jane Parker of Browsholme   108
8. Descendants of Robert Foster of Charnock Richard and Jenett   109
9. Descendants of John Wright of Ploughland Hall, E. Yorkshire, and Alice Ryther   117
10. Foster, Charnock, Crichlow, relationships   127
11. Descendants of Richard Holden of Chaigley Hall, Lancashire, and ? Margaret Loud   139
12. Descendants of Sir Thomas Tunstall, Knt., of Thurland, Lancashire, and Eleanor Fitzhugh   140
13. Pedigree of Robert Robinson (1721 – 1809) of Hutton Hall Hypothesis 1   161
14. Pedigree of Robert Robinson (1721 – 1809) of Hutton Hall Hypothesis 2   162

Illustrations

1 Gordon and John at Green Gates
2 Ushaw College
3 Our Lady and St Kenelm, Stow-on-the-Wold
4 Dr Robert Tate
5 Christopher Flanagan and Uncle Thomas
6 Holderness Hunt group
7 Eveline Robinson née Botterill
8 Daisy Cardwell, BEM
9 Thomas Botterill Robinson
10 Gladys Margaret Botterill, (1882-1975)
11 William Joseph Robinson, (1862-1938)
12 Sarah Ford née Robinson
13 James Francis Ford, 'Fritz Ford'
14 Catherine Robinson
15 Dr Henry Robinson
16 Agnes Eeles née Robinson
17 Richard Botterill of Tathwell Hall
18 Fanny Botterill née Leonard
19 Sarah Wright Ford
20 Thomas Robinson (1823-1880)
21 Tathwell Hall
22 Helen Botterill's wedding
23 The older Botterill children
24 The younger Botterill children
25 Elizabeth Foster (1804-1876)
26 John Leonard (1807-1890)
27 Richard Botterill as a young man
28 Fanny Leonard as a young woman
29 Ryhill Manor
30 Hutton Hall
31 William Robinson of Hutton Hall
32 William Robinson's letter, 1867
33 Canon John Thompson
34 Cuthbert Watson of Ovington

35 English College at Douai
36 John Lingard (1771-1851)
37 Rev. James Foster
38 Ashton Hall
39 Dr Richard Challoner
40 Cuthbert Tunstall and Elizabeth Heneage
41 Dr James Smith
42 William Tunstall
43 Accounts of raids at Fernyhalgh
44 Tanhouse Farm, Charnock Richard
45 John Foster takes the Oath
46 John Foster and Ellen conform
47 Euxton House
48 Captain Robert Charnock (1604-1653)
49 Astley Hall
50 The Battle of Brill
51 Greengore Farmhouse
52 Mary Ann Wright (1800-1883)
53 Mary Ward (1585-1645)
54 Christopher and John Wright
55 Ashby St Ledgers
56 Ripley Castle
57 Francis Ingleby
58 William Allen (1532-1594)
59 English College at Douai, 1627
60 Brasenose College
61 Hoghton Tower
62 Sir Thomas More
63 Cuthbert Tunstall (1474-1559)
64 Browsholme Hall
65 Cardinal John Fisher
66 St Mary's, Cricklade

ACKNOWLEDGEMENTS

The people who have helped me on this journey of discovery are too numerous to mention by name. Those who helped me in specific ways appear in the footnotes; but there are many others whose more general help was often equally valuable. I have made some wonderful friends and benefited greatly from a generous sharing of research.

My constant companion in the early stages of searching graveyards and archives was my good friend Kevin Hodgers who has never ceased to encourage me. My Cardwell cousins, with their understanding of our family culture, proved invaluable time and again. My old school friend, Father Frank McManus, with his understanding of the religious culture has provided a similar service in that field. Frank introduced me to the late Bishop Brian Foley, D.Litt., retired Bishop of Lancaster and long-standing President and Vice-President of the Catholic Record Society. Together, the three of us toured North Lancashire and relived those Catholic struggles of long ago. Although the Bishop was in his nineith year his enthusiasm was unabated; he suggested that we should have a pub lunch – just beer and a cheese and onion sandwich – so as not to waste time! A truly wonderful day and I felt very privileged. It was Brian Foley who urged me to publish my work.

I doubt whether my research would ever have got to this stage had it not been acknowledged en route by Michael Gandy, BA, FSG, Chairman of the Catholic Family History Society. Michael Gandy, together with Tony and Margaret Butler, form the Editorial Committee of Catholic Ancestor in which five of my articles (on which Chapters III, V, VI, VII, and VIII, are based) have appeared. I am most grateful to the Committee for allowing me to reproduce the substance of these articles in book form.

I am grateful for the ready assistance which I have received from professional bodies: West Yorkshire Archive Service; Lancashire Record Office; County Archive Service at Beverley; Mrs. Christine Frost of the Theresian Trust; University Library Archives and Special Collections, University of Durham; Borthwick Institute of Historical Research, University of York; Public Record Office; Bodleian Library; Summertown Public Library, Oxford.

I am deeply indebted to the professional historians and their publishers from whose works I have, as an amateur, quoted so liberally.

Numerous friends have read parts of this script and I value their critical comments. In this regard, I am especially grateful to my long-standing friend Joe Boyle and to my cousin Michael Cardwell for reading the whole book and for their invaluable suggestions. I alone stand responsible for any remaining errors.

When I was seeking the advice of my nephew, David Robinson, on the production of the book, he immediately offered to do the typesetting and artwork. I was delighted to accept this generous contribution from the son of my brother, Gordon, who always took such an interest in my research. I am indebted to my cousin Richard Robinson for introducing me to his old school friend, Richard Barnes. I could not have had a more approachable and encouraging publisher and I have benefited greatly from his sensitive pragmatic guidance. I am honoured that Timothy Radcliffe so graciously agreed to write a foreword.

One's family is inevitably involved in a project of this kind. Their good humoured tolerance and help, each in his of her own way, have made this a enjoyable journey. I particularly appreciate my wife Catherine's generous support throughout and her ever helpful remarks.

Foreword

John Robinson first became interested in the origins of his family when his father died in 1938. Death makes one aware of how precious are the oral memories of one's ancestors, and how easily lost. So this book is a wonderful gift for John's relations and descendants. It will help them to discover who they are and where they come from. But it is of much wider interest than that. It begins with a delightful, warm evocation of John's own childhood, which introduces us to eccentric relatives, and friends such as George the impoverished and whisky drinking French Count. I was also delighted to learn of John's early desire to become a nun!

Each chapter takes us further back into the past, into an ever wider network of ancestors. I came across lots of ancestors of my own, linked with this story not only by a shared Catholic faith, but by Yorkshire roots. Our families even shared a common devotion to the Zetland hounds! It is explicitly the story of the survival not only of a family but of a faith, which is why the story's roots are in the Reformation and the shattering of the unity of Christendom.

John ends by reflecting on this link between family and faith: 'My researches have led me to reflect that accidental factors seem to play a big part in determining religious faith; or, perhaps more truly, the form that such faith takes. And, perhaps, these factors are not so accidental after all?' This is a fascinating question. Ever since the Enlightenment it has been pointed out frequently that if a Catholic had been born in India, then he or she would probably have been a Hindu, or if in Saudi Arabia, a Muslim. So is one's faith just a cultural accident, like one's taste in food, and thus without profound importance?

This book suggests that at least there is something right and fitting that one's faith often, though not always, derives from one's family. As Christians we believe in a Saviour who was born into a particular tradition, Jewish, and at a particular time. The Word of God found a lodging in all of human history by birth into a particular network of blood relationships. Reading this book intensifies one's awareness that one owes one's very existence to a great spreading tree of ancestors. Each of us only exists because millions of people have fallen in love, pledged themselves to each other and begotten children. Life is a gift that we have received not just from our parents, but from innumerable ancestors. And so it is fitting that they may also be involved in the transmission of our life's deepest meaning, eternal life. God gives us life and its deepest mystery through other people. We are the fruit of so many loves, and from them also receive some inkling of the full mystery of love that is God. Might there even be a link between a weakening sense of the mystery of life in Europe, and its tumbling birth rate?

In this book John has gathered up memories of the past. It is good that we remember our ancestors, for this strengthens us to face the future. When we are aware of the vast changes through which our ancestors have lived, then we can have courage for the changes that we and our descendants must live through, and even delight in them. And at the heart of this memory is an ancient memory of the one who said, 'Do this in memory of me'. The recollection of the past gives us courage and hope for a future that we do not know.

This is a thoroughly and consciously Catholic story. It tells of fidelity in the midst of suffering and persecution. But this does not make it partisan or divisive. It is only if all denominations can tell their stories that we can hope to come to mutual understanding. We will find deep Christian unity when we can recognise ourselves in the complex interweaving stories that all Christians can tell about the past five hundred years of this country. John ends with the wise words of Pope John XXIII at the beginning of the Second Vatican Council: 'In the present order of things, Divine Providence is leading us to a new order of human relations which, by men's own efforts and even beyond their very expectations, are directed toward the fulfilment of God's superior and inscrutable designs. And everything, even human differences, leads to the greater good of the Church'.

In the new world that is emerging today, we are faced with the fascinating challenge of listening even more widely, and hearing the histories of other families, which start far away on other continents, and of their fidelity in the transmission of other faiths. If we can have the heart and imagination to open our ears to hear what they have to say, then when their descendants write the stories of their families in five hundred years time, God willing, it will not tell of persecution and suffering!

Timothy Radcliffe, OP
Blackfriars, Oxford
2003

Introduction

I was born into a family which, according to the oral tradition, traced the continuity of its Catholic Faith beyond the Reformation into mediaeval England. The fragmented story of its survival, in the face of religious persecution, has become attenuated with the passing of generations and the danger that it may be lost forever has prompted this personal study.

Roman Catholic history in the British Isles since the Reformation has attracted a great deal of research, notably under the aegis of the Catholic Record Society, with its edited transcriptions of original documents and its scholarly historical analyses. In attempting to apply information from such valuable sources to the story of my own family I hope to make a small original contribution to the history of the subject.

The scope of this investigation is threefold:

To examine the validity of the oral tradition of our family.

To develop the authentic aspects of that tradition.

To provide a resource for further enquiry.

My aim has been to trace our family back as far as possible, in order to provide an historical framework which other researchers may then extend and fill out with more comprehensive accounts of specific topics and people, rather than delay by researching details of our more recent history.

Throughout the study I shall attempt to shed light on such questions as the following:

Why did we remain Catholics?

Was this determined by conviction or by social circumstances?

How did we remain Catholics?

Were we sheltered by a powerful Catholic nobility?

Did we seek refuge in a Catholic stronghold?

Did we seek refuge in a remote area where persecution was less vehement?

Were we protected by non-Catholic friends?

To what extent were we penalised?

What was our attitude to social intolerance and religious persecution?

The fact is that we exist. The question is how did we come to be?

The method adopted begins with a short account of the childhood context in which I absorbed our family tradition and in which I became aware that we were rather unusual in being an old English Catholic family. The method then involves fieldwork in Yorkshire, where, in addition to personal communication, information was gained from the exploration of terrain, buildings, and graveyards. Armed with this information and relevant literature, recourse was had to pertinent documents including wills and baptismal registers and certificates.

Here, the term 'Recusant' refers to Catholics who fell within the following definition given by Terrick Fitzhugh, in his Dictionary of Genealogy: 'A recusant was one who absented himself (or herself) from the services of his parish church. Under the Act of Uniformity, 1559, he was fined 12 pence for each absence. In 1581, the fine was raised to £20 per lunar month, and under Acts of 28 & 29 Elizabeth I, and 3 & 4 James I (their regnal years), he was liable to forfeit all his goods and two-thirds of his real property'. The actual practice of Catholics who survived the Reformation was usually not so clearly defined and it is often obscure unless they appeared in the courts.

I have tried to narrate a story about our family as truly as possible – just one among other possible stories. Sometimes the specifying of people and their relationships from registers makes for rather arduous reading but it has, on those occasions, seemed to me a necessary way of bringing our forebears into the tale; and often little else is known about them. The verification of this story is usually worked out in the notes which, consequently, are often rather lengthy. Relevant charts are placed at the end of a chapter. The Appendix constitutes a working paper on continuing research.

The emphasis is on the Robinson side of the family because my interest in our family history lies in the context of English post-Reformation Catholic history. I believe that all the members of our extended family are equally important and interesting, each in his or her unique way; but here it is only possible to give a brief sketch of those who have a bearing on this particular story.

The account is written as an investigation, from the known and usually more recent facts, backwards in time towards increasingly remote and vague family history; so that questions which arise early may often be answered as the story progresses.

'If I preach the truth of Christ, I hope that will find an echo in the hearts and minds of my listeners. That may lead them into the Church or it may help them to find a new significance to their own religious tradition. In both cases, that is contributing to our pilgrimage towards unity'.

Timothy Radcliffe, OP, in answer to the question: 'In fact, many Catholics see interfaith dialogue as renouncing the commandment "make disciples of all nations". How would you answer them?'

Timothy Radcliffe, OP, *I Call You Friends*
(London and New York: Continuum, 2001), p. 63.

CHAPTER I

The Oral Tradition and Childhood Interest

*'Where is the wisdom we have lost in knowledge,
and where is the knowledge we have lost in information?'*
T. S. Eliot

My interest in our family origins had already been established when my father, William Joseph Robinson, died, at the age of 75, on 14th September 1938.

My father had enjoyed good health until about three months before his death. During the last day or two of his illness, my brother, Gordon, and I stayed with Auntie Hilda in Cheltenham. Hilda was my mother's elder sister, the one next to her; and she was my mother's favourite among all the Botterill girls.

I was aged 10 and I was due to go away that same September, for the first time, to a boarding school in the North of England. The school was Ushaw College, where my father, his brothers, his father, and his uncles had all been educated. I had even heard that an ancestor had helped to found the College. After the funeral, a meeting was held to discuss my future schooling in these changed circumstances. It was a warm sunny day and we were seated around the garden table on the Cotswold stone paving at the back of our house. Besides my mother and myself and, I think, Gordon, there was Philip Ford, who was my godfather, and also a priest, I believe a Father Bilsborrow. It was suggested that, perhaps, I should go to school nearby, at Cheltenham. I was given the choice. But I had no doubt that I wished to accompany Gordon on the two hundred and fifty mile journey to Durham. He had already been at Ushaw for four years. What influenced my decision?

When my father took me on bird nesting walks in the woods around our home at Lower Slaughter, or, on cosy winter evenings in front of the fire where my father smelt reassuringly of tweed and tobacco, he had, in his mild Yorkshire accent, often told me about his school days; when Doctor Robert Tate was President of Ushaw and Monsignor Francis Wilkinson was Rector of the Junior House. He used to recall, with amusement, how, when 'Daddy Wilkinson' asked two new boys what their names were, one of them spoke up in a broad Lincolnshire accent: 'Ma naime is Joe Jaooker and ar cum from Market Raasen, is naime is Billy Claaver'. My father wore bracers, never a belt. He recounted how Daddy Wilkinson always told them to hold their breeches up with bracers rather than by a belt around the waist, which was bad for the health.

I used to listen attentively while my father enjoyed telling me about many things: his farming days at Burton Pidsea; his companionship with the legendary Father Flanagan; the mischievous pranks he used to get up to; and especially about his exploits with the Holderness hounds, in the good company of his friend Clive Wilson and on his favourite hunter, 'Dorothy'. We discussed such intriguing matters as: the uses of tarred band and bee's wax; how to make a whipcord; the habit of chewing tobacco; and how to charge a muzzle loading shotgun.

Each evening, I used to wait for my father to finish his pipe before he read to me such books as: Masterman Ready, Mark Seaworth, Swiss Family Robinson, and Pickwick Papers. I would urge him on with, 'Wake up Daddy' as his voice slowed down with impending sleep. He told me how Dickens, who, he said, used to like to talk with educated farmers, once visited his family.[1]

When I asked my father what his own father died of, he told me there was something wrong with his throat and that he had a short neck, which my father regarded as an unhealthy feature. I don't remember hearing anything about my father's mother except that she was said to have painted a beautiful flower picture which hung up the stairs. Once, when I asked him about our ancestors, he replied, with a twinkle in his eye, 'I think we were related to Guy Fawkes'.

My mother and father slept in a large mahogany four poster bed. Every morning, in his night shirt, my father knelt down beside the bed and, with his brass rosary ring on his finger, devoutly said his prayers. He would finish by turning round to face a picture of the Blessed Virgin which hung on the wall beside his chest of drawers. He always prayed for his son 'Tommy' who died after the First World War.

We were the only Catholics in the village. My mother, who was Church of England, taught me to say my prayers. On Sundays, before attending her own service in the parish church at Lower Slaughter, she used to drive my father to Mass at Stow-on-the-Wold. One Saturday, when, I presume, he must have been going to confession, I accompanied my father. I was fascinated by the atmosphere of the little church with its altar and statues; and I said that I would like to go with him on Sundays.

After Mass, my father used to repair to the 'Unicorn' with a farmer called David Young; and they would be joined by George de Serionne.

George had founded the church. He was a bachelor and a French Count. He used to protest, 'What is the good of being a Count if you are as poor as a rat'.

George used to keep sheep in various fields around the Cotswolds. He knew every lane and undulation among the beautiful hills; so much so, that my mother sometimes used to wonder whether he might be a spy. There were times when she used to drive him in her car to the more distant reaches of his sheepfolds and, as he urged her along some muddy downhill lane, her protest, 'I don't think we should go any further, George', would simply meet with the reply, 'Go on, Gladys, it will be quite all right'.

George used to join us, every year, for Christmas dinner. He took in good part the practical jokes which Gordon and I always played on him – a small balloon, inflatable with a remote puffer, under his plate to make it waddle, or a bread roll made of untearable fibre. He often visited. My father had to resort to the expedient of pouring only a prudent measure of whisky into the decanter because it was always empty by the end of the session.

To George was assigned the unrewarding task of teaching me my catechism. I regret that this early theological excursion, in the company of a scholar of the Sorbonne and of Oxford, was not high on my list of priorities. It was only after his death, years later, that I learnt about the great achievements of my childhood catechist from an article in the Ampleforth Journal entitled 'The Apostle of the Cotswolds'.

I sometimes feigned sickness to get out of Mass. But I was greatly impressed by the kindly, chubby, little Dutch priest, Father Biesen, with his round bald head and short grizzly beard. He used to visit his flock on a grey pony. Father Biesen, in conversation with my father, following a delicious tea with apricot jam and 'Mrs. Wilkins' butter,' used to wriggle in his armchair to such an extent that the little flowers on my mother's beautiful chintz cover would be wrinkled to a frazzle. I remember his being congratulated by everyone after Mass one Sunday; I believe he had received a doctorate in Hebrew studies.

Young Jesuits used to motorcycle over from Heythrop College to help out. I found their sermons very interesting. Two nuns sometimes came on a begging expedition and my mother helped them by taking them in her car. On hearing from my father how I could remember the sermons, they said they wished they could do the same because they were asked to write about them. When, from the back of the car, I expressed my resolution to become a nun, my father chuckled that it would not be possible but that I might become a monk. That seemed to me to be some sort of monkey.

Once, I was ushered into a room at the 'Unicorn' to meet the Bishop of Clifton. My father had told me that I should kiss his ring; a task I didn't relish. My impression was of black suits, a long white tablecloth, and yellow mustard. I didn't quite manage the respectful gesture in which I had been instructed; but the good-natured and portly dignitary dispersed my shyness when he ordered that the substantial remainder of a large tin of toffees should be given to me. Hence I came to view bishops favourably.

Captain Philip Wright Ford, my cousin and godfather, was the same age as my mother and so he liked me to call him 'Cousin Philip'. He was a well groomed, smallish man of good proportions, usually wearing a neat grey suit and highly polished brown leather shoes. He presented a round, invariably good-humoured face, with smiling rather protruding eyes. He sported a closely clipped moustache in one side of which nestled a small, pink, sessile, wart. His short straight mousy hair was divided by a slightly off centre parting and, when outside, he wore a soft, brown, felt, trilby hat.

Philip was an old Stonyhurst man. The Jesuits, for his retirement, allowed him to build a large bungalow in the beautiful park of Heythrop College. He lived there with his wife, Joan, and their servant Josephine, who had been with them since she was aged fourteen and was more a member of the family. Philip was innovative. He was especially proud of the bungalow's roof of cedar wood tiles and the fireplace which he had coloured to his taste by stippling the bricks with a brush dipped in inks, mainly red. His home told the story of his life, with scarlet hunting coats, leather straps and cases, swords, polo boots, and endless fascinating things to find; some of which he gave to me.

Philip had many friends among the Jesuits, including such characters as Father Paul and Father Robert de Trafford, both of whom were his contemporaries. I was with Philip in Oxford, one day, when we met Father Paul in St Giles. He was a tall, rather gaunt, distinguished looking elderly man, garbed in black. His eyesight was seriously failing behind his thick spectacles. My cousin's hearty greeting met with rapid recognition and a warm response. Philip said they used to play rugby together. He told me how his old friend would knock on a door and, when the unsuspecting parishioner answered, announce himself, 'I am Paul', as if straight out of the New Testament. Years later, when I was a Senior Registrar at Littlemore Hospital, Father Paul, aged about ninety and still in harness at St Aloysius' Church, looked exactly the same. This was the background which quickened my decision to follow my ancestors to school.

Ushaw was steeped in the tradition of the English College at Douai with which it was continuous. John Lingard, the historian, who had arrived at Douai in 1782, returned to England with the College in 1793, and became Vice-President, first at Crook Hall and then at Ushaw.[2] The old College breathed the spirit of the Douai martyrs and, listed among them, I noticed a John Robinson. I often wondered whether he was an ancestor of ours. William Allen, Fellow of Oriel College, Oxford, and, later, Principal of the neighbouring St Mary's Hall, refused to take the Oath of Supremacy; Queen Elizabeth I had been reigning for three years.[3] Seven years later, in 1568, Allen founded the English College at Douai, as an Oxford on Flemish soil, where English Catholics could be educated and return as priests and laymen to keep the faith alive at home. He was joined in this endeavour by both students and fellow dons from Oxford. As boys we became imbued with the spirit of this venerable place.

Neither my brother, Gordon, nor I was addicted to the prescribed form of scholarship. Latin and Greek, especially, were foreign to our taste. My brother had a great variety of interests, ranging from crystal sets to postage stamps, all of which competed with the acquisition of required knowledge. My mother and father, expressing their concern about this to George de Serionne, one day, were reassured, 'You have no need to worry, Gordon has character'. For my part, if there was a chance that the President might give 'Studies Off', on being approached by the 'Censor', I preferred, during 'First Hour', to say the rosary (a considerable penance) in support of that Philosopher's endeavour on our behalf, rather than apply myself to the allotted tasks of: 'catechism, by heart, vocabulary, and translation'. In my father's time, a good omen for 'Studies Off' was a patch of blue sky big enough to make an elephant a pair of trousers.

Before I went away to school, my dear and respected governess, Miss Ward, who had been induced to come out of a well deserved retirement to educate me, would occasionally admonish me with the exclamation, 'you duffer John', accompanied by a rap on the knuckles with her knitting needles; there was one little French poem which I simply could not master. At Ushaw, we had to learn long ballads. Gordon had prepared me in good time for this ordeal. While we were sitting together in a leafy pit in the woods near home, he taught me the first verse of 'Lars Porsena of Clusium…'; the only verse I ever knew. I believe, however, that I was considered to have a certain rustic wisdom untainted by excessive book learning, because my school mates would call upon me for an opinion on controversial issues; everybody had a part to play. Gordon and I used to win elocution and debating prizes, and he won first prize in mathematics in 'Underlow', the 'school' in which boys started, at the average age of eleven.[4]

The pursuit of pleasurable objectives, alternative to scholarly activities, occasioned my introduction to Yorkshire. Gordon and I were returning mournfully to school after the vacation and we had to change trains at York, a task which we accomplished without difficulty. As we sat opposite each other waiting for the train to pull out, Gordon chose to share with me his enlightened thinking that, perhaps, we might stay in York for the weekend, supported by our pocket money for the term. The plan was to be facilitated by a strategic telegram to the President to the effect that we had missed our connection. Gordon was four years older than me and his advanced ideas invariably carried weight. When we got to the post office neither Gordon nor the girl behind the counter could think how to spell 'Monsignor'. Otherwise, all went well. We stayed in a small establishment which rejoiced in the status of the 'City Hotel'.

We explored York and rowed on the Ouse. Gordon, as was his wont, went into innumerable technical shops, especially camera shops, where he asked endless questions which almost invariably met with kindly, interested, and instructive responses. I tagged on while he looked at everything and bought nothing. We thoroughly enjoyed our adventure, but had only put off the painful return to school. We were received with serious concern, as propriety demanded; but I came to learn that the masters were secretly amused by Gordon's exploits of this kind.

Such stolid independence of attitude found Gordon in 'Popski's Private Army' to which he had transferred from the Tank Corps, in North Africa, during World War II.[5] In about 1944, as the War was approaching its end, he transferred to the Palestine Police in which he served in the Criminal Investigation Department; and it was then that his abiding interest in photography was stimulated by experience in forensic photography. Ultimately he rose to be head of Kodak in India and the associated part of Asia. When my brother died, I made the following note:

> Gordon had a great capacity for friendship and for getting on well with and appreciating all sorts of people regardless of their race and creed and this, combined with a lively, enquiring, and wide interest, and an amazing ability for knowing how to get around the world, made him a universal sort of man.
>
> I always admired my brother, but never more than in his last illness the serious nature of which was suddenly sprung upon him three weeks before he died. I stood in wonder, in awe, and in joy, before the courage,

the fortitude, the humility, the concern for others rather than for himself, and even the humour, which he showed through those weeks and through his death. What a wonderful example to the rest of us; what a sharing in Christ's victory over death!

I saw much more of Yorkshire when, on the way to or from school, I sometimes stayed for a few days with Auntie Ada and Uncle Will at Garton-on-the-Wolds, where they farmed at Garton Manor. Auntie Ada was very warm and kind. I noticed, in her house, taste similar to that of my mother and the other Botterills: duck-egg-blue walls, attractive flower prints, chintz covers on the chairs, and antique furniture and ornaments. When Tathwell, their old family home, broke up, the beautiful china tea services were each divided; consequently one saw the same cups and saucers and plates in their different houses.

We visited Percy and Ethel at Norton House, Malton. Uncle Percy, the third of my mother's five brothers, was always immaculately dressed and in the best style, as were they all, with a well cut tweed suit, starched white collar, and shining brown leather shoes. He was slim and fairly tall, with twinkling eyes flanked by crow's-feet and shaded by huge bushy eyebrows, 'dog like', as my father described them. I always thought that his moustache was so close cropped as to be hardly worth growing. Like my father, and many country people of that generation, he took great care of things; he would tell me, with pride, that he had possessed his belt for forty years, or his shoes for twenty years.

Uncle Percy, with cap on head and walking stick in hand, showed us around his garden, pigsty, and paddock; and he would keep turning round, expostulating, 'What, what?' in seeking our response to his commentary. He bred, trained, and raced horses. I have a photograph of his twelve-year-old, Sir Picton, winning at Newcastle in 1934. George Formby's father was his groom. Even in his eighties, Uncle Percy still attended all the main race meetings in Yorkshire and was so well known that he got in free of charge. His son, Jack Botterill, was an auctioneer of thoroughbred horses and his grandsons developed this business into the top rank as Ascot Bloodstock; Uncle Percy would be truly proud.

Auntie Ada bought me my violin in a second-hand shop. She also paid for my first lessons which I had, when staying with Auntie Hilda in Cheltenham, under the excellent tutorship of Miss Cohen. Back at school, the patient efforts of Mr Cross, the music master, failed to revitalise a dwindling interest compounded, perhaps, by chilblains and cracking skin on swollen red fingers, in the cold northern winter.

I first met my father's elder brother, Thomas, when he visited the College in 1939. I was immediately struck by the marked resemblance between them; they were separated by a year. While Uncle Thomas talked with the President, Monsignor Charles Corbishly (known by us as 'Boxer'), and other masters, his son Arthur, who had driven him there, took Gordon and myself into Durham.

We visited the Cathedral and I remember Arthur saying a quiet prayer at the tomb of St Cuthbert. I was unaware of the weight that might have been on his mind. As an officer in the Territorial Army he was called up at the outbreak of war and had to leave his young wife, Betty, and their little daughter, Diana, and his farm attached to Magdalen House, near Hedon, in Holderness.

Arthur was taken prisoner at Tobruk in June 1942. While in Italy, he escaped. He was sheltered by an Italian family with whom he lived and he helped them on their farm. As the Germans approached, rather than be found with this family and get them into trouble, he left and made his own way as best he could. He was recaptured and remained a prisoner for the rest of the war.

Arthur's elder brother, Thomas, had died from the wounds he received in the First World War. Their sister, Daisy, was decorated by King George VI with the British Empire Medal for her bravery. On 8th July 1940, she captured, single handed and unarmed, a German parachutist whom she saw land just beyond the hedge at the front of her garden, at East Carlton Farm. He was a Luftwaffe officer from the aircrew of a bomber. He had jumped when it was shot down. He was armed with a pistol. The farm was on the East coast, and a German invasion was expected any day. Winston Churchill said about this courageous act, 'the propaganda alone was worth a flotilla of destroyers'.[6] Many years later, Daisy's son, Norman, discovered, by chance, that Tony Lovell, his schoolfellow at Ampleforth, was one the fighter pilots who had shot down this bomber.

Uncle Thomas was a great raconteur, with a keenly developed sense of history and with a great knowledge of Yorkshire people and affairs, all of which he readily and enthusiastically shared with his listeners. He still held a captive audience on our return to the College.

I next met Uncle Thomas at the funeral of his brother, Henry, in 1943. Uncle Harry graduated MB CM at Edinburgh University, on 1st August 1887, when he was aged twenty-one and nine months. He became a legend as a general practitioner surgeon in Hull. He retired to the Morritt Arms at Greta Bridge and his last days were spent in a nursing home in Durham where I used to visit him. Uncle Harry's son Frank and Uncle Frank's son Harry, whose corpulence was attributed to a relatively sedentary life following a distinguished athletic career as a boy at Stonyhurst, arranged with the President for me to attend Uncle Harry's funeral. The graveyard was full of Robinsons and it was suggested to me that there would be a good deal of talk and argument going on. I did not realise, at the time, that it was the graveyard surrounding St Mary's Church at Hutton Magna.

After the funeral, the ham sandwiches at a hotel in Barnard Castle were a schoolboy's dream. It was there that I was able to have my first conversation with Uncle Thomas. He told me how one of our ancestors was among the best swordsmen of his day. He also told me that we were involved in the Jacobite rebellions. As the story developed, I suggested, rather light-heartedly, that, perhaps, we were even related to St Thomas More. Uncle Thomas did not regard this hypothesis as impossible because, he said, we had an ancestor in the household of Henry VIII.

On this occasion I also met my father's cousin, also Thomas, whom I later visited at Newsham Grange in North Yorkshire where he farmed. He bore a marked facial resemblance to Uncle Thomas and my father. He was a bachelor, and impressed me as a very gentle and pious old man. I noticed that he was unable to straighten his left arm. I remember little about our conversation except that he was educated at Ampleforth and he told me something about his brothers.

After the funeral, my cousin Frank gave me Uncle Harry's wooden stethoscope, one of my most treasured possessions. I was told he used to carry it tucked in between the buttons of his waistcoat like a huntsman would carry his hunting horn.

In my day at Ushaw, training for the priesthood took thirteen years for a boy entering the school of Underlow. He then proceeded: through Low Figures and High Figures; and then, in Little Lads, through Grammar and Syntax; and, in Big Lads, through Poetry and Rhetoric; and then through first and second year Philosophy; followed by four years Divinity. No distinction was made between church students and lay students. The latter usually left school in Little Lads or Big Lads.

The dawn of learning was beginning to light my way a little by the time I went into Grammar at the age of fourteen. Ushaw fostered a patient and merciful culture in which education was not to be subservient to the production of good examination results; though a high success rate in the latter was usual. Apart from Mr Cross, all the masters were either secular priests, the majority, and were referred to as 'Professors', or they were 'Divines', seconded to teaching for about three years, and referred to as 'Minor Professors'. Nobody was called 'Father', they were all addressed, indirectly, as 'Mister' and directly, as 'Sir'.

Mister Fleming, a good and pious priest known to us as 'Phlegm', because he tended to froth slightly at the corners of his mouth, first engaged my interest in Greek history which he taught superbly; that was in 'Low Figures'. Bob Carson, a minor professor, certainly fired my interest, if not my industry, in English. He reintroduced Shakespeare, in cleverly edited productions. It proved a great success. I played the part of Antonio in Twelfth Night, which I thoroughly enjoyed. 'Tommy' McGoldrick, a corpulent man, fresh from Cambridge, certainly had a way of making history interesting. He held classes in the History Library and he used to 'expand' on the art, science, and other aspects, of the period in question. He also organised debates to analyse personalities and events. As public examinations approached, Tommy took us for tutorials in what we needed to know. 'Barney' Payne was our essay master and, with patient encouragement, he marked each weekly essay in a very personal way; he would read out to the school what he considered to be the best works. Basil Kershaw, who taught classics, was a very talented 'all rounder' and was always ready to coach and advise a young aspirant. Besides his involvement in the usual games, he skated beautifully, conducted the College orchestra and taught us boxing and fencing; he even righted the sound post which had collapsed in my violin. 'Alf' Smith, who taught mathematics and who interested us in astronomy, reintroduced athletics in which I discovered that I had some skill. The man, however, who detected and understood my difficulties, when I hardly knew how to express them, was 'Sos' Malone.

Father Wilfrid Malone was one of the finest men I ever met. He was an eminently cultured and good man and showed great sensitivity. He taught Classics in 'Little Lads'. Sos was of shortish, well proportioned stature, with a quick walk, fair curly hair, alert blue eyes, and a large nose with a bump on the bridge which he had the habit of rubbing with his right index finger; rumour had it that his nose had been run over by a skate! He admired John Henry Newman for his character and his theology; he also regarded him as a master of English literature. Sos gave unstintingly of his time to tutor me and to be my spiritual guide. If I have listened patiently to people as a psychiatrist, it is probably because he listened so patiently to me.

At Ushaw I soaked up years of tradition and I learnt as much from the personalities and example of the masters as I did from their formal teaching. I also learnt much from the spirit of my school and the companionship of my school mates. Towards the end of my six years I had discovered that to work hard and to play hard were rewarding and I had begun to do my best at both. My results were far from good;

but I was confirmed in my faith and I had learnt how to learn. I left Ushaw in the summer of 1944 when I was 16 and attended Kingston Technical College to study science in preparation for a medical degree. In January 1946 I was called up into the Royal Air Force.

In the summer of that year my interest in our family history received a further boost under the willing tutelage of Uncle Thomas. I was stationed at Binbrook in Lincolnshire and I used to visit Uncle Thomas and Auntie Eveline in their bungalow at Hedon to which they had retired from Nuthill. Uncle Thomas suggested to me, teasingly, that the family used not to produce anything as common as doctors, lawyers, perhaps, but not doctors. He also told me that he had a cousin who was a Jesuit priest at Stonyhurst; he was put in charge of the farm.

My grandfather did not want any of his sons to follow him as farmers. Uncle Frank was a solicitor in Hull; Uncle Ted also went to Edinburgh and became a doctor; and my father was destined to be a land agent; Uncle Thomas was allowed to farm because he had a 'gammy foot'. But farming was in the blood; they all ended up with farms.

My father was one of eleven children. He told me how his father used to take out his penknife and divide a Pontefract Cake between them. Another important source of information was my father's youngest sister, Mary Agnes. William was her favourite brother, he was always kind to her; she was Gordon's godmother. As a child, there were three regal ladies in my life: Queen Mary; Mrs Whitmore; and Aunt Agnes.

Mrs Whitmore was the lady of the manor at Lower Slaughter. With pearls dangling from her ears and her snow white hair surmounted by a black hat, her dress reaching down to pointed black shoes, she would occasionally stride, with haughty look and slightly halting gait, majestically, though the village. She was attended by her two cairn terriers and her lady's maid, 'Waugh', who, with short bandy legs, waddled slightly behind the main parade.

One day, Aunt Agnes arrived at Green Gates, holding on to a strap in the back of a large, square, black, car driven by her chauffeur, Cecil, the son of Buckfield, her gardener. She descended from the vehicle, straight, tall, and dignified, wearing a long sky-blue taffeta dress and broad-brimmed hat to match. I had never seen such an elegant visitor before. She had no significant moustache but, otherwise, the features of older Robinsons were unmistakable, a sharpish chin and nose, a rather ruddy complexion, and prominent brown eyes.

Aunt Agnes lived in Sutton, Surrey. Her husband, Tom Eeles, a widower with a previous family, had died. Later, I came to know her well. I used to visit her when I was attending Kingston Technical

College and, later, when I was a medical student at St Thomas' Hospital. Aunt Agnes was a charming old lady, with a great sense of etiquette, tempered with humour and a good sense of proportion. She kept abreast of the times and in tune with younger people by her interest, her reading, and by her correspondence through which she kept the members of the family in touch with one another.

From Auntie Agnes I learnt a little more about her father Thomas, and life at Nuthill. Her brothers, apparently, had to sow the fields early in the morning before they were allowed to go to Doncaster races. I think it was her, or my father, who told me that Uncle Harry, as a boy, was given the task of looking after a sick lamb. Even then, his curative skills were in evidence because it recovered, whereupon he sold it and pocketed the money; which practical interpretation of the value of his services secretly amused my grandfather.

One of Aunt Agnes' elder sisters decided that she wanted to become a nun. Her father insisted that she should not join the noviciate straight from school but come home for a year to think about it.

Auntie Agnes used to tell me how our family had lived and farmed at Hutton Hall in the village of Hutton Magna, North Yorkshire, for three hundred years. Her father's father was also called Thomas, and she could go back as far as her great grandfather, Robert Robinson. Their three silhouettes were hanging beside the fireplace in her drawing-room. When I pressed her knowledge beyond Robert, she used to relate how either her father, grandfather, or Robert himself – I am not clear which – used to say some such thing as, 'We are what we are' or, 'We have what we have'; and he was disinclined to go back further. She did, however, tell me that, in penal times, an ancestor of ours was carried in a butter basket down one side of a hedge, while the priest walked down the other side, and the infant was baptised across the hedge. She was also clear about the fact that the family name was originally Vane. I surmised that we sought obscurity in a commoner name and in the remoteness of North Yorkshire to escape religious persecution.

My cousin, Philip Wright Ford, was the son of my father's eldest sister, Sarah, who married 'Fritz' Ford. They owned 'Brown's Hotel' which was favoured by country gentlefolk when visiting London. Holmes, the head waiter, used to come to work in a chauffeur driven Rolls-Royce. The story is told how, one day, some young lord turned up for dinner and on his arm was a voluptuous young lady whose general demeanour failed to satisfy the canons of that genteel establishment. Uncle Fritz called Holmes over in dismay, to be reassured, 'Leave it to me Sir'; whereupon Holmes diplomatically approached the young gallant, 'Will you dine now My Lord, or will you await the arrival of His Grace'. Exit the startled young man. Sarah and Fritz also had two daughters: Theresa, who married Major Chan Bassett and lived on the Isle of Wight; and Monica, who married a Major Culver. My Aunt Sarah's only grandchild was Bernard Culver. My childhood impression was that Bernard presented a source of some concern to the rest of the family.

It was in 1976 that my knowledge of our family history took a leap, albeit, perhaps, a rather speculative one. I was summoned to the Radcliffe Infirmary and there, resplendent above the white sheets, was a ruddy face sporting modified Robinson features surmounted by a greying military moustache – my first sight of Captain Bernard Joseph Francis Culver. I was immediately reminded of Alec Guinness in the hilarious film 'Kind Hearts and Coronets', where the path to the family fortunes was cleared by a series of convenient events: the Admiral, saluting, went down with his ship; the General was blown up by a bomb in his caviar; and so on. Bernard quickly dispatched any interest I might have shown in his deviation from our family's Catholic norms, in taking two or three wives, by declaring that he became a Muslim.

Bernard had been educated by the Jesuits at Beaumont; the 'Crows' as he called them. He had put much work into researching his family history and, on the Robinson side, he had enjoyed the advantage of conversation with his grandmother, Sarah. He was kind enough to give me two papers in which he recorded the result of his labours. Latterly, he had discussed these matters with my cousin Arthur who developed a considerable admiration for Bernard.

Bernard's thesis was, broadly, as follows. The family name was originally Vane and they came up from Monmouthshire to live in Kendal in Westmoreland where the Robinson branch arose. Around the time of the Reformation, the Robinsons divided: a branch went to Hutton Hall, remained Catholic and was Royalist; a branch went to West Layton; a branch went to Rokeby, it was Protestant, Parliamentarian, and fared well; and a branch, also Protestant, went to Newby and also fared well. There are some inconsistencies in his account and his sources are not always quoted.

In the same year, 1976, I attended the funeral of my cousin Agnes, Uncle Thomas' youngest child. She was buried in the family vault at Burstwick, East Yorkshire. I think it was on that occasion that I first heard of our descent from the Wrights of Ploughland Hall. The same Wrights who were implicated in the Gunpowder Plot.

In 1977, Michael Cardwell, Uncle Thomas' great-grandson, came up to Oxford to read Classics. It was through our friendship which developed over the next four years that my interest in our Yorkshire origins received new life. It was from his father, Norman, that I learnt that an ancestor of ours founded the Institute of the Blessed Virgin Mary, but her name, Mary Ward, meant little to me. Neither did I realise that her mother, Ursula, was the sister of John and Christopher Wright, the Gunpowder Plotters.

I now know enough to know what questions I should have asked Uncle Thomas. Understanding of our origins was changing from passive reception to active investigation.

CHAPTER II

Nuthill

*'History is a high point of advantage from which alone
we can see the age in which we live'.*
G. K. Chesterton[1]

My grandfather, Thomas Robinson, left Hutton Hall, the family home at Hutton Magna in North Yorkshire, in 1845, and came, by invitation, to Holderness in the East Riding to be a tenant farmer at Nuthill on the Burton Constable estate.[2] He was aged 22.

On the 18th November 1852, Thomas married Sarah Wright Ford of Burton Pidsea, a village about two miles away. He was aged 29 and she was 25. The marriage was solemnised at the Parish Church in the parish of Drypool 'according to the Rites and Ceremonies of the Established Church, by license' with W. G. Gibson, incumbent, officiating; and the witnesses were Francis Wright and Sarah Ann Wright.[3] This ceremony was probably to comply with the Hardwicke Marriage Act of 1753 in order to make the marriage legal for, on the same day, they were also married in the Catholic Chapel in Hull.[4] This precaution was not strictly necessary because, after 1836, marriage in a Catholic chapel in the presence of a registrar was regarded as legally valid – but perhaps Thomas and Sarah Wright wanted to make sure.

I had always taken it for granted that my grandmother, Sarah, was a Catholic. After all, her sons went to Ushaw and one of her daughters became a nun. It was through her that we were, reputedly, descended from the Wrights of Ploughland Hall. Sarah Wright Ford may well have been a Catholic at the time of her marriage, but she seems to have been baptised into the Church of England, in the Parish of Burton Pidsea on 4th March 1827 by 'Isaac Dixon, Curate'. Her father was 'Thomas Ford of Burton Pidsea, Farmer' and her mother was 'Mary-Ann Ford'.[5] Her mother, furthermore, appears in the Baptism Register of the Parish of Humbleton on 27th November 1800: 'Mary Ann Daughter of Robert Wright of Fitling Farmer by Sarah his Wife bap.d'[6] When Mary Ann was aged 20 she married 'Thomas Ford of the Parish of Burton Pidsea Bachelor 27 years' in Humbleton Parish Church on 22nd February 1821, in the presence of Robert Wright and Hannah

Cobb; 'Jonan Dixon, vicar' officiated.[7] The evidence is not conclusive but it is highly suggestive that this branch of the Wright family was Church of England. Whatever about her family background, Sarah died a Catholic, 'Fortified with the Rites of Holy Church'.[8]

Thomas and Sarah Wright Robinson had eleven children, but I could only ever count ten of them. Their baptisms, apart from that of the second youngest, Mary Agnes, are all recorded in the register of the Catholic Church of St Mary and St Joseph, at Hedon, which lies about two and a half miles west of Nuthill.[9]

Thomas and Sarah's first child, Sarah, was born on 20th September 1853 and baptised on the 21st by Joseph Fisher.[10] Her godparents were Thomas Robinson, almost certainly her grandfather, and 'Catrina Cecilia Robinson', her grandfather's sister, her great-aunt Cecily. Sarah's photographs and her portrait which was given to me by her son Philip suggest that she developed into a woman of considerable beauty. Her grandson, Bernard Culver, described her as 'a most intellectual and sweet old lady'; and, again, 'She was a very sweet and gracious old lady – an "Aristocrat" – and justly proud of her lineage, but she never mentioned it except to me when we were talking of family affairs; a completely different person to her utterly vile French mother-in-law'.[11]

I have, in my possession, a little holy picture entitled 'Mois de Marie' with the message 'With Sallie's best love to dear Willie on his First Communion Day April 2nd 1874'. This refers to my father when, at the age of 11, he made his First Communion 'in the Church of Saint Aloysius at Ushaw this second day of April 1874'.[12] Sarah was aged 20 at the time.[13]

'Marie Anna', Thomas and Sarah's second child, was born on 9th January 1855 and baptised on 11th. Her godparents were Cuthbert Watson, her father's uncle by marriage, and 'Anna Chambers'. Mary Ann married Henry Aloysius Rockliff and they had one daughter, Mary Alice, my cousin 'Clytie', who never married and whom I met once at Aunt Agnes' house.

Their third child, 'Cecilia Maria', was born on 21st October 1856 and baptised on 23rd. Her godparents were 'Gulielmus Robinson', almost certainly William Robinson, her father's brother, and 'Anna Maria Johnson'. Cecily married James Robert Rockliff, a cousin of her sister's husband Henry and they also had just one daughter, Frances Sarah, my cousin 'Fanny', who never married.[14] I have a vague childhood memory of Fanny's visiting, once, at Lower Slaughter. She was small, dressed all in black and, I seem to remember, carried a large black bag. No doubt Clytie accompanied her. These two cousins were often thought to be sisters. They lived in London, I think in adjacent flats, at 59, Oxford Gardens, off Ladbroke Grove, and they were, I believe, very pious ladies and great supporters of the local Catholic Church.

Thomas and Sarah's fourth child has turned out to be the one that I could never count, 'Thomas Ford', who was born on 26th June 1858. William Thompson, his father's cousin, and his wife, Maria, were the godparents; they had probably just moved from Lane Head, Hutton Magna, to South Park, about one and a half miles from Nuthill. This little boy evidently died; and his name, which included the maiden name of his mother, was given to my Uncle Thomas.

Thomas and Sarah's fifth child, Catherine Mary, was born on 21th July 1859 and baptised on 24th. Her godparents were 'Gulielmus Stickney' and 'Maria Stickney'.[15] Catherine, in her photograph, was a stylish girl. She was the one who became a nun.[16] I do not know what became of my aunt Catherine. Uncle Ted tried to find out about her but without success. According to Uncle Ted's daughter, Cecily, he thought she became an Ursuline. The evidence is, however, that she became a Carmelite. My cousin Dick had in his possession a photograph of a young Carmelite nun and his widow, Doris, recalled that this was the daughter who became a nun.[17]

On 3rd July 1861 my Uncle Thomas was born, Thomas Ford Robinson. His godparents were 'James Richardson and Maria Champney'. Thomas was aged only 19 when his father died and he took over the management of Nuthill. When I knew him he was referred to as 'The Boss' or 'The Manager' and his grandson Norman thinks this title derived from his role in the family at that time. I am sure that Uncle Thomas and Auntie Eveline would forgive me my urge to share their youthful love and charming correspondence with my friends. Shortly before they were married, Eveline wrote the following letter to her younger sister, Beatrice:

> Wednesday
> What the dickens
> does this mean

My dearest old Glofesh Iflow,

I was very pleased to get your letter on Monday. Tom came on Saturday and went away yesterday morning by 10, train I did cry when he went and am awfully miserable it is simply wretched without him. We do so want Mama and Papa to let us be married this year in the Autumn but Mama does not want us to. I think she might it is simply cruel keeping us when there is no <u>earthly</u> thing to wait for we should be <u>so happy</u> if only she would say we might as it is we are both miserable about it. I have

hardly done anything but cry since he went and have not given them the pleasure of much of my company – I hope you wont get Influenza. I like Mrs. Robinson and Agnes and all of them awfully and they all like me very much – I am so glad – We have had two very heavy thunder storms here this morning Tom and I write to each other every day. I may get to Aunt Mary's for a day or two with Mama next week, and Tom is coming here again a week on Friday I think all the kids are out I am writing upstairs. I have just written to Ethel. Helen is going to Aunt Lizzie's on Friday good business
   Written in haste
    I am just going to
    write to Tom
     E. B.
    I hope you can read it
     Yes.[18]

Eveline was the fifth of thirteen children and she was the first of the girls to get married. Her sister Helen, referred to in the letter, was the eldest, and my mother, one of 'the kids' referred to, was the eleventh. Beatrice was the seventh and was at Cheltenham Ladies College at the time of the correspondence and, no doubt, she was closest to Eveline, separated from her only by Uncle Oswald.

Their home was Tathwell Hall in the little village of Tathwell, near Louth, in Lincolnshire. My impression is that the charm and humour, the respect for everything and everybody, the laughter and fun in this family, of which my mother was one of the sweetest members, radiated from the household to include the village and the countryside beyond. 'Papa' was Richard Botterill whom they all idolised and 'Mama' was Fanny whom they deeply loved.

My grandfather, Richard Botterill, was one of the most successful race horse breeders of his time. His stud book of 1890 refers to such as 'Quicklime' which: 'as a three-year-old won £6782, proving himself the best colt of his year, winning the Epsom grand Prize, the Prince of Wales's Stakes at Ascot [etc.]'.[19] His racing colours were yellow with a red cap. Fanny was the daughter of John and Elizabeth Leonard. My mother told me that the Leonards were of Huguenot stock and she proudly wore a gold signet ring with their crest – the head of a lioness surmounting a crown.

Richard Botterill of Garton Fields, on the Sledmere estate, and Fanny Leonard of Ryhill Manor, both in East Yorkshire, were married on 17th November 1864.[20] Their ages were very similar to those of Thomas and Eveline when they were married: Richard was 32, Thomas was 31; Fanny was 19, Eveline was 21. My mother told me that her father was so concerned about his daughter Eveline marrying a Catholic that he felt it necessary to obtain permission from the Bishop of Lincoln. Perhaps that was the reason for the delay, or perhaps her mother thought that Eveline was too young. In any event a letter arrived addressed to:

>   Miss Beatrice Botterill
>   Miss St John
>   Fairholme
>   Montpellier
>   Cheltenham

from the 'Grand Hotel, London' dated Nov. 6th 1892

My dearest old Fat,
   I thought I must just write a few lines to you – tell you I am married and done for now – and jolly happy I am too – All passed off very well last Wednesday morning at 9.30 and we came to London by the 10.18 from Leybourne with a carriage full of nice old slippers Everybody knew what we were – On Friday we went for a coach drive down to Oatlands Park 22 miles it was so lovely, we did enjoy it. We went to the Crystal Palace yesterday and saw some grand fireworks. We have been to three theatres and to [----------] I think we may go on to Brighton for a day or two this week. I think we shan't go to the Isle of Wight now. I got some lovely presents but they will tell at home what they were. I have no time now.
   Love from Tom and me
      Your loving sister
         Eveline Robinson.[21]

Auntie Eveline was a keen member of the Holderness Hunt. She rode side-saddle. It was said that her first child, Eveline Mary, my cousin 'Daisy' – whom we met capturing a German parachutist – was almost 'born in the saddle'. Daisy certainly inherited her mother's love of horses and of every sport in which they were involved. Her son, Norman, still subscribes to keep her racing colours in the family; they are the colours of her grandfather, Richard Botterill, but with olive green collar and cuffs.

Daisy married Norman Cardwell, a man of great culture, charm and talent, whom she lovingly referred to, rather to the surprise of new acquaintances, as 'Dog'. He read Classics at Oxford, was a competent artist and cellist, and served as a Captain in the King's Own Yorkshire Light Infantry during the First World War. He then adapted successfully to life as a farmer at Carlton in East Yorkshire, and fully supported Daisy in her sporting enthusiasm. Though I seem to remember the odd complaint, tempered with humour, that Daisy's horses were cropping grass designated to his bullocks! During the Second World War Norman was a Major in the Home Guard and his First World War uniform fitted him without any alterations.

Norman and Daisy had one son, Norman, to whom I often refer as one of my main sources of information and from whose family I have received such kind and enthusiastic encouragement for my genealogical research. Norman's wife, Sheila, enjoyed the benefit of many a dialogue with Uncle Thomas who, while describing details of the agricultural land drainage of Holderness, would encourage her that if he did not tell her these things the information would be lost for ever. Uncle Thomas '…had been one of the Commissioners for Keyingham Level Drainage authorities and yearly, "rode the drains" by boat for the traditional inspection of the canals'.[22] As an old man, during the War, he used to sit outside his bungalow at Hedon in readiness to discuss a variety of matters at some length with an interested passer-by, a category to which he considered Sheila belonged, while on her way to work. She guiltily confesses that, sometimes, she had to resort to the expedient of crouching low behind his garden hedge as she hurried past to catch her train! On meeting with an affirmative answer to his question, 'Have I ever told you about so and so?', Uncle Thomas was liable to reply, 'Well, I'll tell you again'. Sheila includes among her distinctions a London University degree in Physics, taken at a time when this was most unusual for a woman. She is also a direct descendant of John Gully, the famous prizefighter, who later became a well known racehorse owner and Member of Parliament for Pontefract; Norman and Sheila have several portraits of his winning horses. We shall have occasion to refer to John Gully again.

Norman was educated by the Benedictines at Ampleforth where he distinguished himself at sport, much to his mother's satisfaction. His father once told me that, although he himself was not a Catholic, he had a considerable admiration for the monks. During the Second World War Norman served as an officer with his father's old regiment. A hand grenade that had not gone off deprived this sportsman of a foot and deafened him for life. His even greater distinction lay in his courageous acceptance of these disabilities, despite which, he pursued an eminently successful career as agent to Sir Richard Sykes at Sledmere. Norman managed the Sledmere estate, including the stud, not only to a high standard of orderliness but, also, with human sensitivity and consideration for everybody's needs. The standard set by

Cuthbert Watson at Wycliffe was maintained and possibly surpassed! We shall hear more about Cuthbert Watson later. I have never heard Norman complain in spite of these constraints; though he did tell me, once, with a twinkle in his eye, that he was out shooting when his leg fell off in the middle of a turnip field!

Thomas and Eveline's second child Thomas Botterill Robinson was born on 5th May 1899. He was educated by the Jesuits at Stonyhurst. Life at Nuthill, vibrant with good humour and companionship, parties and sport, was overcast by the sombre shadow of the First World War; but a shadow penetrated by the light of heroism, as shown in the following account:

Lieut. Thomas Botterill Robinson, 2nd Northumbrian Brigade, Royal Field Artillery.

At Stonyhurst Tom Robinson is remembered as a good-natured young giant, very popular with everyone, and withal possessed of a strong, independent character. Like the rest of his schoolmates who were approaching military age during the war, he was full of eagerness to join up at the earliest possible opportunity.

His time came when he left College, in July, 1917, and applied himself immediately to the realisation of his ambition – a commission in the Artillery, an arm for which his marked ability in mathematics peculiarly fitted him.

He received a commission in the R.F.A. in September, 1917, after a preliminary training at Exeter, where he passed his examinations with honours, being amongst the first three on the list. His training was completed at Bordon Camp, Salisbury Plain.

On August 24th, 1918, he crossed to France with the 2nd Northumbrian Brigade. He took part in some heavy fighting during the great advance. His favourite work in the line was the interesting and dangerous rôle of Forward Observation Officer to his battery. Owing to his marked efficiency in this work he was frequently detailed for it. It was while thus employed and occupying an observation post in the front line of the advance that he was severely wounded by a shell on October 24th, 1918, sustaining a double fracture of the lower jaw.

His recovery was slow, necessitating four months in hospital before he was again fit for active service. After a short leave he volunteered for service in the East, and was sent to Turkey in May, 1919, where he was stationed at Constantinople.

During his sojourn there he contracted dysentery, returning to hospital in England. After leaving hospital, he came to live with his family in Holderness, where he contemplated adopting the career of farming on his father's estate there.

He was devoted to country pursuits, a bold and enthusiastic rider to hounds, and a keen, all-round sportsman.

Friends who met him but a few weeks before his death, and even the members of his own family in constant association with him, could not have realised beneath all his outward energy and apparently strong abundant vitality how the after-effects of his severe wound, added to the inroads of the malady contracted in the East, were sapping his strength. Towards the middle of January he was taken ill with inflammation of the spinal cord (myelitis), and died after a week's illness, borne with characteristic pluck and cheerfulness. He retained consciousness up to the very end, asking for the Last Sacraments himself, and receiving them with calm courage and devotion.

At the very end he sent for the priest again, begged to be excused for disturbing him, and received Holy Communion.

He died on Friday evening, January 23rd, 1920, aged 21.

We have inserted this – a memoir and portrait – as the illness of which he died was medically certified to be due to the wound he received in action.

Tom was the eldest son of Mr. Thomas Robinson and Mrs. Robinson, of Nuthill, Preston (Hull), members of an ancient Catholic family of Yorkshire, whose ancestors were among the founders of Ushaw College.

Tom's death was much regretted in his own neighbourhood, where his family is so well known. He was a devoted son, and his simple, unaffected character and genial good nature won him many friends.[23]

Thomas was buried in the family vault in the graveyard at Burstwick. A brass plaque in St Mary and St Joseph's church in Hedon commemorated his death and referred to the altar which was erected there in his memory 'by his sorrowing family'.[24]

Thomas' brother Arthur, whom we first met when he brought his father, Uncle Thomas, on a visit to Ushaw, was born in 1903. He also went to Stonyhurst. Arthur, as a confidant of his father, was an important and eloquent exponent of the oral tradition. After the Second World War, he took up life again as a very successful farmer who also played his full part in public affairs. He was the Chairman of the Cereal Committee of the National Farmer's Union which office necessitated regular visits to London. Whenever I met him his engaging extroverted personality belied his traumatic war experiences. He used to go to Italy to visit the family with whom he stayed when he escaped from being a prisoner of war.

Arthur seemed much the same even when, in his eighties, he was dying from carcinoma of the oesophagus. He and Betty welcomed Catherine and myself with their usual hospitality and Arthur walked around the house, with the help of his thumb-stick, enthusiastically showing us some humorous hunting prints he had been collecting. While we were there a nun came to visit him and we were privileged to join them in a humble prayer. Arthur chose to avoid the family vault at Burstwick and, instead, to be buried, where there would, he considered, be less argument, with the nuns in the graveyard at Marton. There, he would also enjoy the company of 'Flanny', the old family favourite.

Father Flanagan is commemorated by a plain granite cross, strong and beautiful in its simplicity, and on the granite block which supports it is this inscription:

>PRAY FOR THE SOUL OF
>REV. DEAN
>CHRISTOPHER FLANAGAN
>FOR 39 YEARS PRIEST IN CHARGE
>OF MARTON CATHOLIC CHURCH
>AND PRIVATE CHAPLAIN TO
>BURTON CONSTABLE
>DIED AT MARTON JUNE 14TH 1939
>AGED 70 YEARS
>R. I. P.

My mother spoke in most affectionate terms about 'dear old Flanny'. She used to tell the story of how they were sitting next to each other at a dinner party and each of them, rather embarrassingly, suspected that the pervading smell emanated from the shoes or feet of the other, until, simultaneously, they recognised the source of their consternation: a strong Gorgonzola cheese on the table before them. Greatly relieved, they confided in each other about their suspicions, 'Well, do you know Gladys…'.

Sometimes, in a moment of secular inspiration, Uncle Thomas would send word to Flanny who duly turned up for a game of cards and a talk. They used to become so preoccupied with the business on hand that lunch would have proved a rude interruption and Uncle Thomas had sandwiches brought out to the garden where they sat at the card table. At about four o'clock in the afternoon the whiskey decanter and soda-water siphon would arrive. I believe they found it difficult to complete any rubber or set because of the urgency of discussion over a wide range of topics. As the intensity of the conversation stole the night away, Father Flanagan would reflect that he had to say Mass at eight o'clock in the morning and, reluctantly, a horse and trap would be organised to take him home. Flanny enjoyed a drop of whiskey and my father told me how, when he and another practical joker were serving his Mass one day, the other suggested that they should put whiskey in the cruet that held the wine, but my father prevented this as going too far. Flanny was pastor and friend to everybody, whatever his or her beliefs; it seems that his starting point was the unconditional love of God for everyone, without exception.

Next came Arthur's brother 'Dick', he also went to Stonyhurst. My mother was very fond of Richard. She used to tell the story of how, as a boy, he climbed a tall tree in quest of a bird's nest but, just as he was about to achieve his objective, in his excitement, he was overcome by a pressing need of nature and had to return to earth forthwith! Richard and Doris have a delightful family of children and grandchildren; the sort of people for whom I am recording this history.

Thomas and Eveline's youngest child was Agnes, born in 1912. She was referred to as 'Little Agnes' to distinguish her from Aunt Agnes who was known as 'Big Agnes'. My earliest memory of Agnes was when she stayed with us at Lower Slaughter. I was still wearing 'smocks' and she made me a hat to go with one of them. When Catherine and I had children of similar age she was in charge of catering at Somerville College and we used to meet her on Sundays at St Aloysius' Church.

When 'Little Agnes' died on 11th September 1976, I drove up to Yorkshire, to attend her funeral, with 'Dickie', my cousin Richard Botterill. As the small funeral procession drove through the countryside, from Hedon to the interment at Burstwick, a man working in a field nearby stopped his tractor, doffed his hat, and stood respectfully while we passed. Dickie turned to me and said, 'You would never see that in England, would you?'!

To return to my grandparents Thomas and Sarah their seventh child was my father. William Joseph Robinson was born on 6th November 1862. His godparents were 'Carolus Johnson and Susanna Curtis'. At the age of nine he went away to Ushaw and he was probably accompanied by his elder brother, Thomas, and his younger brother, Francis, because they are all listed as entering the College in 1872. He remained there until 1878. My father was a keen sportsman and, no doubt, his interest was kindled at school. He continued to play cricket after he left. He also skated and he used to go swimming at Hornsea; indeed, he gave me my first demonstration of the strokes.

My father was aged 14, he told me, before he learnt to ride but he became one of the best horsemen in the Holderness Hunt. Uncle Thomas used to hunt in a silk top hat whereas my father wore a bowler hat; though he referred to the greater protection afforded by a top hat if you fell on your head. As a young man he appears very dapper in his photographs; yet he was frequently up to mischief. He used to tell me how, while the guests made merry at a big country party, he and a friend stole out into the night, unhitched all the patiently waiting horses and hitched them back into their carriages the wrong way round! He was widely known as 'Holderness Bill'.

My father took over his grandfather Ford's estate at Bramhill House, Burton Pidsea. At one time he went into partnership with his brother, Thomas; but, evidently, this did not work out satisfactorily and, once, while walking down from Stow, he told me that, 'You should never go into partnership with your brother', it was not a good idea.

My father's first wife, 'Nellie', Helen Rockliff, died on 15th March 1911 at the age of 51. She is buried in the graveyard at Burton Pidsea and on the same gravestone are commemorated their little daughter Dorothy Mary who died on 18th October 1892 when she was nine months old, and their son Thomas who died at the age of 34 on 15th August 1924, largely, I believe, as a result of his experience as a soldier in the First World War. Thomas is listed in the Ushaw College Diary as entering at the age of 15 in 1905 and he left in 1907. Otherwise I know nothing about 'Tommy' except that he enjoyed shooting but was quite unable to pick up the bird that he had shot. The only survivor among the three children of my father's first marriage was Mary Helen who married Charles Clement Wreathall. They farmed at Cottingham and had two children, Henry and Ann.

My father remained a widower for ten years. By all accounts he was a very popular man who enjoyed a vigorous sporting and social life with his many friends. My mother had known him for years because, of course, her sister Eveline was married to his brother, Uncle Thomas. She told me, in fact, that she used not to be very keen on him. But then, people began to notice that they seemed to be together a lot, and she had, on such occasions, apparently, been out shooting with him.

My mother, Gladys Margaret Botterill, was born on 4th September 1882. Her own account of her childhood at Tathwell Hall was quaint and full of charm; a little girl, so enchanted by a happy family life in the heart of the Lincolnshire countryside, who was full of wonder about everything and who loved everybody. Brought up in the nursery with the 'kids' as Eveline described them – these would have been Mildred, Hilda, my mother, Lilian, and Douglas – her pleasures were simple and beautiful. She had two little pot dolls that she carried with her in her pocket and, if things went wrong, she could always get comfort from holding them. One of their greatest joys was in choosing and receiving those old fashioned Victorian Christmas cards with colourful pictures of children and flowers and birds, often framed in paper lace.

My mother delighted in the Kate Greenaway books, with their delicately painted pictures of engaging children and pretty cottage gardens with green gates and hollyhocks, neatly clipped evergreen hedges, and little steeple shaped trees. She loved trees of all kinds. One of her favourite colours was 'wagon red', a shade somewhere between the red of old bricks and plant pots and the living colour of a robin's breast. The birds brought her the greatest pleasure and she always fed them, 'cake crumbs for the robin'. I think her favourites were the robin with his faithful friendliness and sweet song, and the hedge sparrow, or 'Cuddy' as she called her, with her little eggs of light greenish blue, another of my mother's favourite colours. All the girls were likened to birds. I believe my mother was a hedge sparrow, Auntie Beatrice, I think, was a partridge, and Auntie Lilian, the impact of whose approaching presence customarily called forth the exclamation 'Eleven is coming', was a bull finch!

My mother's favourite flowers were wild yellow primroses, with their 'perfect scent', growing in a copse or on a mossy bank. The kind lady in the village shop would give them a few sweets in exchange for rather unusual pieces of white wood which they used to find under the trees and present across the counter. The sweets would be parcelled in little bags fashioned from a square of paper rolled into a cone shape and sealed with a twist. There were red squirrels in the woods around Tathwell. My mother was an avid reader and her favourite sister Hilda, who was not so inclined, once became so fed up with her nose being constantly between the pages that she kicked the book out of her hands!

They loved the servants and would go and visit 'Cook' to receive a treat. Years later my mother took me to see 'dear old Fletcher' who, as a servant at Tathwell, perhaps the cook, had married either the footman or the butler. The servants were an extension of the family, one big family. She told the story of the butler who tripped up, tray in hand, with 'Mama's' very best china crashing to the floor. 'Oh dear, oh dear' exclaimed Mama. 'It is quite all right, Madam, I am not hurt', came the reassuring reply.

My mother went to boarding school in London and she was home sick. After the holidays she returned with an unsuspecting and unexpected Lilian: 'Please Madam I have brought my sister'. Douglas, as a small boy, also, evidently, had reservations about current plans for his education. He writes:

My dear Lilian
I got your letter the other morning how did you like going to the bible class by yourself did you enjoy yourself when you went to Mrs Patchelle. I am

writing to mother and Gladys and you. Those fruits Gladys sent me are very good I have had another tooth pulled out it was a second dubble one it hurt fit to kill me I have had all my dubble teeth pulled out now at the bottom. I saw Papa on saturday on black cob but not to speak to I saw Druc he said he saw Oswald and Percy in the sledge at hallington yesterday.

Do you sledge much Have you got a pare of skates yet we are bound to write to our Mothers every sunday Mrs Hapwood plays chess with me nearly every night last tuesday Margaret Davy told Arnold to meet her on tuesday because we had a half holiday every tuesday at the begining of the month and I went with him Margaret davy said you were all wriding in the sledge and the poney galaped away and again Beart was drivigt it and it galaped away with her and threw you all out and broke the sledge all into atthoms I must stop now to work

With best love from
Your loving Brother
Douglas Botterill

Enclosed is an additional note with a line drawing of a large circular head on two small legs: 'I am nearly <u>dead</u> with <u>work</u> look at the other side' and on the other side is written: 'Please will you send my long sailors trowsers and direct them to <u>me</u> look at the other side'.[25]

On Sundays, all thirteen of them and Mama and Papa walked together from the Hall to attend divine service in Tathwell church where their spiritual needs were attended to by the vicar, Canon Foster. Doctor Foster's only child, Julia, was like a sister to the Botterills. Tragically, her mother had suffered a nervous breakdown and was a permanent patient in Littlemore Hospital. Doctor Foster was a man of great culture and learning. I remember Julia showing me his impressive Shakespeare library, a subject on which he was a considerable authority. He was revered by them all, but especially by Auntie Beatrice. His great friend was the Catholic priest in Louth.

Many years later, the family gave a stained glass window to Tathwell church in loving memory of their mother and father. On one side stands Our Lord welcoming little children to himself and on the other side stands St Vedast, the patron of the church. Below each image is a small square, framing two horses; the animals which gave them both their livelihood and their recreation and whose intelligence and strength, grace and beauty, they all so much admired.

My mother was imbued with Christian wisdom in the tradition of the Church of England. Sustained by hope, her faith was deep as was her charity; I venture to say that her life was saintly. At one time she used to attend Mass with my father; but she found our ways strange, many of those practices which went out with the Second Vatican Council. Although she regarded the Catholic Church as the 'original Church', she derived more help from the observance which was so much part of her background. One of her sustaining dicta, as old age crept on, was that 'You have to do as well as you can for as long as you can'. She would also sometimes say that, 'You owe it to other people to look as well as you can'. She certainly lived up to both these standards. She was 92 when she died.

My mother was artistic and, I think, had exquisite taste. Her art master, whose studio she attended in Lincoln, considered that she should exhibit her paintings, but she was unduly modest. Over the years, people enjoyed visiting her, not least, because she created a simple homely beauty wherever she went, a beauty in keeping with her gracious personality. She admired old things, especially antique cottage furniture, and quaint little cottages too. If they passed some dilapidated structure her brother Percy would joke, 'House for Gladys'!

The greatest joy of dawning romantic love dwelt in a look. My mother told me how she and one of the stable boys used, shyly, to catch each other's eye, nothing more, it was enough. Her great friend at school was Helen Bewsher and she fell for Helen's handsome brother, Fred; but it was not to be.

At the outbreak of the First World War all the available Botterill girls joined the VAD and they were stationed at Netley Military Hospital. I think the others were nurses but my mother elected to be a cook and worked under a 'Cordon Bleu'. At Netley they made lifelong friends. My mother had already shown a pioneering spirit in being the first in the family to have her hair cut short and, when the war was over, she ordered a motor car. I believe it was about three years before she took proud possession of a Bullnosed Morris.

She married my father on 21st September 1921, when she was aged 39 and he was 58, at St Mary's Catholic Chapel at Hedon, in the presence of Leonard S. Botterill, her eldest brother, and Thomas, my father's brother; the celebrant was Fr J. Griffin.[26] My father had already allowed her to clip his rather untidy walrus moustache into a neater appendage and this initiative was followed by other modifications to his person aimed at delivering him from a rather careless widowed state; improvements with which, I think, he readily complied. Life at Burton Pidsea was hectic in its social demands and difficult to change. Farming was entering a low ebb. My brother Gordon was born on 18th August 1923. My mother saw that this life was no longer conducive to their happiness. My father decided to retire and she brought him to the Cotswolds.

Hilda, the sister to whom my mother was so close, was already living in Cheltenham; she had married Charles Kynaston, a widower and retired farmer. Uncle Charlie was a short, rather portly man with a clipped grey beard and, like my father, he wore a bow tie. A great attraction for Gordon and myself was Uncle Charlie's large shed down in the orchard. I seem to remember he had some sort of engine installed in it. He had rigged up a fine swing from the beams in the roof and I can see him now as he swung to and fro singing 'The Blue Bells of Scotland'. The shed was full of all sorts of interesting tools and machinery. He also made excellent rhubarb wine which we discovered some years after he died.

Auntie Beatrice was probably the first link with the Cotswolds through her school days at Cheltenham Ladies College. My mother had also accompanied Julia Foster and her father when he did locums in Oxfordshire and they used to go off exploring on their bicycles. I remember her telling me how they bought bags of delicious apricots in Aynho where the apricot trees are still trained up the walls of the houses.

It was a hard decision for my mother. Everybody said that she was taking my father away from the life he knew and away from all his friends. Uncle Charlie wanted my parents to buy a certain house in Northleach; but my mother had spotted the charm of Lower Slaughter, a village which was not so well known in those days. She saw great potential in a butcher's shop and its outbuildings, all of Cotswold stone. It was separated from the river only by the small road running through the village and by a patch of grass where, under a tall lime tree, children would gather on nostalgic summer evenings when house martins and swallows swooped on flies swarming over the water. Sometimes a kingfisher would perch on the little white wooden bridge which we used to cross to collect the milk from old Mrs Wilkins who lived opposite. The ducks quacked their way up and down the stream and 'Jack', the lone swan, would pay us a visit. My mother consulted an old man about whether the river had ever flooded within his memory. Reassured, she bought the old stone butcher's shop and engaged an up-and-coming builder in the village, a man called Wheeler, to help her to convert it into the home of her dreams. Green Gates was born. Soon afterwards I was conceived. Away from the rather hectic social scene of Holderness, she prepared me for life, in serene contemplation of the tranquil beauty of the Cotswold hills; and that was the world which I entered on 17th October 1927.

To return, again, to my grandparents Thomas and Sarah Robinson their eighth child was James Francis. He was born on 11th June 1864. His godparents were 'Gulielmus Robinson', probably his uncle, and

'Elizabeth Porter', a cousin of his father. According to the Ushaw Diary, he was a student at the College from 1872-80, he entered when he was only 8 years old.[27] As a solicitor, commissioner for oaths, and clerk to the Sculcoates Rural District Council, he practised from 4, Parliament Street, Hull. He and his wife, Edith, had four children: Henry Francis, whom we have already met, farmed at Skeffling; William Francis died in infancy; Edith Monica, who married Robert Pinder; and George Francis who entered Ushaw, as a lay student, at the age of 12, in 1921, from Burstal Garth, the farm at Skeffling bought by his father in 1915.[28] Years later, a schoolfellow of George recalls:

> In the junior seminary we had to hand in our pocket-money and six old pence were doled out to us weekly for 'pop shop'. Moreover our letters home were read by the Minor Professor. George wanted to keep his own stock of pocket money. To achieve this, when he was short of money, he used to stick the stamp on his letter home upside-down, as a sign to his parents…He had no liking for study,…He was a large gangling man – loved to play goalkeeper at football – was always smiling, very likeable and amusing, always ready for a bit of boyish mischief. He was certainly a character!…He left Ushaw at the end of the school of Grammar, in July 1926. His luggage arrived back at Ushaw in Sept. 1926, but no George![29]

Uncle Frank negotiated that, in part, the Elizabeth Langstaff Fund – which will be explained later – could apply to 'members of the Robinson family who were not preparing for the Ecclesiastical state'; and Gordon and I benefited from this.

Then came the ninth child, Uncle Harry. Henry was born on 27th October 1865. His godparents were Robert Dale Middleton and Teresa Middleton. He entered Ushaw at the age of 11 in 1877 and left in 1879, his birthday is given as October 27th. One of his testimonials, that 'From J. Bell Esq. M.D., F.R.C.S., President of the Royal College of Surgeons, Edinburgh,…' dated August 1887, states: 'From the completeness of his education and excellence of his qualification, my old dresser, Mr. H. Robinson, M.B. C.M., has proved himself to be a successful student, and I have no doubt he will be also a successful and useful practitioner'.[30]

This newly qualified doctor's success was not confined to medicine. When he won the Lonsdale Cup, a race which was run only at the accession of a new Lord Lonsdale, Uncle Harry, on receiving the trophy from the new peer, unwittingly declared that he hoped to be winning it again soon.[31]

Uncle Harry had one son, referred to previously, Harry Francis

Nixon Robinson. My impression was that Uncle Harry's advice was frequently sought and readily given when members of the family were ailing. One of his dicta was said to be, that if a man under 40 complained of his heart it was his stomach that should be suspect and if a man over 40 complained of his stomach it was his heart that should be examined. He also considered that a little dirt was no harm and helped to build up resistance to disease. I heard he had such a poor sense of rhythm that, when marching with the police, to whom he was surgeon, he would be out of step far more often than could be accounted for by chance alone. He went back into practice at the age of 74, as his contribution to the war effort, and drove around Hull in a large old car which was substantially dependent on string to maintain its integrity.

I should feel privileged if my visits to Uncle Harry in the nursing home in Durham brought him a little comfort. He received spiritual consolation from Fr Meagher, a pleasant man, who was chaplain to Durham gaol. He was the brother of Dr Meagher, Vice-President of Ushaw. 'Bob Meagher' was a highly intellectual and, at the same time, very human man who used to enter into bargaining sessions with Gordon over swapping postage stamps from his valuable collection; he also looked after the goldfish in 'Prof's Parlour'.

Mary Agnes, the tenth child of Thomas and Sarah, was born at Nuthill on 14th November 1867. Her name does not appear in the baptismal register at Hedon; she must have been baptised elsewhere. I wonder whether this related to events in 1866 when:

> …an epidemic of rinderpest broke out and the Privy Council ordered all Fairs and Markets to close. When the cattle plague finally died out the Holderness farmers had lost the habit of patronising Hedon and preferred the Markets of Hull and Beverley. …If Hedon suffered because of the cattle plague it was a much greater loss for the unfortunate farmer. Some of the bitterness is revealed in an address given by Tom Robinson [my grandfather] to the Society at Hedon in 1867.
>
> "I have been deputed by the Committee of this Society [the Holderness Agricultural Society] to bring before your notice for discussion the subject of C.P.
>
> The subject is an all important one, exciting the anxiety of all classes of the Society at this present moment.
>
> We might begin from the commencement of the disease, trace its arrival from Revel, follow it in its course as it was allowed to disseminate itself through the length and breadth of the land, condemn the Government for the apathy with which they first looked on, and

afterwards in the abortive orders they issued or the Powers delegated to Inspectors and Legal Authorities, how such powers were abused, so that the Inspector Plague became almost as great a nuisance as the C.P.

I would however rather look at the present, and allow things that are past to be done with, and that the discussion we have here today may be as to what is the best course to pursue under existing circumstances. Perhaps the two great questions of the present time are the Poleaxe and Compensation. As regards the stamping out system, my opinion leads me to think that the day has long gone past when that course could have possibly been adopted with any benefit to the Country, the disease has gained such a hold in the land that the indiscriminate slaughter of all infested animals will entail such a loss to the nation as it will take many years to recover, and then there is the Power delegated to Local Authorities to order even the slaughter of healthy animals which may have been in any way in contact with those tainted by disease, truly a Stockowner holds no enviable position between the Inspector and Local Authorities.

I very much doubt if perfect isolations in infected animals, and prohibition of transit of live cattle, except for breeding and grazing purposes, were adopted, we should not be in a much better position at the end of 12 months than under the present stamping out system.

Look again at the blunder committed by inspectors. We have all read and heard of many, and this is not always made by the ignorant village farrier, but by men high in their profession. When such men as Prof. Simonds, Mr. Worms and Mr. Lipper are at variance as to what is, and what is not C.P. may we not tremble for the safety of our own herds, especially when we consider the class of men whom of necessity in many instances must be appointed Inspectors, and the terrible powers with which such men are armed – only 280 out of the 900 Inspectors appointed are members of the Vet. College. Is it not monstrous that these men can intrude themselves upon your property at any time and order the indiscriminate slaughter of your cattle? The loss already to the Country has been enormous, not so much in cattle that have died, as in those that have been slaughtered, and in those that have been sent to market as fat stock, which certainly had no pretensions to anything of the sort.

I will state to you what has been done with the disease in my own instance – I had 41 beasts at my Burton farm when the disease broke out. My Vet. farried about 10, which all died. I had the others well nursed and attended to, and without the aid of either Vet., Surgeon, Prof. Simonds or Mr. Worms we recovered 19 out of the remainder or something like two thirds, and every beast had the disease. Again at Mr. Stickney's at Ridgemont, one animal was taken ill which they immediately took clear away from the others. Three more were afterwards taken ill, in all of which they pursued the same course of isolation, the result was that one of the animals died and that although nearly three months ago, they have not had another case of C.P. I could enumerate many instances attended with equal success.

Gentlemen, I think you will agree with me that I have every reason to condemn the stamping out system, and need not wish for the interference of Inspectors and Local Authorities. All that we want from the Government is a reasonable law, and we the Agriculturists of England will obey the law, as we do other laws, without so much interference from Inspectors and Local Authorities. We as little like to be interfered with in the management of our business as any other class of men, and think we know as well how to manage it, through the treatment we sometimes meet with from inspectors and Local Authorities would lead us to infer that those Authorities are not of the same opinion.

Now Gentlemen, we come to the subject of Compensation. Compensation is truly a misnomer, we are not compensated. The Inspector comes and takes possession of our Property Stock and says if you will allow us to destroy this quietly we will pay you one half or three fourths of its value as the case may be, and this is what is termed compensation. In what manner paid? Paid by a County rate of which the tenant Farmers of England pay 9/10ths. No doubt at some future day the Government will turn round and say how liberally they treated the Farmers. After such liberal treatment how can we ever ask anything more about the Malt Tax. But if this wholesale slaughter is allowed to go on this system of compensation will never be able to meet it, and I much doubt if the Country will long submit to so dangerous and ruinous a power, placed in the hands it now is. The Government may look upon the cattle as a class question, but it is no class question, it is a Government question, for the welfare of the Nation is at stake.

The contagion has already got too great a hold of the Country for any one to imagine that its effects will be confined to Farmers. We may see their mind one after another, but at the same time commerce must lose its confidence, Landlords will look in vain for rents, and Tradesmen for customers, whilst panic and Cattle Plague stalk side by side through the land.

One word on Local Authorities. I would remind those to whom these powers are delegated to use them tenderly. A universal law issued by Act of Parliament is a very different thing from a law emanating from Local Authorities in Petty Sessional or other divisions. Englishmen have hitherto considered House, Premises and Property their own, without interference from the Government, now things are changing, our premises are entered and our cattle taken and slaughtered against our will, whilst the poor suffering heartstricken owner receives base courtesy at the hands of the Powers that be, and his family are expected to stand quietly by and witness the destruction of their property."[32]

During the recent scourge of foot and mouth disease many farmers of our own time would, no doubt, have agreed with the sentiments so eloquently expressed by baby Agnes' father. Wherever she was baptised, Aunt Agnes was certainly a staunch Catholic. Besides contributing generously to the education of Gordon and myself, Aunt Agnes was also a great source of encouragement to me in my interest in our family history and in my striving to be a doctor.

Thomas and Sarah's eleventh child, Edward, was born on 2nd January 1870. His godparents were John Richardson Johnson and Maria Anna Robinson, almost certainly Edward's sister. The Ushaw Diary lists him as entering in 1880, aged 9. Uncle Ted and I have it in common that we were both aged 10 and nearly 11 when our fathers died. He, like Henry, studied medicine in Edinburgh and subsequently he practised at Stonely in Huntingdonshire where he lived in a beautiful old thatched house. He and his wife had two daughters: Mary, who married Stanley Measures by whom she had Ann and Robert; and Cecily who married Philip Bradley and went to live in Jersey.

Cecily wrote, 'My mother was a Protestant and Mary and I brought up to be Church of England too, if we had been sons we were to be Catholics – all very amicably worked out!'. Cecily's husband, Philip, was a Catholic and he was educated by the Benedictines at Belmont. Philip's sister, Olive, was an Ursuline nun, Mère Marguerite, and she 'was in the Congo and was killed by the Simba in the uprisings, …She bravely put herself between the priests and the Simba to protect them but instead they (the Simba) threw their spears at Philip's sister and killed her… She had devoted her life to the Congolese and they in their turn were devoted to her'.[33]

I remember meeting Cecily at Aunt Agnes' when I was a student, and I was struck by her beauty. Comments which she made in a letter to Norman Cardwell, dated 28th August 1991, give a glimpse into Bramhill House in my father's widowed days:

> …Mary and I stayed with Uncle William and Mary (before she married Wreathall) and enjoyed it so much but I remember being rather in awe when taken the round of all the uncles and Aunts! We were very young and in fact our nurse came with us to help in the house – Bramhill was a lovely house… We were very fond of Mary and I kept in touch with her until she died, she stayed with my mother and father at Stonely – Uncle

William and Gladys, Gordon and John all stayed at Stonely on their way to Lower Slaughter and Philip and I went to see Aunt Gladys in her dear little house in Cheltenham how very nice she was and so artistic... Mary and I also stayed at Nuthill with Uncle Tom and Aunt Evelyn when in our teens, also rather in awe and overwhelmed by so many Uncles Aunts and Cousins!!! Uncle Tom mounted us and we had a day with the Holderness clothed in Aunt Evelyn's riding things!! We also went to a Hunt Ball – Our forebears must have owned so much land at one time and been a family of great stature – We have a snapshot of the five brothers (Uncle Tom down to my Father) all mounted on lovely horses at Nuthill, my Father being the youngest of 10 used to be very much teased! My mother who was so gentle was in awe, too, of them all when she was taken up to meet them! All long ago now but I am glad I remember it all. It must have been quite something when my Father broke away from Yorkshire to live in Huntingdonshire and marry my mother! Daddy and all of us were very fond of your mother and I have a newspaper cutting of your Mama taken after she was awarded the O.B.E. [B.E.M.] – how very nice looking she was – She also stayed at Stonely as also did Agnes many times. Agnes used to tell us how scared she was when sent out hunting on her pony, with a Mother, Father and brothers and sister who went so well and so much expected of her.[34]

And now we shall leave Thomas and Sarah's children and introduce those children's second cousin: 'Fr. "Solid" Robinson was sturdily and heavily built, so much so that Fr. Frank Irwin once alluded to him as the missioner "at whose footfall the college estate trembled" '. Thus, has Father Robert Robinson SJ walked out of his obituary and into this account![35]

Uncle Thomas described Robert, this cousin, to me as a blunt Yorkshireman who, during a visit to a house with which he was not acquainted, asked, 'Do I go upstairs or down the garden?'! Robert's father and Uncle Thomas's father were first cousins, they shared the same grandfather, Robert Robinson of Hutton Hall; and farming was in the blood. When Catherine and I visited Stonyhurst, in about 1972, to offer our two sons Shaun and Timothy to that educational establishment, the headmaster, Father Bossy, told us the story that, once, at the same time, there were three Jesuits called Robinson on the staff of Stonyhurst and they were referred to as 'Grub, Grass, and Grace'. I later learnt from Father F. J. Turner SJ that: 'Grace' was the Spiritual Father, Fr James Robinson; 'Grub' was the Minister, Fr Jim Robinson; and 'Grass' was the Procurator, my father's cousin, Fr Robert Robinson. I learnt, moreover, from Fr Holt, the Jesuit archivist, that, in the account of himself which he gave when he joined the Society, Fr Robert wrote that he was a year at Ampleforth before going on to Stonyhurst, and that his father was Thomas Robinson and his mother was Isabella Naylor. They were both Catholics and they were alive in 1885 when, on 7th September, aged 19, he began his noviciate at Manresa House.[36] His obituary by Fr de Trafford, my cousin Philip Wright Ford's old school friend, states that Robert was born at Ovington in the North Riding of Yorkshire on 23rd July 1866 and that he entered Stonyhurst College in December 1878. Fr de Trafford writes:

> Anyone who lived with Fr. "Solid" Robinson, as he was always appropriately called, could not fail to be impressed by his steady regularity, whether in spiritual duties or the monotonous routine of book-keeping. He took great pride in the accuracy of his books with his neat handwriting and he was always ready to help to disentangle the inaccuracies of others. He was a thorough Yorkshireman, outspoken at times and always to the point. His replies were brief and emphatic. When Minister at the seminary he visited a scholastic late going to bed. *Fr. 'S.'* "Go to bed". *Schol.* "But, Father, I can't sleep". *Fr. 'S.'* "Go to bed". *Schol.* "Really, Father, it's no use, I can't go to sleep". *Fr. 'S.'* "I didn't tell yer to go to sleep, I told yer to go to bed": ...His sermons were much appreciated by his Lancashire congregations at Stonyhurst where he was deservedly popular. Of his sermon 'The Christian Warrior', which he maintained could be adapted to any special occasion, he was very proud. To one of the community who asked, "Are you going to give them the 'Christian Warrior'?" he would reply with a chuckle, "Nay, that's only for big occasions"..., he was a successful farmer and very appreciative of any praise of his crops and cattle... When, in 1936, he left Stonyhurst and retired from the R.D.C. [membership of Clitheroe Rural District Council] the *Clitheroe Advertiser and Times,* referring to his departure, wrote: "Throughout the countryside – and that means the entire Ribble Valley – Fr. Robinson is known and deeply respected. His outstanding trait is an equable temperament, a capacity to take the broad view of things and a vision which enables him to grasp the effects of the benefits to be derived from modernity while holding tenaciously to tradition and to the preservation of everything handed down from the past that is worth preserving. A couple of phrases are enough for Fr. Robinson to express himself at district council meetings and they are usually not only to the point but full of worldly wit and wisdom".

My grandfather Thomas Robinson having made provision for his wife and all his children and for his wife's mother, Mary Ann Ford, died at Nuthill on 18th December 1880; he was aged 57.[37] The year before, he had won a handsome silver cup on which was engraved:[38]

HOLDERNESS HOUNDS
LARKSPUR
PRIZE DOG PUPPY
8th August, 1879.

The cause of death on the certificate appears as '[? Intent] Pneumonia 1 year, Phthisis, certified by John J. Hayes M.R.C.S.', and the informant is given as W. J. Robinson his son – my father, aged 18 at the time – who was present at his death. This fatal illness was probably pulmonary tuberculosis, with much wasting of his body. It is understandable that my father thought that there was something wrong with his throat. Two years later, in 1882, the year of my mother's birth, the German bacteriologist, Robert Koch, discovered the causative organism but many years were to elapse before effective treatment was discovered. Thomas' will was proved at York on 18th February 1881, 'Under £30,000'.

Thomas' widow, Sarah, my grandmother, was resident at 18, Cambridge Gardens, Notting Hill, with her daughter, Cecily Mary Rockliff, when she made her will on 1st August 1893. In it she refers to 'all my lands, tenements and hereditaments at Elsternwick and Lelley in the parish of Humbleton'. She directed that ten pounds yearly be paid 'to my old servant Jane Blenkin'. who was, no doubt, related to Christopher Blenkin, my grandfather's shepherd at Nuthill, whose photograph appears in the family album, 'Parterre', and who was obviously greatly esteemed. Sarah died at the age of 68, on 26th February 1895.[39]

In 1845, Thomas Robinson came to Nuthill to become a successful farmer and a wealthy man. His life, 1823-1880, spanned a period of social reform and, for Catholics in England, Newman's 'Second Spring'. In that same year John Henry Newman, who had been persuaded by his scholarship that he should belong to the Catholic Church, was received by the saintly Dominic Barberi at Littlemore. In the same village, the following year, social enlightenment brought into being the 'Oxfordshire Pauper Lunatic Asylum'; the hospital where I worked for 28 years.

But such enlightenment spread only slowly. In Ireland the potato famine, combined with social injustice, and augmented by disease, including tuberculosis, ravaged the population.

Thomas Ledwith, a convert to Catholicism, my wife Catherine's great-grandfather, died in 1866, at the age of 56, and his widow, Bridget Murray, with her five children, was evicted from their home at Knockdomney in the County Westmeath. She returned to the little thatched house where her family farmed for 300 years, Ballymurray, the land of the Murrays.[40]

Daniel O'Connell, that great statesman, described as 'The King of the Beggars', educated at the English College at St Omer and the English College at Douai, had achieved the Roman Catholic Emancipation Act of 1829.[41] Leys comments, 'it was owing to an Irishman that in 1829 the Catholics of England gained the freedom to be truly Catholic and wholly English – a freedom for which they had prayed for 270 years'.[42]

More important, in some ways, however, than the Emancipation Act, was the second Relief Act of 1791, whereby Catholics were no longer obliged, as they had been under pain of punishment since the Act of Uniformity of 1559, to attend the services of the Church of England on Sundays and holy-days.[43] This Act also 'gave legal existence to registered Catholic places of worship, and Catholics were admitted to the professions'.[44] When Father Joseph Swinburn laid the foundation stone of the Catholic Church of Saint Mary and Saint Joseph, at Hedon, on 12th August 1803, advantage was being taken of this reform.

Father Swinburn had entered the English College at Douai in 1788 and had been a prisoner at Doullens in 1794. He returned to England and was ordained at Crook Hall, the precursor of Ushaw, on 3rd April 1800. The next year he came to the mission at Hedon where he remained for 39 years.[45] He was succeeded by: Henry Newsham; William Parsons; Francis Trappes; and, in 1851, by Robert Tate DD who became President of Ushaw and whose photograph appears in our family album 'Parterre'.[46] On 14th April 1853 he, in turn, was succeeded by the Rev. Joseph Cottam Fisher, a well-known Ushaw priest, who was just in time to baptise my aunt, Sarah Robinson, on 20th September that year.[47] He remained at Hedon until 1885 and, no doubt, baptised her younger sisters and brothers. He also appears in the album 'Parterre' where his photograph suggests a man of considerable refinement.

Perhaps the opportunity afforded by this Relief Act also contributed to my grandfather's decision that his sons should enter the professions rather than become farmers. The University of Oxford would not have been available to them. Although Oxford had excused religious Tests and opened its doors to Catholic students in 1854, the English Catholic hierarchy, which had been restored in 1850, 'retained its own ban so that as a general rule (broken only by a dozen or so students at any time) Catholics were still not formally permitted to become members of the University. Only in 1896 after prolonged wrangles, was this ban grudgingly lifted, allowing a full Catholic return to Oxford'.[48] Alberic Stacpoole, quoted here, goes on to say that in the same year 'a house was purchased at 36, Beaumont Street and at length a resident chaplain was secured, Canon Arthur Kennard of University College. Sir Everard Radcliffe Bart., who arrived in Oxford in 1901, recalled him'.

The Radcliffes are a distinguished Yorkshire family and I am proud to count among my friends Father Timothy Radcliffe who has recently been Master General of the Dominican Order. Evidence will later emerge which is suggestive that there were previous friendships between our two families. The Dominican Friars returned to Oxford in 1921. They had first arrived in 1221, when the Order 'conscious that their special work was to preserve Catholic doctrine against heretics, determined to make foundations as soon as possible in every university in Europe'.[49]

The families which converged to give birth to these, my immediate ancestors, must now be traced along their divergent ways into Mediaeval England.

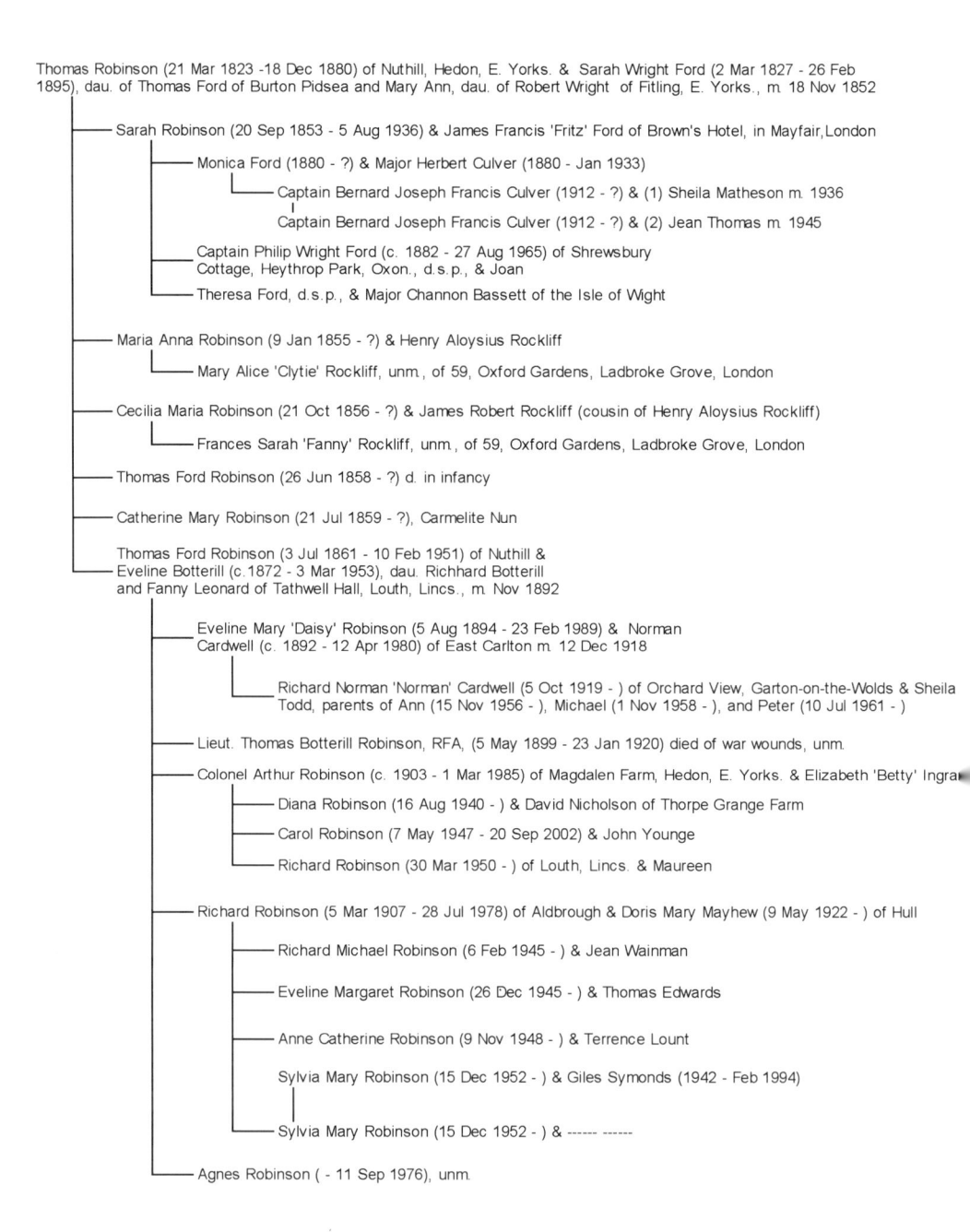

1. Descendants of Thomas Robinson and Sarah Wright Ford, of Nuthill, E. Yorkshire (1)
down to the Thomas Ford Robinson branch

Thomas Robinson (21 Mar 1823 -18 Dec 1880) of Nuthill, Hedon, E. Yorks. & Sarah Wright Ford (2 Mar 1827 - 26 Feb 1895), dau. of Thomas Ford of Burton Pidsea and Mary Ann, dau. of Robert Wright of Fitling, E. Yorks., m. 18 Nov 1852

- Sarah Robinson (20 Sep 1853 - 5 Aug 1936) & James Francis 'Fritz' Ford of Brown's Hotel, in Mayfair, London
  - Monica Ford (1880 - ?) & Major Herbert Culver (1880 - Jan 1933)
    - Captain Bernard Joseph Francis Culver (1912 - ?) & (1) Sheila Matheson m. 1936
    - Captain Bernard Joseph Francis Culver (1912 - ?) & (2) Jean Thomas m. 1945
  - Captain Philip Wright Ford (c. 1882 - 27 Aug 1965) of Shrewsbury Cottage, Heythrop Park, Oxon., d.s.p., & Joan
  - Theresa Ford, d.s.p., & Major Channon Bassett of the Isle of Wight
- Maria Anna Robinson (9 Jan 1855 - ?) & Henry Aloysius Rockliff
  - Mary Alice 'Clytie' Rockliff, unm., of 59, Oxford Gardens, Ladbroke Grove, London
- Cecilia Maria Robinson (21 Oct 1856 - ?) & James Robert Rockliff (cousin of Henry Aloysius Rockliff)
  - Frances Sarah 'Fanny' Rockliff, unm., of 59, Oxford Gardens, Ladbroke Grove, London
- Thomas Ford Robinson (26 Jun 1858 - ?) d. in infancy
- Catherine Mary Robinson (21 Jul 1859 - ?), Carmelite Nun
- Thomas Ford Robinson (3 Jul 1861 - 10 Feb 1951) of Nuthill & Eveline Botterill (c.1872 - 3 Mar 1953), dau. Richhard Botterill and Fanny Leonard of Tathwell Hall, Louth, Lincs., m. Nov 1892
  - Eveline Mary 'Daisy' Robinson (5 Aug 1894 - 23 Feb 1989) & Norman Cardwell (c. 1892 - 12 Apr 1980) of East Carlton m. 12 Dec 1918
    - Richard Norman 'Norman' Cardwell (5 Oct 1919 -) of Orchard View, Garton-on-the-Wolds & Sheila Todd; parents of Ann (15 Nov 1956 -), Michael (1 Nov 1958 -), and Peter (10 Jul 1961 -)
  - Lieut. Thomas Botterill Robinson, RFA, (5 May 1899 - 23 Jan 1920) died of war wounds, unm.
  - Colonel Arthur Robinson (c. 1903 - 1 Mar 1985) of Magdalen Farm, Hedon, E. Yorks. & Elizabeth 'Betty' Ingram
    - Diana Robinson (16 Aug 1940 -) & David Nicholson of Thorpe Grange Farm
    - Carol Robinson (7 May 1947 - 20 Sep 2002) & John Younge
    - Richard Robinson (30 Mar 1950 -) of Louth, Lincs. & Maureen
  - Richard Robinson (5 Mar 1907 - 28 Jul 1978) of Aldbrough & Doris Mary Mayhew (9 May 1922 -) of Hull
    - Richard Michael Robinson (6 Feb 1945 -) & Jean Wainman
    - Eveline Margaret Robinson (26 Dec 1945 -) & Thomas Edwards
    - Anne Catherine Robinson (9 Nov 1948 -) & Terrence Lount
    - Sylvia Mary Robinson (15 Dec 1952 -) & Giles Symonds (1942 - Feb 1994)
    - Sylvia Mary Robinson (15 Dec 1952 -) & ------ ------
- Agnes Robinson (- 11 Sep 1976), unm.

2. Descendants of Thomas Robinson and Sarah Wright Ford, of Nuthill, E. Yorkshire (2)
below the Thomas Ford Robinson branch

Thomas Robinson (21 Mar 1823 -18 Dec 1880) of Nuthill & Sarah Wright Ford (2 Mar 1827 - 26 Feb 1895) of Burton Pidsea m. 18 Nov 1852

- William Joseph Robinson (6 Nov 1862 - 14 Sep 1938) of Bramhill House, Burton Pidsea, E. Yorks. & (1) Helen 'Nelly' Rockliff (c. 1860 - 15 Mar 1911)
  - Mary Helen Robinson (17 Apr 1887 - ?) & Clement Wreathall of Cottingham, E. Yorks.
    - Henry Clement Wreathall
    - Patricia Ann Wreathall & Basil Thompson m. 1952
  - Thomas 'Tommy' Robinson (26 Feb 1890 - 15 Aug 1924) d. largely as a result of World War 1, unm.
  - Dorothy Mary Robinson (29 Dec 1891 - 18 Oct 1892)
- William Joseph Robinson (6 Nov 1862 - 14 Sep 1938) & (2) Gladys Margaret Botterill (4 Sep 1882 - 1 Jan 1975) dau. Richard Botterill and Fanny Leonard of Tathwell Hall, Louth, Lincs., m. 21 Sep 1921
  - William Gordon Robinson (18 Aug 1923 - 15 Nov 2001) of 6, Malvern Priors, Malvern Place, Cheltenham, Glos. & Joan Marian Eustace (18 Jan 1924 -)
    - Susan Mary Robinson (1 Mar 1956 -) & Clifford Paul Sherman (28 Apr 1955 -)
    - David Eustace Gordon Robinson (23 Jan 1958 -) & Christine Patricia Sampson (6 Apr 1959 -)
  - Doctor John Richard Robinson (17 Oct 1927 -) of 480, Banbury Rd., Oxford, & Catherine Josephine Ledwith (24 Mar 1938 -), dau. of John Ledwith of Ballymurray, Co. Westmeath, and Margaret Keegan of Kinnegad, Co. Westmeath, m. 16 Sep 1961
    - Margaret Mary Robinson (23 Jun 1962 -) & Cornelius Francis O'Connell (16 Jan 1962 -) of Cork m. 3 Aug 2002
    - John William 'Shaun' Robinson (31 May 1963 -) of Norwich & Tuula Nicholson (20 Jul 1963 -)
    - Timothy Paul Robinson (15 Jul 1964 -) of Oxford & Helen Louise Guyatt (31 Jan 1967 -) m. 17 Feb 2001
    - Nicola Frances Robinson (4 Dec 1966 - 7 Sep 2000), unm.
- James Francis Robinson (11 Jun 1864 - ?) of Burstal Garth, Skeffling, E. Yorks.
  - Henry Francis Robinson of Burstal Garth & Joan, parents of James
  - William Francis Robinson, died in infancy
  - Edith Monica Robinson & Robert Pinder
  - George Francis Robinson
- Doctor Henry Robinson (27 Oct 1865 - c. 1943) & ------
  - Harry Francis Nixon Robinson & ------
    - Douglas Saville Robinson
    - Brian Nixon Robinson
- Mary Agnes Robinson (14 Nov 1867 - ?), d.s.p. & Thomas Eeles (second wife), of Sutton, Surrey
- Doctor Edward Robinson (2 Jul 1870 - ?) of Stonely & ------ Welstead of Stonely, Huntingdonshire
  - Mary Robinson & Stanley Measures
    - Ann Measures
    - Robert Measures
  - Cecily Robinson & Philip Bradley of Jersey

CHAPTER III

Hutton Hall: a Nursery for the 'Second Spring'

*'In a higher world it is otherwise, but here below to live
is to change, and to be perfect is to have changed often'.*
John Henry Newman[1]

An old man was approaching his death.

At Hutton Hall the new life of spring was now maturing in the warmth of long summer days and Thomas Robinson my great-grandfather, in his eighty sixth year, was rallying from illness. His son, William, wrote to the Very Reverend Robert Canon Thompson:

> Hutton Hall
> June 25th 1867
>
> My Dear Cousin
>
> At my Father's request I enclose your cheque for £10-16-4 for the Dalton rent after the property tax has been deducted, the receipts for which I enclose along with the cheque. My Father I am glad to say is going on as well as we can expect and the Docter [sic] says he has no doubt but he will so far recover as to be able to walk about. It is really wonderful at his advanced age. He is now able to sit up an hour or two every day. It is a long time since we have had the pleasure of seeing you in this neighbourhood, I can only say that we shall be very glad indeed to see you. Mrs R. I am glad to say is well and joins me in kind regards to you and believe me
>
> Your affectionate Cousin
> W. Robinson
>
> The Revd R. Thompson[2]

Thomas would live to hear, once again, the angel's 'good tidings of great joy', but then, as his reflections on his long life were coming to a close, a man of his disposition may well have said, with St Paul, 'For I am even now ready to be sacrificed: and the time of my dissolution is at hand'.[3]

Thomas was well acquainted with death. The fifteenth anniversary of the death of his wife, Sarah, would come up in January and the following month the anniversary of the death of their daughter Mary Ann when she was only 15. Their eldest son, Robert, had died in 1847 from 'General Dropsy' when he was only 33. Thomas and Sarah's little son James had died when he was only 5 years old.[4]

James was baptised at Wycliffe on 21st January 1822 and his godfather Cuthbert Watson was, no doubt, well qualified for the task. He was nicknamed the 'Pope of Ovington' because of his ardour for the old faith; a pragmatic enthusiasm expressed, not only in bearing the main cost of building St Mary's Catholic Church at Wycliffe which opened in 1849, but, also, as indicated by the following inscription on a tablet above a public water tap in Hutton Magna village:[5]

> This supply of water
> was brought here from near
> Warden Hill
> a distance of 1,200 yards, at the sole expense of
> Cuthbert Watson Esq.
> of Ovington who, for 60 years has been the
> confidential agent of the Wycliffe Estate
> for which great boon the inhabitants of
> Hutton
> erect this tablet to express to him their
> gratitude and heartfelt thanks

Cuthbert Watson was a household name in our family. As my old Uncle Thomas used to say when asked whether he was actually a relation, 'Well, he was nearly related'; apparently he nearly married one of the Robinson girls. Cuthbert had lost his first wife, Ann Dale, the autumn before James was christened; they had only been married eight years.[6] James's godmother was his aunt Anne Brown, his mother's sister, who was to become Cuthbert Watson's second wife; and by whom he had a son William who died when he was fifteen months old. Anne, herself, died on 17th January 1850, at the age of 64; and Cuthbert died on 19th February 1859, he was 81.[7]

Thomas Robinson of Hutton Hall lived to be 86. He died from 'Debility and Erysipelas' on 10th February 1868.[8] A common factor to the causes of the deaths of himself and his children may have been the virulence, at that time, of the haemolytic streptococcus.

Richard Brown my great-great-great-grandfather, who was described in the Returns of Papists for the Diocese of Chester, 1767, as a 60 year old farmer of Aldbrough who had resided there for twenty-two years, provided a kind of ancestral glue for our family.[9] His daughter Ann married Lawrence Thompson of Lane Head and their son Lawrence married Elizabeth, sister of Thomas Robinson of Hutton Hall.[10] Richard Brown's other daughter, Dorothy, married Robert Dale of Hutton Fields; and Richard Brown's son, James, married Robert Dale's sister Ann.[11] James Brown and Ann Dale had two daughters, Sarah and Anne. Sarah Brown married Thomas Robinson of Hutton Hall and, as we have seen, Anne Brown was Cuthbert Watson's second wife.

The life and humour of those days are well illustrated in a picture entitled 'The Crack Team of 1858'. It depicts a crested carriage dashing past Burton Constable. There are four in hand: fine high spirited horses with cocked ears and nostrils flaring, their coats glistening over rippling muscles; the expression of each is different, painted with intimate knowledge. Two liveried grooms sit on the pillion. High up on the front of the carriage are five elegant gentlemen, the oldest and most upright of whom is Cuthbert Watson, all in black silk top hats, except one which is grey. Careful scrutiny reveals that the owner of the grey hat appears to be missing! Had he failed to turn up? The team was the property of Major T. C. Constable of Burton Constable.[12] I have in my possession an invitation whereby the Major's great-nephew, Lieut. Colonel Chichester-Constable and his wife Mrs Chichester-Constable request the pleasure of the company of Mr and Mrs W. Robinson, my father and mother, on the occasion of the marriage of their daughter Blanche to Major Lancelot Arthur Eddis, RFA, at Marton Church, and afterwards at Burton Constable.

Lieut. Colonel Chichester-Constable's great-grandfather was Thomas Hugh Clifford of Tixall in Staffordshire. Joseph Ward of Tixall, an Agent for the Cliffords, makes the following entries in his diary under 1838:

June 8th
…my father went with Mr. Watson round the Haywood side & dined with him & Mr. Clifford & Mr. Robinson.

June 9th
…Mr. Robinson that is Mr. Watson's nephew went to Stafford with my father on the hack horse.

June 11th
Went with Mr. Robinson to see Oscott college.

June 12th
My father dined with Mr. Watson & Robinson at 3 o'clock.

The Mr. Robinson in these entries was almost certainly Robert Robinson, aged 25 at the time, the eldest son of Thomas Robinson of Hutton Hall and Sarah Brown who, of course, was Cuthbert Watson's sister-in-law.

Thomas Hugh Clifford was a great nephew of Amy Clifford, the wife of Cuthbert Tunstall, son of Francis Tunstall of Wycliffe and Cecily Constable, who changed his name to Constable (as did those who followed him) on inheriting the Burton Constable estate in 1718. Thomas Hugh Clifford died in 1823 and the Mr Clifford of the diary was probably a relative.

Cuthbert Watson wrote to Joseph Ward, from Ovington, near Wycliffe the home of Charles Clifford, on 19th June 1842, as Joseph was about to embark for New Zealand:

Dear Sir,
I arrived safe at home on Tuseday [sic] night, I left London on Tuseday morning and got home a little after ten o'clock that night therefore you see I can come from London sooner than I can come from Staffordshire. I did not see Mr. Chas. Clifford which I was sorry for, he called on Monday at my Hotell [sic] & left his card with invitation to breakfast with him next morning, but I was obliged to come away at six o'clock & of course did not see him… I hope you were merry on the Thursday after I left you,… There has not been any rain here since I left home, we want it very much but I think crops are looking much better here than about Great Haywood, but it will be sometime before we can begin to mow, the grass has to grow first. …Do you think your Brother will have time to look after the Tenants at Haywood &c. – Do you think Francis Ward could do it as he would have more time than your Brother.
    I am Dear Sir
    Yrs. most truly
    Cuthbert Watson[13]

It would seem that the Robinson involvement with the Tunstalls of Wycliffe, which we shall hear about later, continued with their descendants who came into Burton Constable. It is not surprising that several members of our family had a print of 'The Crack Team of 1858'.

In more recent times, Uncle Thomas' grandson Richard enquired of me: 'Did you know the fine portrait of him [Cuthbert Watson] by Sir John Watson Gordon which hung on the stairs at my parent's farm at Magdalen? He frightened us to bed as children'.[14]

Thomas and Sarah's two youngest sons, Thomas Robinson of Nuthill, my grandfather, and William Robinson of Hutton Hall, lived to be successful farmers with families of their own; and, what was more important, they 'kept the faith'.

Thomas was baptised, according to the Wycliffe Register, on 23rd March 1823 and his sponsors were Adam Dale and Ann Chambers.[15] William was baptised on 26th August 1824 and his sponsors were Lawrence and Elizabeth Thompson.[16]

These two brothers must have wondered about the lives of their older Thompson cousins who lived half a mile down the road, at the Lane Head. Thomas and William's aunt Elizabeth, their father's sister, and her husband, Lawrence Thompson, had five children whose ages, when Thomas was born, were: Robert, aged 15; James, 13; William, 12; Ann, 10; and John, 8.[17] Robert and James, who were away at Ushaw, would only be seen during the summer vacation and John, when he was aged 13, went to join his brothers in training for the priesthood.[18] Robert and James were ordained in 1835, the year that Thomas himself went to Ushaw, and James taught there until 1836. John was ordained in 1839, the year that Thomas left school.

William Thompson is not listed in the Ushaw College Diary. He, evidently, continued farming at Lane Head. William married Maria, the eldest daughter of John and Sarah Robinson of South Park in Holderness, in 1844; he was 34 and she was 35.[19] Maria had been educated at the Bar Convent in York.[20] William and Maria lived at Lane Head where they were joined by Maria's mother, Sarah, after the death of her husband, John, who was interred in the Catholic Chapel at Hedon on 4th August 1846.[21] Maria's brother Samuel continued to farm at South Park. Sarah, herself, died on 12th October 1856 and she is buried in Hutton Magna graveyard.[22] The next year, on November 15th, Samuel died; and William and Maria moved to South Park, where they would have been close neighbours of Thomas, at Nuthill, just over half a mile away as the crow flies.[23]

When Lawrence Thompson, the future father of the three priests, Robert, James, and John, and husband of Elizabeth Robinson, was baptised at Wycliffe on 4th March 1777, his godparents were his uncle James Brown and his aunt Dorothy Dale and supplying for James Brown, on that occasion, was Anthony Langstaff.[24] Anthony's wife, Margaret Langstaff, and Adam Dale were the godparents of Lawrence's brother Richard when he was baptised. Furthermore, Anthony and Margaret Langstaff appear as godparents to Robinson children of that generation. Thus, the mind is prepared for finding a Charitable Trust called 'Elizabeth Langstaff's fund' the terms of which are as follows:

The Foundation

1. In this scheme the expression "the Foundation" means the Foundation of Elizabeth Langstaff for the education and maintenance of youths for the ecclesiastical state, held in connection with St. Cuthbert's College, Ushaw, in the County of Durham for the benefit of the respective descendants of William Pratt, late of Richmond, Yorkshire, wine merchant, and of James Brown the elder, late of Aldborough near Richmond aforesaid, which Foundation is comprised in a Declaration of Trust dated 16th. November 1818.[25]

There appear to have been no further vocations to the secular priesthood after Robert, James, and John. Uncle Thomas was one of the Trustees and his brother James Francis Robinson, acting as solicitor, in a letter to the Board of Education dated 22nd July 1937, gives the following information: The Pratt family had become extinct; of James Brown's three children, a son died without issue, and Ann who married Cuthbert Watson left no issue; only his daughter, Sarah, who married my great-grandfather, Thomas Robinson of Hutton Hall, had issue.

Thomas and Sarah sent their sons to school at Ushaw. Robert went there when he was 14, in 1828, during the Vice-Presidency of the young Robert Tate; but he was only there from May until December.

The Ushaw Diary lists the entry of Thomas to the College, 'from Wycliffe', at the age of 12, in 1835. Why was Thomas listed as coming from Wycliffe? This may simply have been because Hutton Hall was on the Wycliffe estate. Other possibilities are: that he was staying with his godfather at Wycliffe Grange, perhaps to further his education; or he may have been there in relation to the death of his sister Mary Ann in February that year.

When Thomas went to Ushaw, John Briggs was President and Joseph Cottam Fisher, was Prefect of Studies. As we have seen, Joseph Cottam Fisher, later, as the parish priest of Hedon, baptised Thomas' children: my father and his brothers and sisters. Before Thomas left in 1839, the famous Charles Newsham, who was to achieve so much in the embellishment of the college during his long reign of 26 years, had become the sixth President.

As Thomas left, so William went to Ushaw and the diary lists him as aged 15 at entry from Hutton Hall.[26] He remained there two years. In his second year, Robert Tate, who was then chaplain to Sir Walter Vavasour at Hazlewood Castle and missioner to the local community, where he was also able to pursue his sporting interests of hunting and fishing with the local gentry, returned to Ushaw for his second period as Vice-President, albeit a little reluctantly, at the invitation of Charles Newsham.

A glimpse into life at Hutton Hall in those days is caught between the stone gateposts: on one is carved 8 and on the other 9; apparently the work of Thomas and his brother William. When their father might ask, 'Now then, when did you two lads come in last night', they could truthfully reply that they returned between 8 and 9![27]

The census of the parish of Hutton Magna, on 9th June 1841, finds Thomas and William at Hutton Hall together with their mother, Sarah, and also: Elizabeth Glover, aged 20; Sarah Green, aged 15; Genny Buckle, aged 15; and Anthony Mitchell, aged 15; all of whom are likely to have been servants.[28]

The census of 6th August 1851 no longer includes Thomas but the following names appear: Thomas' father, Thomas Robinson, aged 69, Farmer, 445 acres, born Hutton; Sarah, aged 66, his wife, born Aldbrough; William, aged 26, born Hutton, working on the farm; Sarah Green, aged 26, and Mary Rowell, aged 27, both house servants; and Henry Hall, aged 20, Charles Roper, aged 17, and John Eeles, aged 14, all farm servants.[29]

Robert Tate again left Ushaw for the mission in 1849 and in 1851 he went to Hedon where Thomas, my grandfather, had been farming at Nuthill for six years. Perhaps he had an occasional day's hunting with my grandfather? Robert Tate certainly had a prominent place in our family photograph album.

William Robinson of Hutton Hall married Elizabeth Hunt. They had five children and must have felt that the future of their branch of the family was assured; but it was not to be so.[30]

On 28th April 1928 an article appeared in the Darlington and Stockton Times, entitled, 'Tudor house to change hands after 300 years. Hutton Hall – The home of the Robinson family. A story in stone'. Thomas, the third of William and Elizabeth's children, the elderly bachelor whom I met at Uncle Harry's funeral, was interviewed for the article:

> The present occupier (of Hutton Hall) Mr. Thomas Robinson, who has upheld the prestige of his forefathers in regard to the manner in which he has cultivated the holding, has decided to relinquish it in order to concentrate his energies on his own property at Newsham Grange –... After his father's death in 1884 Mr. Robinson, in conjunction with his brother, William, carried on the farm until the latter's death in 1914 since when he has carried on single handed. He is an all-round sportsman and in his younger days he was a keen follower of the Zetland hounds. His well known horse "Silvertail" ridden by its owner proved an easy winner of the farmers race for the Zetland Cup in 1892, upsetting the calculations of many of the knowing ones.

Mr. Robinson's father had a wide reputation as a breeder of coach horses. He was a prominent figure at markets and fairs in the district, and his services as a judge of horses were in constant demand in agricultural shows.[31]

In his will of 19th February 1879, William Robinson of Hutton Hall refers to, 'my freehold estate called Newsham Grange consisting of a dwelling house and one hundred and fifteen acres of land or thereabouts…' He also refers to, 'my freehold cottage situate in Queen Street Barnard Castle…' and to, 'the several farms now occupied by me under Sir Frederick Augustus Talbot Clifford Constable Baronet and Christopher Cradock Esquire'. Referring to a codicil to this will, made on 5th November 1884, the witnesses, William Eaton and M. E. E. Hodgson, state, about William Robinson, this successful farmer educated at Ushaw, that he 'appeared fully to understand the same and made his mark [a simple X – no doubt too ill to sign] thereunto in our presence'. Thirteen days later, on 18th November 1884, at the age of 60, and just one month short of four years after the death of his brother Thomas of Nuthill, he died. The gross amount of his personal estate was £9,520-16-1. His wife, Elizabeth, died on 18th April 1902 at the age of 75. They are commemorated together on a gravestone in Hutton Magna graveyard. I have been told, about Elizabeth, that she would tolerate nothing short of spotless white sheets after they had been laundered.[32]

William, the eldest brother of Thomas Robinson of Newsham Grange who was interviewed, was unmarried; he died in 1914. Thomas' second brother, Robert, who was a doctor, was married but he died without issue. In his will of 26th July 1946, Thomas states, 'I give devise and bequeath all the rest and residue of my real and personal estate…to pay and divide the same equally between the widow of my brother Robert and my said housekeeper Ethel Jane Alsop absolutely'. Thomas' sister, Mary Elizabeth, died unmarried at the age of 46 on 27th December 1916. On her death certificate she is described as 'Domestic housekeeper (Farm House)'; and the cause of death was: '1. Schirrhus of Breast. 2. Operations Recurrence. Certified by Robb. Robinson M.B.' Under the heading 'signature, description and residence of informant' appears the entry 'F. J. Robinson, Brother, Present at the death, Wycliffe, Warkworth'. Francis James Robinson was married but without issue.[33] Thomas, himself, died on 22nd November 1950 at the age of 82. He and his sister, Mary Elizabeth, share a gravestone in Hutton Magna graveyard.[34] But, now, we must return to William of Hutton Hall's letter to his to his cousin the Rev. Robert Thompson.

Robert Thompson had been the missioner at Nun Monkton, seven miles north-west of York, since 1862 when the mission of

Linton-upon-Ouse, two miles further north, was moved there; and he was building a new church in the Gothic style. He had come there from Bishop Thornton, which lies two miles north-west of Ripley Castle, and, prior to that, he had served at: Aiskew, Bedale; Ackworth Grange, Pontefract; and St Patrick's, Leeds, following his ordination at Ushaw in 1835.[35]

Elizabeth, the mother of the Thompson cousins, was born on 3rd February 1773 and baptised by the midwife the same day because she was in danger; and the official ceremony was on 13th February. Her godfather was Hugh Tootell, steward to Marmaduke Tunstall Esq. Lord of the Manor of Wycliffe. Her godmother was Sarah Dale, wife of the older Adam Dale of Wycliffe Grange.

All the Thompson cousins were baptised at Wycliffe Hall. Robert, the eldest, was baptised on 1st July 1807; and his godmother was Mrs Ann Brown of Aldbrough, Sarah Brown's mother, a daughter of Adam Dale of Wycliffe Grange. He went to school at Sedgley Park in 1820 and proceeded to Ushaw in 1822, when the college was well established under its second President, John Gillow.

The following year, Robert was joined at Ushaw by his brother James, who went to Sedgley Park in 1822. His godfather was Ann Brown's husband, James Brown of Aldbrough. James Thompson was also ordained in 1835 and remained teaching at Ushaw until 1836. But, the next year, on 31st August, he died.

The godmother of William Thompson, who did not go to Ushaw, the third of Elizabeth's children, was Dorothy Robinson, his mother's eldest sister.

Elizabeth then had a little girl, Ann. Her godfather was Thomas Robinson of Hutton Hall himself; and her godmother was his second eldest sister, Mrs Ann Chambers.

Robert and James Thompson were joined at Ushaw by Elizabeth's youngest child, John, in 1827. John was born in 1814, just under a year before the Battle of Waterloo. His godmother was his aunt Cecily Robinson, the sister next to Thomas; she was aged 35 at the time.

The following sketch gives a glimpse into John's childhood:

> His excellent parents, the Catholic type of past generations, assiduously guarded him from evil. He was a sprightly child, stout, robust, active, fearless of danger. Once when walking out with his Aunt and godmother Cecily Robinson, he broke his bounds and ran into the middle of the road, thoughtless of the danger to which he was exposing himself. A horse at full gallop tore down the road where little John remained; the horse leaped over the child, leaving him untouched. The feelings of his Aunt and of his

Gordon and John at Green Gates in 1929. The head of Nurse Luty can just be seen above the wall. Nurse Luty was from Louth in Lincolnshire. She looked after Gordon as an infant, at Burton Pidsea, became a great family friend, and used to come on holiday with us to Southsea. Nellie Forty used to look after us at Lower Slaughter. Our mother would affectionately describe them both as 'Treasures'.

2 St Cuthbert's College, Ushaw: where, over the course of three generations, fifteen members of my family went to school.

3 The Catholic church of Our Lady and St Kenelm at Stow-on-the-Wold, in 1988. The church was founded in 1918 by Count George de Serionne and it was based on a disused Church of England school.

Dr Robert Tate: Vice-President of Ushaw from 1828 to 1830 and again from 1840 to 1849, the latter period overlapping with the time when my great-uncle, William Robinson of Hutton Hall, was there (1839-41). In 1849 Robert Tate left Ushaw for 'the mission' and in 1851 went to Hedon where William's brother, my grandfather Thomas Robinson, had been farming for six years, at Nuthill. Robert Tate returned to Ushaw as President in 1863 and remained there until his death in 1876. Thus, he was President during the first four years of my father's time at Ushaw (1872-78). He had a prominent place in our family album.

Father Christopher Flanagan playing cards with Uncle Thomas at Nuthill. 'Flanney' was Parish Priest at Marton and Chaplain at Burton Constable. It must be towards evening – the whiskey decanter has been brought out!

6 A Holderness Hunt group, taken in about 1925. Left to right: my father's elder brother, Thomas; Charlie Littleworth, the huntsman, mounted; my father; my brother, Gordon, in the arms of my mother; Uncle Thom[as'] eldest daughter, my cousin Daisy, with her son, Norman Cardwell, on his pony.

7 Aunt Eveline out hunting: my mother's sister, Uncle Thomas' wife.

8 My cousin Daisy (fourth from the right): in the presence of Queen Elizabeth and Princess Elizabeth. Daisy has been decorated with the British Empire Medal for her gallantry. She captured, single handed and unarmed, an armed Luftwaffe parachutist who landed near her house, on the Yorkshire East Coast, in the summer of 1940, when an imminent German invasion was expected.

9 Lieut. Thomas Botterill Robinson RFA: my cousin, eldest son of Uncle Thomas and Aunt Eveline. He died of his war wounds at the age of twenty, on 23rd January 1920.

10 Gladys Margaret Botterill, (1882-1975): my mother, when she served as a cook in the VAD (Voluntary Aid Detachment) at Netley Hospital, in World War I.

11 William Joseph Robinson, (1862-1938): my father.

12 Sarah (1853-1936): my father's eldest sister, grandmother of Bernard Culver who used to discuss family history with her. Bernard described her, in later years, as 'a most intellectual and sweet old lady'.

13 James Francis Ford, 'Fritz Ford': husband of my father's sister Sarah. They owned 'Browns Hotel' in Mayfair – an establishment favoured by country gentlefolk when they came up to London.

4 Catherine: born in 1859, my father's sister; before and after she entered the Carmelite Order which she joined in 1876/7.

5 Uncle Harry (1865-c.1943): my father's brother Henry, when he qualified MB CM at Edinburgh University at the age of 21.

16 Mary Agnes (1867-c.1965): my father's youngest sister, with whom I used to discuss family history.

17 Richard Botterill (1831-1911) of Tathwell Hall: my mother's father. The photograph is autographed and dated January 1st 1909.

18 Fanny Leonard (1844-1923): my mother's mother.

19 Sarah Wright Ford (1827-1895) of Burton Pidsea, East Yorkshire: my father's mother.

Thomas Robinson (1823-1880) of Nuthill, Yorkshire: my father's father.

21 Tathwell Hall, Louth, Lincolnshire: the gardener and two of the Botterill girls, I think Mildred and Lilian

22 Helen Botterill's wedding when she married David Herbert, 'Cheena', who was a clergyman at Llanfairpwllgwyngyll, on the island of Anglesey. Cheena used to bathe in the Menai Strait daily, winter and summer. Left to right, back row: (between central pillars) Leonard; unknown man; Percy; middle row: unknown cleric; Oswald; Harold; Richard Botterill; David Herbert with Helen; Fanny Botterill; Ada; Doug; unknown cleric; front row, seated: Mildred; Lilian; Gladys, my mother; Hilda; unknown little girl; Beatrice.

The older Botterill children with their parents, from left to right: Helen, the eldest, nursing Ada, (...ard the second eldest is missing and was probably away at school); Eveline; Harold in front of the ... Oswald; Percy in front of the pillar; Richard Botterill my grandfather; Fanny Botterill (née Leonard) ...andmother with Beatrice on her knee.

The younger Botterill children, left to right: Douglas, the youngest; Hilda; Lilian; Mildred; Gladys, my ...er; Ada.

25 Elizabeth Foster (1804-1876): wife of Richard Botterill (1802-1855) of Garton Fields, East Yorkshire; my grandfather Richard Botterill's mother (not to be confused with the Fosters of Charnock Richard).

26 John Leonard (1807-1890) of Ryhill Manor, E: Yorkshire: Fanny Leonard's father.

27 Richard Botterill: my mother's father, about the time of his marriage to Fanny Leonard, 17th November 1864.

28 Fanny Leonard of Ryhill Manor: my mother's m

hn Leonard and his wife, Elizabeth, outside their home, Ryhill Manor.

30 Hutton Hall: the Tudor Manor House of Hutton Magna on the Wycliffe Estate, North Yorkshire, which came into the hands of the Tunstall family in 1614; the home of the Robinson family for 300 years The photograph was probably taken around 1880.

[William] Robinson (1824-1884) of Hutton [Hall,] my father's uncle.

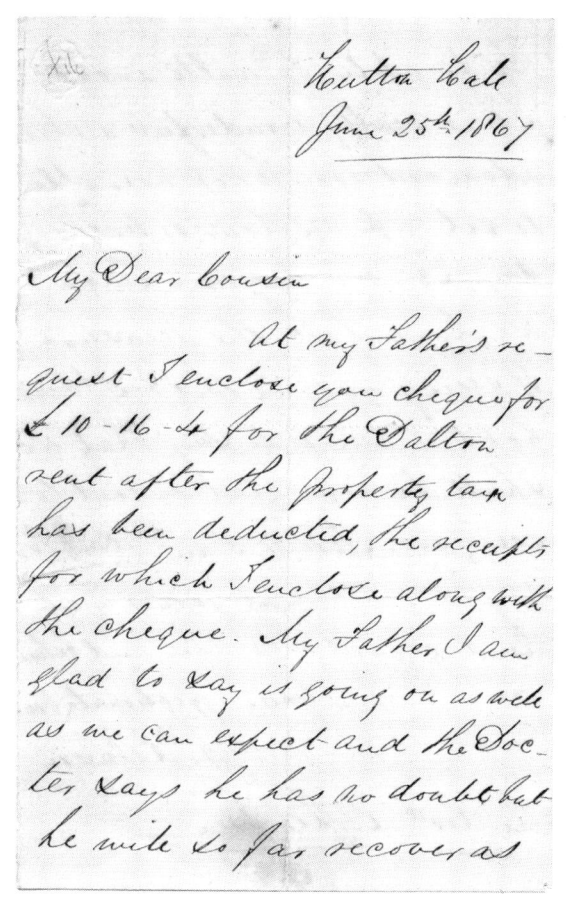

32 A letter which William Robinson of Hutton Hall wrote, in 1867, to his cousin Robert Thompson (1807-1875), on behalf of his father, Thomas Robinson of Hutton Hall. Thomas, aged 86, was recovering from illness – he lived for a further seven months. Robert Thompson was the priest at Nun Monkton, at the time, where he built a little church 'in the Gothic style'.

33 Canon John Thompson (1814-1884): brother of Canon Robert Thompson, both Ushaw priests and cousins of my grandfather Thomas Robinson of Nuthill. John Thompson was chaplain to the Bar Convent in York for 43 years. The Bar Convent was established, discreetly, in penal times, in 1686, by Mother Frances Bedingfield of the Institute of the Blessed Virgin Mary, forty-one years after the death of Mary Ward, their foundress. John Thompson was greatly esteemed by the nuns and he is buried in their graveyard.

34 Cuthbert Watson (c.1777-1859) of Ovington by Sir John Watson Gordon: confidential agent of the W
Estate for 60 years. Cuthbert Watson was a household name in our family and, when asked whether he v
related, Uncle Thomas used to reply that he was 'nearly related'; he was a brother-in-law of my great-
grandfather, Thomas Robinson of Hutton Hall; he nearly married one of the Robinson girls.
(The portrait used to hang on the stairs at Magdalen) Photograph kindly given to me by my cousin Richard Robinson.

Parents, when they heard of what had happened can be better understood than described. In mature years, John recognised in his wonderful preservation, the action of his dear Angel Guardian... One of his masters [at Ushaw] affirms that his life there was innocent, blameless, and uniform. So equable was his course through the college, that it affords little for record or observation.... His delicate health obliged him to restrain his natural ardour for studious pursuits and prevented a fuller development of gifts, which were of a high order – Music, drawing, painting, poetry could not receive the desired cultivation, though he knew how to appreciate the beautiful in nature and art.[36]

Cecily was in the habit of making notes about people whom she wished to remember on the blank pages of her prayer book; and she made this entry about her godson:

> Ushaw College
> Oct. 21st 1839
> Mr John Thompson ordaned [sic]
> Priest. 26 January 1840
> said Mass at Wycliffe

The sketch continues:

On the 16th of that month [February 1841] he became Chaplain to this Community which then numbered within the walls of the "Old Bar Convent" fourteen Choir Nuns and six Lay Sisters.
His personal appearance at this time was prepossessing. Tall of stature, priestly bearing, a countenance beaming with Angelic innocence, with gentlemanly manners. He soon won the confidence of his flock, nuns and children. His visits to the school were hailed with joy by the children, for he was so kind, considerate and affable to all.
A great admirer of church ceremonial, ...His sermons were well prepared; his language was sometimes flowry [sic], but the truths he wished to inculcate were unmistakably told. His selection of subjects showed how carefully he studied, not only the spiritual needs of those whom he addressed, but likewise their tastes and position.
As a Confessor, he was gentle, kind and firm; he did not say much, but the few words he did say were full of unction and deeply impressive.
His catechetical instructions were carefully prepared and clearly delivered but he had not the gift of questioning the children.
At an early stage he began the study of our Institute and so persevering were his efforts that we think that allows us to affirm, that no one laboured

more earnestly and perseveringly in this intricate matter as he did. He literally wound himself up in this favourite pursuit and allowed no opportunity to escape of increasing his store of information.

John Thompson was canon penitentiary of the diocese from 1851 to 1880. He was chaplain to the Bar Convent for 43 years; and there he died on Thursday 17th July 1884 at the age of 69. '....the solemn High Mass of Requiem was sung in the presence of the Bishop of Leeds by the Very Rev. Provost Browne, of Leeds, the Rev. T. Van Zon and X. De Vacht being deacon and sub-deacon; Very Rev. Canon Gordon, D.D., assistant priest; Canons Walshaw and Watson, deacons at the throne; and Mgr. Goldie master of ceremonies. Nearly all the canons of the diocese, all the clergy of the city, and many from the neighbourhood were present to offer their tribute of reverence and prayer around the bier of their beloved brother in the priesthood'. This contemporary account continues:

> ...the funeral discourse was preached by the Very Rev. Canon Mottor [Motler], who, in eloquent and impressive language, dwelt upon the saintly life of the departed and his diligent and faithful ministry... The procession was then formed, and advancing through the avenue of venerable limes that had guarded the funerals of so many generations of nuns, the grave was reached and the last words of supplication offered for the eternal rest of the good and faithful priest.– And while the earth is yet loose upon those honoured remains, it may be well to recall a few memories of one of those good old priests who connect us with the names of Lingard and Gillon [Gillow], Bishops Smith and Gibson and Briggs. Self-denying and priestly in their lives, intellectual even in their recreation, they seem to stand as models for our own times, and reminders of more earnest and truly Catholic days. John Thompson was born seventy years ago, near the banks of the Tees, where the fair scenery of that beautiful river shows the fairest, and where, through generations of persecution, the practice of the old faith shone the brightest. He was baptised on St. John Baptist's Day, August 29th within twenty-four hours after his birth, in the old chapel of Wycliffe Hall. Catholic memories indeed cling abundantly around the site, for there Cuthbert Tunstall, the last Catholic Bishop of Durham was born; and flying from the persecution of the revolution of William III., Bishop Smith, the first vicar-apostolic of the north, ended his saintly days in peace within the same venerable walls; while somewhat lower down the Tees, another ancient church holds the ashes of a venerated bishop and of a celebrated doctor of divinity, both members of the Witham family. There the old faith has never been destroyed, and the fervour of the old Catholic

life wonderfully preserved. Fasting and self-denial were not then nominal practices; the writer well remembers how uncles and aunts of the deceased between eighty and ninety years of age fasted most vigorously, and when remonstrated with, and assured that they were dispensed by reason of their great age, considered themselves insulted, and persevered to fast and abstain to the last. Under the care of parents and relatives such as these, it is not wonderful that John, with his brothers Robert and James, were privileged to receive a holy and happy vocation to the priesthood. At St. Cuthbert's College, Ushaw, the three brothers were looked upon as models of what the life of ecclesiastical students should be. John was respected and loved alike by masters and fellow-students. Innocent, docile and amiable, he was compared with St. Aloysius, whom, with St. John Baptist, he chose as his patron. Intelligent and persevering, he was most successful in his studies, and while still a college student, exercised his pen, during hours of recreation, in writing for the Orthodox Journal; displaying even thus early a gracefulness of diction and thorough Catholic spirit well worthy of imitation. Having been ordained priest in 1839, his first labours were at Stalybridge and Leeds, but in 1841 he was appointed to St. Mary's Convent, which was to be his field of work and merit till the close of his days. Fervently and regularly, while health permitted, those unobstrusive [sic] duties were discharged, as the faithful director of the large community entrusted to him. To the end he retained the affectionate regard of the inmates of St. Mary's, and the respectful reverence of his brethren of the clergy. R.I.P.[37]

Thomas Robinson of Hutton Hall and his sister Cecily would have been among the aunts and uncles referred to in this account. Cecily had been baptised at Wycliffe Hall by the Rev. Thomas Penswick, who knew the family so well and always stated relationships in his register, on Saturday 16th May 1779 – a year before the Gordon Riots. Her godfather was Adam Dale, the younger, of Wycliffe Grange. Adam Dale and Cecily's father, Robert Robinson of Hutton Hall, were to be Mr Penswick's executors. Her godmother was Adam's sister-in-law Dorothy Dale of Hutton Fields.

Cecily, never married. She lived at Newsham Grange and that is where she died at the age of 82 on 13th April 1861. She had made her will on 13th March the previous year. She left: £100, together with her household furniture, except the plate and linen, to her brother, Thomas; £100 to her other brother, Robert Robinson of Rokeby Close; and £50 to her sister Elizabeth's husband, Lawrence Thompson, who was living at South Park. To Lawrence's two priest sons, Robert and John, she left £250 each. To her nephews: William Thompson of South

Park, the brother of the two priests; Thomas Robinson of Nuthill; William Robinson of Hutton Hall; and Thomas Robinson of Ovington her brother Robert's son; she left £300 each; and to the last named she also left her copy of 'Rees Cyclopedia'. To her brother Robert's daughters, Cecily, Ann, and Elizabeth, she left £250 each; and, in addition, she left her watch chain and seal to Cecily and her wearing apparel to Ann. She left £30 to each of her godchildren, who were: my father's eldest sister, Sarah, who was aged 8 when her great aunt Cecily died; Frances Mary, daughter of William Thompson; and Joseph Bell, son of her brother Robert's daughter, Ann. She left her farming stock, cows, horses, carriage, plate, linen, and all other possessions, to her three nephews, Thomas of Nuthill, William his brother, and William Thompson, to be equally divided; and she made them her joint executors. Her estate was valued at under £4,000.[38]

Cecily's elder sister, Ann, married Ralph Chambers on 16th June 1809.[39] In 1840 Mrs Ann Chambers was living at Newsham Grange, which she owned, and her nephew William Thompson, the brother of the priests, was also living there and farming the 115 acres of land.[40] This was four years before William married Maria Robinson of South Park.

Thomas Robinson of Hutton Hall's elder brother, Robert of Rokeby Close, died in 1865, his ninetieth year, at Ovington, the home of his son Thomas who was married to Isabella Naylor, both Catholics, and, at the time of his death, they had two daughters and a son.[41]

Vocations to the religious life were to continue into the next generation. The year after the death of Robert of Rokeby Close, his namesake, Robert, was born to Thomas and Isabella; the little boy who was to become known as 'Fr. Solid', whom we met at Stonyhurst.

In conclusion, as we have seen, Catherine Mary, one of Thomas of Hutton Hall's own granddaughters, my father's elder sister by three years, became a Carmelite nun, probably during my father's penultimate year as a lay student at Ushaw, in 1877. Catherine had her eighth birthday the month after William wrote to his cousin Robert Thompson.

And next we must examine the background of Robert's 'excellent parents, the Catholic type of past generations'.

3. Descendants of Robert Robinson and Cecily Foster, of Hutton Hall, Hutton Magna, N. Yorkshire
godparents (sponsors) are mentioned

Robert Robinson (1721 - 27 Oct 1809) of Hutton Hall & Cecily Foster (1733 - 1804), dau. of James Foster of Euxton House, Euxton, Lancs., and Elizabeth, dau. of Robert Holden of Leagram, Lancs., m. 16 Jul 1767

- Dorothy Robinson (19 Jun 1769 - ?), sponsors (sps): Mr Collingwood and Sally Dale stood for Mr Dale (Adam Dale of Wycliffe Grange) and Mrs Tootell
- Ann Robinson (3 Mar 1771 - ?) bp 3 March, sps: Robert Dale (Robert Dale of Hutton Fields) and Ann Robinson the Aunt
- Elizabeth Robinson (3 Feb 1773 - ?) bp 3 Feb, emergency, and 13 Feb, sps: Mr Tootell and Mrs Dale (Sarah, wife of Adam, above) & Lawrence Thompson (- 12 Apr 1865) of Lane Head, Hutton Magna, later of South Park, bp 4 March 1777, sps: James Brown, uncle, supplied by Anthony Langstaff, and Dorothy Dale (sister of Robert D., above), m. 4 Feb 1806
    - Very Rev. Canon Robert Thompson (Jul 1807 - 8 Nov 1875) bp 1 Jul 1807, sps: Robert Robinson and Ann Brown
    - Rev. James Thompson (Dec 1809 - 1837) bp 19 Dec 1809, sps: James Brown and Mrs Brougham
    - William Thompson (Sep 1810 - 2 Oct 1887) of Lane Head, later of South Park, bp 5 Sep 1810, sps: Adam Dale and Dorothy Robinson, & Maria (24 Feb 1809 - 3 Jan 1875) bp 27 Feb 1809, sps: Robert Tichborne and Mary Robinson (of South Park, her aunt), dau. of John & Sarah Robinson of South Park, m. 1844
    - Ann Thompson (Apr 1812 - ?) bp 11 Apr 1812, sps: Ann Chambers and Thomas Robinson
    - Very Rev. Canon John Thompson (Aug 1814 - 17 Jul 1884) bp 28 Aug 1814, sps: Cecily Robinson and James Foster
- Robert Robinson (29 Jul 1776 - 4 Nov 1865) of Rokeby Close, bp 30 July 1776, sps: Tom Robinson, uncle, and Mary Dale (sister of Robert Dale, above), & Isabella ------ (- 22 Oct 1873)
    - Cecily Robinson (Mar 1811 - ?) bp 2 Mar 1811, sps: Lawrence Thompson and Dorothy Robinson (probably Robert Dale of Hutton Field's sister who married Ralph Robinson of Hutton Fields), & John Howell of Middleton Lodge
    - Ann Robinson (Oct 1812 - ?), bp 13 Oct 1812, sps: Thomas Robinson and Ann Robinson & Joseph Bell of Darlington
    - Thomas Robinson (Jun 1817 - ?) of Ovington, bp 29 June 1817, sps: Adam -------- and Isobel Craggs, & Isabella Naylor, parents of Fr Robert Robinson SJ (23 Jul 1866 - 28 Aug 1944), 'Fr Solid,' procurator at Stonyhurst College
- Cecily Robinson (15 May 1779 - 13 April 1861) of Newsham Grange, bp 16 May 1779, sps: Adam Dale (son of Adam Dale above) and Dorothy Dale, Adam's sister), unm.
- Thomas Robinson (30 Jul 1781 - 19 Feb 1868) of Hutton Hall, bp 30 Jul 1781, sps: William Foster of Burton and Ann Brown of Aldborough, & Sarah Brown (1784 - 26 Jan 1853), dau. of James Brown of Aldbrough and Ann Dale, dau. of Adam Dale of Wycliffe Grange, son of Robert Dale of Hutton Hall (and Mary ? Tunstall), son of Adam Daile of Hutton
    - Robert Robinson (Sep 1813 - 14 Sep 1847) bp 28 Sep 1813, sps: Adam Dale of York and Mrs A. Brown, unm.
    - Mary Ann Robinson (Jul 1819 - 20 Feb 1835) bp 14 Jul 1819, sps: Robert Robinson and Dorothy Robinson
    - James Robinson (Jan 1822 - 17 Aug 1827) bp 21 Jan 1822, sps: Cuthbert Watson and Ann Brown
    - Thomas Robinson (21 Mar 1823 - 18 Dec 1880) of Nuthill, bp 23 Mar 1823, sps: Adam Dale and Ann Chambers, & Sarah Wright Ford (2 Mar 1827 - 26 Feb 1895) of Burton Pidsea, m. 18 Nov 1852
    - William Robinson (Aug 1824 - 18 Nov 1884) of Hutton Hall, bp 26 Aug 1824, sps: Lawrence and Elizabeth Thompson, & Elizabeth Hunt (24 Jul 1826 - 18 Apr 1902) parents of Thomas Robinson of Newsham Grange
        - William Robinson of Hutton Hall, d.s.p.
        - Doctor Robert Robinson of Hutton Hall, d.s.p.
        - Thomas Robinson (13 Sep 1868 - 22 Nov 1950) of Newsham Grange, Newsham, N. Yorks., unm.
        - Mary Elizabeth Robinson (14 Feb 1870 - 27 Dec 1916) of Hutton Hall, unm.
        - Francis James Robinson, d.s.p.

4. Descendants of John Robinson of South Park and Elizabeth Troath Caley
A Catholic Robinson family, distinct from ours, into which we married
South Park lies within a mile of Nuthill

John Robinson (1742 - 11 Jan 1814) of South Park, bu. Burstwick, (son of John R. of South Park and Mary, dau. of Leonard Metcalf of Nut Hill; son of John R. of Marton and Elizabeth Cowtas/Coultas; son of John Robinson of Hambleton Hills) & Elizabeth Troath Caley (1740 - 20 Apr 1808), dau. of William Caley of Grimoldby Grange, Lincs., m. 1776

- Dom William Cuthbert (Maurus) Robinson, OSB, (11 Oct 1777 - 31 May 1832) bp 12 Oct, sp: John Robinson snr.; professed at Lampspring 17 May 1792, bu. Lampspring
- John Robinson of South Park (1778 - 1846), interred, 4 Apr 1846, in Catholic Chapel, Hedon, & Sarah Moore (1783 - 12 Oct 1856), bu. at Hutton Magna. As a widow she evidently lived with her dau. and son-in-law, Maria and William Thompson, at Lane Head, Hutton Magna.
  - Maria Robinson (24 Feb 1809 - 3 Jan 1875), bp 27 Feb, sps: Robert Tichborne and Mary Robinson, & William Thompson (Sep 1810 - 2 Oct 1887) of Lane Head and, later, of South Park (1st cousin of Thomas Robinson of Nuthill), m. 4 Jul 1844
  - Frances Robinson (5 Apr 1810 - ?) bp 9 Apr, sps: Francis Meynell of Worlaby and Frances Hardcastle of Yo
  - John Robinson (1812 - 25 Jan 1837) bu. at Burstwick
  - Charles Robinson of Mansfield (10 Aug 1814 - ?), Chemist and Druggist, bp 15 Aug, sps: William Westwood and Margaret Westwood, & Clare Willson
  - Samuel Robinson (7 Nov 1816 - 15 Nov 1857) of South Park, Farmer, bp 11 Nov, sps: Chris Meynell and Elizabeth Robinson. After Samuel's death, William and Maria Thompson moved into South Park.
  - Thomas Robinson (15 Jan 1818 - ?) of Alton Cheadle, Staffs., Surgeon, bp 18 Jan, sps: Thomas Owst and Mary Wilson, & (1) Elizabeth Caley
  - Thomas Robinson (15 Jan 1818 - ?) of Alton Cheadle & (2) Mary Anne Caley
  - Sarah Robinson (1 Aug 1821 - ?), bp 1 Aug, sps: Thomas Hall and Mrs Meynell, & John Leake, the younger, of Lane Head
  - Edward Robinson (17 Mar 1824 - ?) of Limehouse London, Timber Merchant, bp 18 Mar, sps: Seth Agar and Mary Meynell, & (1) Mary Porter (- 1858) of Bedale, N. Yorks.
  - Edward Robinson (17 Mar 1824 - ?) & (2) Mary Priestman (- 1915) m. 1860
- Charles Robinson & ------ Kirkman, no issue
- Samuel Mastin Robinson (1783 - 28 Jul 1811), sudden death from lightning
- Mary Robinson & John Thompson of Thorpe m. 2 Nov 1817
  - William Thompson
  - John Thompson
- Susanna Robinson (6 Feb 1787 - ?), bp 11 Feb, sps: Joseph Denton and Helen Caley, & Christopher Meynell of Hull, Chemist and Druggist, m. 5 Sep 1816
  - Mary Meynell of Hull (- 1866), Presentation Nun, in Manchester
  - Thomas Meynell of Hedon, Brewer, & Sarah Mary Southwell
- Henry Robinson (8 Apr 1788 - 29 Jan 1867) of Sproatley Grange, bp 9 Apr, sps: Hen Wytham and Winifride Hunt, & Elizabeth Grant Robinson (1799 - 29 Jan 1867), dau. of his 1st cousin, William Grant Robinson
  - Elizabeth Robinson (4 Apr 1821 - 1914), Member of the Catholic Record Society, whose pedigree, used here, is recorded in 'Catholic Registers of Everingham Park, Yorks. 1771-1884' CRS Vol VII pp. 266-267
  - Catherine Robinson (1822 - ?) ob. inf.
  - Teresa Robinson, (3 Nov 1823 -), bp 4 Nov, by J.Swinburn, sps: Chris. Meynell and Miss Agar, & Robert D Middleton, Fmr., son of John Middleton and Teresa Ann, dau. of Robert and Dorothy Dale of Hutton Fields. Robert and Teresa M. were godparents to Henry Robinson, son of Thomas and Sarah Robinson of Nuthill.
  - Mary Jessy Robinson (27 Aug 1825 - 2 Feb 1864) & Richard Holden, Chemist and Druggist of York, m. 3 Jun 1851; great-grandparents of Ursula Randall
  - Lucy Grant Robinson (1826 - 1908), Good Shepherd Nun
  - Mary Anne Robinson (1828 - 1868), IBVM Nun, York
  - Francis Mary Robinson (1829 - 1861) & Florent Cruysmans
  - Anna Maria Robinson (1830 - 1883)
  - Clare Robinson (1832 - 29 Jan 1867) who, with both her parents, perished in a fire at Sproatley Grange
  - Agnes Robinson (1834 - 1880) & Florent Cruysmans of Antwerp, Chevalier of the Order of Leopold, her brother-in-law, m. 1863, with dispensation
  - William Grant Robinson (1835 - 1857)
- Elizabeth Robinson (19 Nov 1789 - ?), bp 22 Nov, sps: Will Foster and Rose Caley, Lincs., & Seth Agar of York
  - William Seth Agar, (1815 - 1872), Canon of the Plymouth chapter
  - Charles Agar (- 1849)
  - Mary Ann Agar

CHAPTER IV

The French Revolution: a Family Concern at Hutton Hall

'no hours can be more engaging than those employed in reviewing the deeds of ancestors, from whom we have received the documents of faith, together with inducements to a virtuous life'.
William of Somerset quoted by John Daniel [1]

Robert and Cecily Robinson's little family at Hutton Hall was well established to welcome the new baby boy. His eldest sister, Dorothy, was aged 12; Ann was 10; Elizabeth was 8; Robert was 5; and Cecily was 2 years old. His mother, Cecily, was aged 48 when she had him and his father, Robert, was ten years older.

Thomas, who was to become my great-grandfather, was baptised on Monday 30th July 1781 and Fr Penswick noted that he was half a day old. His godfather was William Foster of Burton, his mother's nephew. His godmother was Ann Brown of Aldbrough, the eldest daughter of Adam Dale of Wycliffe Grange and Sarah his wife, who married James Brown; and who was to be the mother of little Sarah, born three years later, the girl that Thomas was going to marry.

Their home, the old stone Hall of Hutton Magna, lay in the low ground by the brook on the edge of the village, north of St Mary's Church. The H shaped building, much altered over the years, had become a farm house. Just over a mile to the south the parish was bounded by the Roman road, a sign of its ancient origins.

Hutton Hall had sheltered Catholics, through the vicissitudes of history, from Tudor times. Some of its wood carving was from the 16th century. One of the upstairs rooms 'contains a cross of plain bevelled wood, about 2 ft. long, placed in the ceiling apparently for some special purpose and without reference to the structure or timbers of the roof'.[2] The winding staircase turned at right angles as it ascended, curiously sloping down to the left, around a stout rectangular central column. My late cousin Bernard Culver recalled how his grandmother, my father's eldest sister, Sarah, born in 1853, told him 'that about 150/200 years ago, one of the Sons, by accident, discovered a "Priest's secret room" in the walls of a big circular stair-way';[3] and, elsewhere, Bernard says, 'About 150 years ago one of the Sons slipped going downstairs and he put out an arm to try to prevent a base over apex fall. In doing so, he evidently pressed hard on a stone block – this swung on an axis, to reveal a long forgotten inner staircase, which led to a "Priest's hole" of the Reformation days'.[4] My father's cousin, Thomas Robinson of Newsham Grange, who gave up Hutton Hall in 1928, informed the representative of the Darlington and Stockton Times that the secret hiding places in the house were destroyed when it was re-roofed 45 years previously.[5] Some of the farm buildings were as old as the Hall. Such was the stone dovecote which straddled the stream above a primitive water-closet. The old brew-house, with its vaulted brick ceiling, had stepping stones jutting from the outside wall for the hens which roosted in its upper storey.

The cold, crisp, morning atmosphere, between the hayricks and the steaming stables and cow sheds, would be alive with the smells and noises of the farmyard combined with the enthusiastic chatter and laughter of children as they went about their daily tasks: collecting the eggs, feeding the animals; everybody has responsibility on a farm.

After playing in the soft white snow, beneath the frosty branches of the leafless trees sparkling in the silvery winter sun, little hands, so cold and painful, would find the comfort of grown-up's hands to warm them and then: delicious things to eat; the blazing log fire in the hearth; and old folk's talk of times gone by.

One day the snowdrops would appear, then primroses and swelling buds, and shoots of green testing the early spring. The birds would be busy with their nests, someone would hear the cuckoo, the martins and the swallows would arrive. Soon all hands would be making hay and crops would be golden in the heat of summer.

This was, indeed, a refuge from the terrible, dark, damp, dungeons of penal times. What moved men and women like these farming folk to risk such a fate?

Here, at Hutton Hall, behind closed doors, with neighbours gathered in, the central mystery of our faith would be celebrated: the unique sacrifice of the cross, on which Christ died for everyone without exception, would be made present, sacramentally, in the sacrifice of the Mass in which, by the power of the Holy Spirit, when the priest speaks the words of consecration, Jesus, in his humanity and divinity, becomes truly present, body and blood, under the appearances of bread and wine; the sacrifice in which he takes us up with him into his eternal offering to his father; as he, himself, had instructed at the Last Supper; and as it had been down the centuries throughout Christendom.[6] But in this kingdom, in penal times, the lives of these priests and people were united with this holy sacrifice in a special way – because such prayer was punishable by fines, imprisonment, and even by death. It was to keep this, our heritage of faith, alive in their native land that some of the sons and daughters of England were prepared, if necessary, to die.

Thomas Robinson was a boy aged ten when Edward Kitchen returned to his chaplaincy at Lartington Hall in October 1791 after only three months in post as the seventeenth president of the English College at Douai. The responsibility, in such difficult times, for a man of indifferent health had proved too much for him; fifteen months later, aged 45, he was dead.

In France, widespread unemployment and starvation had inflamed public opinion.[7] The Estates-General, primed with the grievances of the populace, had met at Versailles on 5th May 1789; and from this encounter the Third Estate emerged with all the strength which had been sapped from an oppressive feudal nobility. Events moved apace and converged in the storming of the Bastille on 14th July.

The English College had twice been invaded by the mob; and the college printer, Derbaix, accused of loyalist propaganda, had been hanged *à la lanterne*.[8]

Lartington Hall lay only eight miles north-west of Hutton Magna where, no doubt, apprehension at Kitchen's return would now be focused on events across the English Channel. Thomas probably sensed this family concern; and even more so on the nomination, in February 1792, of the Rev. John Daniel, to succeed Kitchen as president of Douai.[9] John Daniel was the nephew of Robert and Cecily's close friend Thomas Penswick. Mr Penswick had been the priest at Wycliffe Hall for five years when Robert and Cecily were married there on 16th July 1767; he had baptised all their children. He had chosen Robert Robinson and Adam Dale as his executors; and he had died at Wycliffe the previous year at the age of 73.

John Daniel, the son of Edward Daniel of Durton and Mary, daughter of William and Grace Penswick of Lytham in Lancashire, was born in 1745. He became a student at Douai on 20th October 1760. Following his ordination, he taught there continuously; and he was vice-president and professor of divinity at the time of his appointment as president. Two sons of John Daniel's cousin, Thomas Penswick who was steward to Lord Gerard of Bryn, were students at Douai at the time: Thomas Penswick in the school of Logic and John Penswick in Grammar. Robert Dale, a lay student, the son of Robert Dale of Hutton Fields and a cousin of Thomas Robinson's future wife, Sarah, was a year ahead of John Penswick, in Syntax.[10]

Milburn considers that John Daniel's appointment was one of expediency and he adds, 'Unfortunately he was not at all the man required for an emergency, being dilatory by nature and a semi-invalid'.

During the next year, however, the college was left in relative peace. But then, on 21st January 1793, Louis XVI was executed. In the following month England entered the war against the Revolutionaries. The college was seized and put under armed guard. The college porter was displaced by three vigilant officials who took up strategic positions. Despite the watchfulness of the 'three spiders', as they were nicknamed, four of the Philosophers, including Richard Thompson, future grand vicar in Lancashire, and Thomas Penswick who became vicar apostolic of the Northern District, under the direction of the prefect (apparently the president was too timorous for this initiative), scaled the walls and hid property outside the town; this was later sold to meet expenses of students released from prison. They also buried church plate in the garden and hid refectory plate under the floor of Low Figures' schoolroom. John Penswick watched through a keyhole while the plate was being buried and was able to locate some of it many years later. Another student, Thomas Stout, hid a box of relics which included the hair shirt of St Thomas Becket, the college patron, and the biretta of St Charles Borromeo.

There was a mass exodus from the other British houses at Douai and, out of 89 collegians at the English College about 25 returned to England; there would have been more but the president was indecisive, weighing up the dangers of staying against the consequences of cutting off the supply of priests to England. By May, the allies had driven the Republicans back, the noise of war was heard in the town; the siege of Douai seemed imminent. Further students escaped and the rest left for their country house at Équerchin. John Daniel remained behind with two students who were too ill to travel. After two months those at Équerchin were ordered back to Douai and imprisoned in the deserted Scots College.

On the 26th October 1793, carts were commandeered to take the prisoners, under guard, to the state prison at Doullens; they were accompanied by John Daniel and by a handful of monks from the English Benedictine house at Douai who had been imprisoned with them. Some slipped away en route. Others escaped in the early days at Doullens; after which confinement became absolute.

The students had been interrogated and, during Robespierre's Reign of Terror which had begun in September, the worst could be expected. Such a fate was probably only prevented when, in July 1794, Robespierre, who, it was feared, had gone mad, was himself sent to the guillotine.

On 24th November 1794, after thirteen months at Doullens, months during which the students kept up their studies and discipline as much as circumstances allowed, the 'trente-deux' – twenty six Douatians and six Benedictines – returned to Douai, but to the ruins of the Irish College; their own College had been taken over as a military hospital. On the 13th February they heard with joy and tears that they were going to England. On 2nd March 1795 they set sail from Calais 'and after an inconvenient and difficult passage, but with joyful hearts, landed at Dover the same evening'.

In the meantime there had been further cause for concern at Hutton Hall. Thomas's mother, Cecily, had two sisters who were Poor Clare nuns at Dunkirk. The Poor Clare convents at Dunkirk, Aire, and Rouen, were daughter houses of the community founded at Gravelines by Mary Ward in 1608.[11]

Elizabeth Foster was professed under the name Agnes Joseph on 21st November 1744, at the age of 19; and in 1776 she became the twelfth Abbess. Her sister Grace was professed under the name Grace Maria on 29th June 1748, also aged 19.[12]

But now it was the year 1793. England had declared war on France; the English nuns in that land and in Flanders were regarded as enemy aliens; and Robespierre had mounted his Reign of Terror. On 13th October the mother house of the Poor Clares at Gravelines was sacked and the nuns were imprisoned in their own convent. On the same day, the Benedictine nuns at Dunkirk were escorted under armed guard to the convent of the Poor Clares in that town. On 17th October the two communities, comprising forty nuns, guarded by fifty soldiers, were embarked for an unknown destination and an unknown fate. The nuns overheard one of the guards propose to the ship's captain that it would save a lot of trouble if they drowned them all. Fortunately, that sailor did not comply with such a barbarous suggestion. After sailing up the coast they landed that evening at Gravelines, whereupon they were imprisoned with the Poor Clares in the mother house. There, under daily insults and threats and knowing that each nun was on Robespierre's list for the guillotine, the three communities endured a miserable existence for eighteen months. Their diet was mainly bread and water and they had to burn the remaining furniture to survive the rigours of an exceptionally cold winter. Many became ill and eleven of them died. The rest were only saved by the downfall of Robespierre.

On 26th March 1795 the nuns were told they were free to go to England. The Gravelines nuns were resolved to return when the war was over. They were held in high regard by the townspeople for the good which they had done and the local officials agreed to their request. On April 19th, dressed in whatever makeshift garments were available, the nuns set out for Calais and for England. On May 3rd the three communities arrived in London, when each went its separate way; an emotive parting of women who had sustained each other through such suffering.[13] The Dunkirk Poor Clares settled at Churchill Wood; and, in the community's necrology, we find the final account of my great-grandfather's two aunts.

Referring to 'Sister Grace Maria alias Foster':

She died February 2nd about one o'clock in the morning 1802 having happily received all the rites [at] the Churchill Wood near Worcester. Being blessed by Divine Providence with cheerful and amiable dispositions she was singularly beloved by the whole Community in the sundry offices she filled in the Convent more particularly as Mis of Novices and the school Infirmarian…

Referring to 'Sr Agnes Joseph alias Foster':

She departed this life Febry 14th 1802 about six o'clock at night happily fortified with all the rites of Holy Church at Churchill Wood 4 miles east of Worcester. She had been Abbess twenty six years three months and nineteen days
              Requiescat in Pace Amen.
The twelth [sic] Abbess much beloved for her tender charity and greatly revered for her prudent and affectionate manner of conducting to religious perfection all committed by Divine Providence to her care. On the eighth of September 1793 the religious of this Convent were forced from their happy abode and conducted in a brutal manner to the Mother convent at Graveline where amidst the most distressing treatment from the infamous revolutionists of that period and privations she by word and example encouraged the Community to humble submission to the ever faithful hand of an all wise Providence.

Elizabeth and Grace, who consecrated their lives to God at the age of 19, and who had been through so much together, died together in February 1802; Elizabeth was aged 77 and Grace was 72. Two years later their younger sister, Cecily Robinson, died and was buried in the graveyard at Hutton Magna; she was aged 71.

Robert Dale was among the students of the English College at Douai who managed to avoid imprisonment at Doullens. He was aged about 18 and in Syntax when, with seven other students, including Daniel O'Connell the Liberator who was in Rhetoric, he left Douai in January 1793.

John Lingard, who was in first year Theology, also avoided

imprisonment. Though he had narrowly escaped being murdered by the mob as early as June 1790.[14] In February 1793 he returned to England with the young Lord Stourton, who was in Poetry, and he became tutor in the Stourton household at Ollerton Hall near York.[15]

Bishop Gibson, in March 1794, had temporarily settled a handful of the Douai students at Tudhoe, near Durham, in a school kept by the Rev. Arthur Story; and Lingard accepted the Bishop's invitation to join them as their master. On 15th October this small community was transferred to Crook Hall, ten miles from Durham, under the presidency of the Rev. Thomas Eyre whose policy is thus outlined:

> President Eyre, conscious of the importance of sound learning in this successor to Douai, showed himself to be an exacting master, and there were those who thought they saw in him the zeal to reproduce in the humble surroundings of Crook the great achievements of *Alma Mater Duacensis* in its early years. And as at Douai the greatest fruits were reaped in poverty, so it was with Crook, for in these austere surroundings John Lingard, president's assistant, procurator, prefect of studies, professor of Poetry and Rhetoric, composed his *Antiquities of the Anglo-Saxon Church,* his first work as a historian, and the product in large measure of lectures to the Divines on winter evenings.[16]

It was to Crook Hall that the northern contingent of Douai students, accompanied by their president John Daniel, made their way in March 1795. Lingard was ordained priest by Bishop William Gibson in the chapel of the Bar Convent at York on 18th August that year.

Two hundred and twenty six years had now gone by since William Allen's foundation at Douai and during the first 210 of those years Catholics in England had been hounded, persecuted, and fined almost out of existence.[17] But then, in 1778, the nineteenth year of the Reign of George III and three years into the American War of Independence, when the British Government needed to attract recruits in the Scottish Highlands where the old faith had survived and was strong and widespread, the first Catholic Relief Act was passed. This Act reversed the statutes of William and Mary whereby: Catholics could neither acquire land by purchasing it nor by inheritance; their priests and schoolmasters could receive a sentence of life imprisonment; and an informant who secured their conviction was rewarded with £100. Also the Oath of Allegiance had been modified to be acceptable to Catholics.[18]

This new Oath, which excluded the denial of transubstantiation, was taken by Thomas' father, Robert Robinson of Hutton Hall, at Richmond on 13th January 1792, in the company of Thomas Sanderson, who had succeeded Thomas Penswick as chaplain at Wycliffe Hall, Adam Dale of Colburin, and Peter Pearson who belonged to an old Recusant family whose history was similar to that of our own.[19] In the previous October, at Northallerton, the same Oath had been taken by James Brown, Thomas's future father-in-law, and Anthony Langstaff whose sister Elizabeth established the Langstaff Trust.[20]

The Relief Act of 1778 met with the inflammatory reaction of the Gordon Riots, in which an anti-papist mob ransacked London from 2nd to 9th of June 1780; and in which 285 people died; in addition to the 21 who were afterwards executed.

The second Catholic Relief Act, of 1791, allowed Mass to be celebrated in chapels provided they were registered and the priest had taken the Oath of Allegiance; and school masters who took the Oath should not be prosecuted. But the legality of establishing a school for clerical students, run by the secular clergy or by a religious order, was ambiguous.

In addition to this barrier, Catholics had grown used to going abroad for their education and they often hoped that they might be able to return to their traditional establishments. The Rev. Robert Banister, a senior and much respected Lancashire priest, in a letter to Bishop Gibson, dated 16th November 1795, wrote:[21]

> When peace is made (and that epoch may not be too distant) we can scarcely doubt but the French will agree to restore to British subjects the property which they had and enjoyed in France before the war commenced. In which case Douay college will return to its ancient walls... My neighbour Mr. Wilson is constantly of one mind, that Douay College will return to its old site. Mr. Daniel tells me, that Gregory Stapleton wishes ardently to return to St. Omers: he therefore ought not to precipitate matters here, but rather patiently wait to see, what new light and order divine Providence may by his omnipotence, draw out of this abyss of darkness, confusion and impiety...the President of Douay College wishes first to wait for the issue of war, and for a more hopeful prospect,...[22]

Public opinion was, however, changing and the no-popery aggression of the Gordon Riots was the last major discharge of anti-Catholic hysteria. England gave generous hospitality to French priests fleeing the persecution of the Revolution. Political and Catholic interests were, after two and a half centuries of division, beginning to coincide.

David Mathew states, 'the movement in favour of political freedom gathered momentum and was assisted by the sense of unity induced in the nation by the long Napoleonic Wars... The widespread atmosphere of co-operation at this period was also fostered by the interest taken in horse-racing by such leading Catholic owners as Edward Petre. John Gully the prize-fighter had married a Catholic and had a rather loud friendliness towards the old religion;...' and here, this boxer, the great-great-great-grandfather of my Cardwell cousins, who also became a successful racehorse owner and Member of Parliament, is quoted, 'I shall try old Lomax', wrote Gully, 'to say Mass for me. What will he charge?'.[23]

On his return from Douai, John Daniel, in fact, found himself at the centre of the controversy between Bishop Gibson and Bishop Douglass, vicar apostolic of the London District, about the location for the successor to the English College at Douai. The outcome was that Old Hall Green became the seminary for the south of England and Ushaw the seminary for the north.

And it was to Ushaw 'a building far from complete,...' that, 'The first contingent of students, a group of boys constituting "Little Lads' Bounds", left their temporary *Alma Mater* at Crook Hall on July 19th [1808] the feast of St Vincent de Paul, and plodded their way through the Lanchester valley towards the steep hillside at Esh, no doubt dressed in their mixed Oxford coats and corduroy breeches, and carrying the best part of their belongings with them'.[24] Thomas Eyre continued as President with John Lingard as acting Vice-President.

That winter, tragedy struck in the cold, damp, unfinished, structures of Ushaw; and typhus fever killed five of the students.

John Lingard left Ushaw on 11th September 1811 to take up his appointment to the quiet country mission of Hornby near Lancaster. In this peaceful setting he worked on his famous History of England. Fourteen miles down the road, Cecily Robinson's half-brother, James Foster, a Douai priest, was chaplain at Thurnham Hall.[25] James appointed his 'Friend Doctor Lingard' executor of his will in 1821; and he empowered 'him my said executor, if he shall think proper to do, to become the purchaser of all my household goods and furniture, books plate silver and other implements of household on payment into the residuum of my estate and effects of the sum of one hundred pounds. And I do give and bequeath unto him ten pounds'.[26]

John Daniel had been, for a short time, president of Crook Hall but he was advised to give this up 'and to retain only the title of president of Douai so as to watch over the interests of that venerable college. For this purpose [after a short break at Kirkham in Lancashire] he took up residence in Paris and spent the rest of his life trying to negotiate the return of the stolen property'. He died there on 3rd October 1823 aged 78 'without attaining his ambition'.[27]

James Foster died at Thurnham where he had been missioner for 40 years, at the age of 78, from a broken blood vessel, on 17th February 1824.[28] John Lingard's signature appears on the document which states that James Foster left under four hundred and fifty pounds; the same handwriting in which is written his well known hymn 'Hail Queen of Heaven' on the back of an envelope preserved in the Big Library at Ushaw.

John Lingard, himself, a scholar respected by Catholics and Protestants alike, who did so much to restore the prestige of the Catholic Church in England, died at Hornby on 17th July 1851 at the age of 80. Lingard never ceased to take a deep interest in and provide every kind of support for his Alma Mater; and it was at Ushaw that he was laid to rest.[29]

Thus, was paved the way for the sons, grandsons, and great-grandsons, of Thomas and Sarah Robinson of Hutton Hall, to receive their education at Ushaw. And, as we are about to see, among other things, this was the logical continuation of an already established tradition.

5. Descendants of John Foster of Charnock Richard and Ellen

John Foster (c. 1640 - 1710) of Charnock Richard & Ellen

- Robert Foster (-1719) of Charnock Richard ' . . . a well-to-do tanner, connected with the Tootells, Daniels, and other good Catholic families . . . ' & Elizabeth Parker (c. 1665 - ?)
  - Helen Foster of Burton Constable, Yorks., baptised 29 Jul 1691, & Thomas Daniel of Whittingham, Kirkham, Lancs.
    - Rev. Thomas Daniel, (20 Mar 1714 - 25 Aug 1770); entered Douai 12 Jun 1730; ordained 16 Jul 1739; founded chapel in Little Blake St. York; died in York
    - Robert Daniel (c. 1716 -1778) of Euxton House, Euxton, Lancashire, & Mary ? Platt
    - Jane Daniel (c. 1720 - c. 1780), spinster. Her will of 10 Aug 1780 refers to her living at Euxton Hall, where her brother William died in 1777
    - Rev. William Daniel (Oct 1725 - 25 Jul 1777), alias Foster; entered Douai 13 Jul 1740, ordained 19 Dec 1750, chaplain to Sir Walter Vavasour at Hazlewood Castle and then to the Andertons at Euxton Hall where he died
  - John Foster
  - Margaret Foster
  - Elizabeth Foster
  - Cecily Foster & ------ Heys
  - James Foster (1705 - ?) of Charnock Richard and, by 1743, of Euxton House, & (1) Elizabeth Holden, only child of Robert Holden of Leagram, m. c. 1725
    - Elizabeth Foster (1726 - 14 Feb 1802), religious name, Agnes Joseph, OSC, professed 21 Nov 1744 at Dunkirk, Abbess, died Churchill Wood, Worcester
    - Sister Grace Maria Foster (1729 -2 Feb 1802), OSC, professed at Dunkirk 29 Jun 1748, died at Churchill Wood, Worcester
    - Robert Foster (c. 1731 - 1794) of Burton Constable (an agent of the Constable estate) & Esther --------
    - Cecily Foster (1733 - 1804) & Robert Robinson (1721 - 27 Oct 1809) of Hutton Hall, Hutton Magna, N. Yorks, m. 16 July 1767
  - James Foster, (1705 - ?), by 1747, tenant farmer of Ashton Hall, Lancaster, & (2) Emerentiana Heys (1718 - ?)
    - Frances 'Fanny' Foster & -------- Lupton
    - Mary Foster
    - Rev. James Foster, (14 Feb 1746/1747 - 17 Feb 1824), b. Ashton Hall; early education at Dame Alice's school, Fernyhalgh; entered Douai 27 Jun 1764; ordained 1 Jan 1775; chaplain at Hazlewood Castle; at Burton Constable 1775 - 1778; at Thurnham in 1785, built church, died there; friend of Dr John Lingard.
    - William Foster
    - Joseph Foster, apprentice with Robert Gillow at Lancaster; later, of Dublin
    - Amy Foster & Angelo Dragetti of Bolognia, Italy
    - Thomas Foster
    - Ann Foster & John Armstrong of Worksop, Notts.
  - Rev. William Foster (c. 1707 - c. 6 Feb 1754) alias Charnock; entered Douai 31 May 1720; ordained Dec 1730; died at York
- -------- Foster & Tootell ? William Tootell (c.1676 - ?), of Euxton, (brother of Hugh Tootell, b. 1671, entered Douai 23 Jul 1688, ordained Lent 1698, alias Charles Dodd the church historian, d. 27 Feb 1743, nephew of Christopher Tootell alias Blacklow, b. 1662, educated at English College, Lisbon, priest at Fernyhalgh c. 1699, d. 18 Nov 1727)
  - Margaret Tootell (c. 1700 - ?)
- Cecily Foster (c. 1670 - ?) & George Cubbon (c. 1670 - ?)

CHAPTER V

Of Roses White and Red

*'We are as dwarfs standing on the shoulders of giants.
That is why we see further than they'.*
Bernard of Chartres [1]

Robert Robinson of Hutton Hall could look back over his 88 years with satisfaction.

It had been a century of continuing persecution for English Catholics, yes, but also a time of consolidation; especially since the birth of his youngest child, Thomas my great-grandfather, who was baptised at Wycliffe Hall in 1781.[2] The story about how a baby of our family was carried in a butter basket down one side of a hedge while the priest walked down the other side and baptised the child across the hedge could be relegated to history. Local tragedies still occurred, such as when William Robinson of Hungry Hall Farm was murdered in 1794 whilst out on Holwick Fell, but that was different.[3] Priests and Catholic schoolmasters were no longer hounded by pursuivants who stood to gain a £100 reward for turning them in.

Catholic farmers, though having to pay double land tax, had been able to get on with their business, excluded by law from the time consuming responsibilities of public office; and farming methods had improved to the extent that the weight of beasts sold at Smithfield market had doubled.[4]

Robert's wife, Cecily, had died five years ago and the next year, 1805, he made his will. He had already given and delivered to his elder son, Robert, 'all my late stock of cattle, sheep other stock and all my furniture and husbandry utensils carts carriages etc: which then were upon the Farm at Dalton fields' and to his younger son Thomas 'I have given all my late stock of cattle sheep and other stock and the furniture and husbandry utensils carts etc: which then were upon the Farm at Hutton hall aforesaid and upon my estate at Newsham the tenant right in which I have given up to him'. He had taken care of his four daughters and appointed his sons his executors. The will is finalised by Robert's confident looking signature witnessed by his friend Adam Dale. His personal estate amounted to less than fifteen hundred pounds.

During Robert's childhood the talk in Hutton Magna would have been about Sir Thomas Robinson who was building Rokeby Hall, about three miles West of Hutton, in the centre of the Park bounded on the North by the river Tees; he came to be regarded as one of the most distinguished early Georgian amateur architects. The manor had been purchased from Sir Thomas Rokeby by his great-great-great-grandfather, William Robinson, in 1611. William Robinson and his son Thomas, the architect's great-great-grandfather, were Protestants and they were both slain fighting on the side of Parliament in 1643.[5] Sir Thomas Robinson put Rokeby up for sale in 1765, the year in which his brother, Dr Richard Robinson, Bishop of Kildare, became Archbishop of Armagh and Primate of all Ireland for the Established Church. Richard wanted to buy the estate but his brother would not sell it to him; and so he built his own 'Rokeby' at Marley, near Dunleer, in County Louth. In 1777 Richard was created Baron Rokeby of Armagh. Now we must return to Hutton Hall.

Adam Dale of Girlington – the grandfather of Sarah Brown who married Thomas Robinson of Hutton Hall – together with his brother Lawrence and their mother Mary, had kept on Hutton Hall Farm since the death of his father Robert Dale of Hutton Hall, at the age of 58 in 1736. In 1760, Adam Dale moved to Wycliffe Grange; and, in the same year, Robert Robinson moved into Hutton Hall; the two largest farms on the Wycliffe estate.[6] Hugh Tootell, attorney to Marmaduke Tunstall, Lord of Wycliffe, registered these messuages at Thirsk Quarter Sessions, in 1765, under Papists Estates, at £165-10 and £133 respectively.[7]

Robert Robinson's contemporaries farming in this part of North Yorkshire evidently formed a tightly knit community. Among them, both the conservation of land and fidelity to the Catholic Faith are, perhaps, best illustrated with reference to Adam's eldest son, Robert Dale of Hutton Fields, whose messuages were valued at £103-15.

Robert Dale, himself, married Dorothy, elder daughter of Richard Brown of Aldbrough. Richard Brown's son, James, married Robert Dale's sister Ann; and their daughter Sarah married my great-grandfather Thomas Robinson of Hutton Hall. Richard Brown's younger daughter, Ann, married Lawrence Thompson of the Lane Head; and their son, Lawrence, married Thomas's sister, Elizabeth Robinson. Robert Dale's elder sister, Dorothy, married Ralph Robinson of Manfield and later of Hutton Fields; Dorothy and Ralph were the parents of Anthony Robinson of Ovington and Matthew Robinson who died in Jamaica. Ralph's father, Richard Robinson of Pecknall House, Romaldkirk, chose Robert Dale as his executor. Robert Dale was also a friend of Ralph's youngest brother, William Robinson, who, with his wife Mary, lived above Smallways. Of William and Mary's ten children, the five youngest: William and his twin George, Richard, Frances, and Rose, were all baptised at Wycliffe Hall; and Robert Dale was godfather to Richard. Anthony Langstaff was the son of Robert Langstaff of East Layton and Mary, daughter of Ralph Wilson of Manfield. Anthony and his wife, Margaret, farmed at Rokeby Close. They, too, were friends of Robert and Dorothy Dale and were godparents to their children. Anthony and Margaret were also godparents to children of Lawrence and Ann Thompson and to grandchildren of William and Mary Robinson above Smallways.[8]

The late Merryne Watson, referring to 'above Smallways near Newsham' states, 'This exactly describes the position of Newsham House' which had 'an imposing Georgian front wedded to an older farm house in the rear. I have heard it said (no written evidence) that a Robinson was responsible for the improvement of Newsham House. Apparently this was a tremendous drain on the Robinson finances and eventually the estate was sold to the Milbank (of Barningham) family'. He also found, in the Newsham Tithe Apportionment, 1840: 'Newsham House. Owner Robert Robinson'.[9] This Robinson was, no doubt, the one who got into financial difficulties. He may well have been Robert Robinson who was baptised at Wycliffe, on 4th April 1796, and whose sponsors were John Rutter and his wife, Mary, daughter of William and Mary Robinson, above Smallways, who were, almost certainly, Robert's grandparents.

My great-grandmother Sarah Robinson, née Brown, of Hutton Hall was related to the Tunstalls of Wycliffe Hall through her grandfather Adam Dale of Girlington and, later, of Wycliffe Grange. The link between the Dales and Tunstalls was William Liddell of Wycliffe who, in his will of 1742, refers to 'my cousin Adam Dale of Girlington' and to 'my dear cousin Marmaduke Tunstall'. William's brother, Thomas Liddell, was a priest, educated at the English College at Lisbon, and he served at Lartington Hall, a Catholic stronghold under the Maires; his sisters Catherine and Mary were Bridgettine Nuns in Lisbon as were his aunts Christina and Mary Tunstall.[10]

William Liddell was married to a Mary Dale and one of their sons, Thomas, was also a Lisbon priest. His first mission, in 1743 when he was aged twenty-four, was at Egton Bridge, Lythe, the birth place of the Venerable Nicholas Postgate. In 1745, because of Thomas's known Jacobite fervour, it was thought best that he should disappear.[11]

Luke Potts, a Douai priest aged twenty-nine, replaced Thomas Liddell and joined Rev. Monox Hervey at Ugthorpe on 12th November

1745. As Bonnie Prince Charlie and the Jacobite rebels retreated northward, pursued by the Duke of Cumberland, the two priests were in danger and hoped for refuge with the Catholics of Egton Bridge. These people, however, were in fear of their lives because of a mob led by Whitby shipwrights, besides constables and local mercenaries; they refused the priests shelter. Luke Potts and Monox Hervey hid up on the moors during the night of December 10th and also the next day; but then, exhausted, they sought food and shelter in Ugthorpe. That evening, they were arrested. The two priests were committed to York gaol, after refusing to take the Oaths of Supremacy and Uniformity, and they were indicted on charges of priesthood which they admitted; but they were discharged. Luke Potts 'set out for Mr. Tunstall's, at Wycliffe, where Bishop Dicconson resided under the alias of Mr. Eaton. He rode post haste and "When called next morning was found booted and spurred, kneeling as he knelt exhausted to say his prayers the night before" '.

William Liddell was the son of Henry Liddell and Mary, a sister of Francis Tunstall, Lord of the Manors of Wycliffe, Hutton, and Scargill. Francis Tunstall was married to Cecily Constable, daughter of John, 2nd Viscount Dunbar, and their son Marmaduke, who succeeded when his father died in 1713, was the cousin to whom William Liddell referred.

Francis Tunstall's cousin, Peter Bryan Tunstall, alias Scargill, the son of his uncle Francis Tunstall of Ovington and his wife Ann, daughter of Sir Thomas Riddell of Fenham, was a student at the English College at Douai.[12]

Bryan Tunstall remained on the College staff after ordination. He was prefect of studies and confessor in 1705, the year Richard Challoner entered Douai, and he held these offices until he returned to England in 1715; the year Robert Witham of Cliff returned to Douai as president; and the year before Challoner was ordained. Bryan Tunstall probably played a significant part in the intellectual and spiritual formation of the 'Venerable Richard Challoner'. Latterly, Bryan Tunstall served St Wilfrid's mission in York and he died in Little Blake Street in 1742, aged 69.

Marmaduke Tunstall, Lord of Wycliffe, was a bachelor and when he died in 1760, aged 88, he was succeeded at Wycliffe by his nephew, Marmaduke Cuthbert Constable, the son of Marmaduke Tunstall's brother, Cuthbert Tunstall. When Cuthbert Tunstall came into the Burton Constable estate in East Yorkshire in 1718, he assumed his mother's name, Constable. On succeeding to Wycliffe, Cuthbert's son Marmaduke resumed the name Tunstall.

Robert Foster, who was to become the brother-in-law of Robert

Robinson of Hutton Hall, was an agent of the Burton Constable estate in 1761 and his sister Cecily was on the payroll of Wycliffe Hall.[13] These positions could well have arisen through friendships forged between the Foster relatives and the Tunstalls and Constables at the English College at Douai. For instance, Cecily's cousin William Daniel was teaching humanities at Douai when Marmaduke Tunstall, Lord of Wycliffe in Cecily's time, was a student there; perhaps William put in a word for Cecily.[14]

Robert and Cecily's father was James Foster whose family had lived at Charnock Richard in Lancashire since, at least, the 16th century. James had been renovating an neglected old Elizabethan house in the neighbouring village of Euxton. When James Foster got married in 1725 it was probably to this renewed home, Euxton House, that he took his bride, Elizabeth, the only child of Robert Holden of Leagram. And it was here that James and Elizabeth brought up Cecily, her brother, and their two elder sisters, Elizabeth and Grace.[15]

Robert Robinson of Hutton Hall and Cecily Foster were married at Wycliffe, where Rev. Thomas Penswick was the Catholic chaplain, on Thursday 16th July 1767.[16]

Their marriage took place just before the 1767 Return of Papists for the Diocese of Chester, which included the Deanery of Richmond. The House of Lords instituted this enquiry because of concern that the Anglican bishops were allowing the spread of Catholicism.

Thomas Penswick, the uncle of John Daniel the president of Douai, was the son of William Penswick and Grace Johnson of Lytham in Lancashire. His sister Mary was married to Edward Daniel of Durton. Thomas was born 24th September 1717. He entered the Venerable English College at Rome 8th February 1732 and he was ordained 9th March 1743.

Thomas Penswick was chaplain to the Maires at Hardwick Hall when, in 1746, they were attacked by a no-popery mob 'resulting in the death a few days later of Ann Maire, the wife of Francis Maire Esq.'. Thomas went to Wycliffe in 1762 and took with him his register which he had started at Hardwick. His entries, which give the ages of the babies at the time of their baptism and their relationship to their sponsors, suggest an intimate knowledge of the families involved. Thomas Penswick died at Wycliffe 7th April 1791 aged seventy-three. Robert Robinson and Adam Dale, the younger, of Wycliffe Grange, to each of whom he left five pounds, were, as we have seen, his executors; among other items he bequeathed to them, in trust, was his horse.[17]

Thomas Penswick's register shows the close relationship between

Adam and Sarah Dale of Wycliffe Grange and Robert and Cecily Robinson, the first five of whose six children had Dale godparents: Dorothy, born in 1769, Sally Dale stood for her father Adam Dale; Ann, 1771, Robert Dale of Hutton Fields; Elizabeth, 1773, Adam's wife Sarah; Robert, 1776, Adam Dale's sister Mary; Cecily, 1779, Adam Dale's son Adam.[18]

Cecily Robinson of Hutton Hall had a cousin, Thomas Daniel. He was the eldest son of her aunt Helen Foster of Burton Constable and Thomas Daniel of Whittingham, Kirkham, in Lancashire.

Thomas Daniel entered the English College at Douai on the 12th June 1730, during the latter part of the presidency of Robert Witham and two months before Richard Challoner left for the English mission. He, himself, left for the mission on the 5th August 1740 and served at Linton-upon-Ouse. In 1742, on the death of Bryan Tunstall, Thomas Daniel took up residence in 'Chapel House', Little Blake Street, as the first Rector of St Wilfrid's mission. Each priest was, in turn, the Bishop's Vicar-General for Yorkshire and Procurator of the Yorkshire Brethren's Fund. In his latter capacity, Thomas Daniel worked very closely with a Catholic lawyer, John Maire, who had been educated at Douai and Gray's Inn and who was the fifth son of Thomas Maire of Lartington and Hardwick; he acted as investment manager.[19]

> Thomas Daniel was very much a man of affairs. He had been concerned with investing clergy funds. He even sold books to his brethren buried in country missions, explaining that "you will find the vast difference between buying books of me and of a bookseller". In his will, apart from £3000 of clergy funds in his care, he disposed of a personal estate of £1370. He left £200 of this and his furniture to his successors in the mission. (His money was invested in the Easingwold Turnpike Co.) At his death there were two maids in the York house. We know nothing of his pastoral methods.[20]

About the time when Robert Robinson moved into Hutton Hall, Thomas Daniel was building the chapel in Lop Lane; apparently, 'as an annex to the house, stretching into its garden, and so concealed from direct view. It was up by 1764 when the churchwardens noted its existence and said that a papist parishioner had proudly told them it was needed for a congregation of 170'.

Thomas Daniel died 25th August 1770 and was buried at St Michael le Belfry. One of his executors was Mr Hugh Tootell of Wycliffe whose wife, a year previously, had become godmother to Robert and Cecily's daughter Dorothy; Hugh Tootell himself, two and a half years later, became the godfather to their daughter Elizabeth. Thomas Daniel, as procurator of the Yorkshire Brethren's Fund, had kept an account-book which gives valuable information about Catholic affairs.

Cecily Robinson's cousin, William Daniel, alias Foster, was eleven years younger than his brother Thomas. He entered Douai 13th July 1740, was ordained 17th December 1750 and stayed on teaching humanities. William taught Anthony Langstaff's brother, Robert Langstaff alias Wilson, from the second class of Rudiments, in 1752, through to Rhetoric, in 1757.[21] Robert Banister was prefect of studies at the time. Years later, when Banister was at Mobreck Hall, Kirkham, in his correspondence with his nephew, Henry Banister alias Rutter, he referred to his neighbour 'Mr. Wilson'. Robert Banister, among other strong opinions expressed, deplored the social frivolities going on at Douai compared with the hard work of their day.[22]

The government may not have been so vigilant about English boys going abroad to become priests as in the previous century; but other perils remained. William Witham arrived at Douai 19th August 1757 'after various accidents at sea: being taken by a French privateer, July 31, and being on board during a sharp engagement between the same privateer and another with 3 English vessels, about 2 hours in the night-time, the second or third of August, it being a little after full-moon: robbed of his money, watch, buckles, etc.'.[23]

Anthony's other brother, Valentine Langstaff alias Marmaduke Wilson, was also a Douai priest; he lived to be ninety-two. Elizabeth Langstaff who founded the charitable trust in 1818 for the education of priests at Ushaw was their sister.

William Daniel left Douai 18th July 1758 to become chaplain to Sir Walter Vavasour at Hazlewood Castle. Thomas used his brother's account 'to conduct mission and family business' such as paying the Douai fees of their cousin James Foster and to send money to Cecily Robinson's sisters Elizabeth and Grace Foster, the Poor Clare nuns at Dunkirk.[24]

Cecily Robinson's half-brother, James Foster, was the son of her father, James Foster, by his second wife Emerentia, 'Eamy', Heyes. James was born 14th February 1747 at Ashton Hall, near Lancaster, where his father was a tenant farmer after he left Euxton House. James went to school at Fernyhalgh, entered Douai 27th June 1764 and was ordained 1st April 1775. He then took over the chaplaincy of Hazlewood from his cousin William Daniel.[25] William returned to Lancashire as chaplain to the Andertons at Euxton Hall where he died on 25th July 1777 at the age of fifty-two. Thomas Penswick was a witness to his will in which he left £200 to Cecily and Robert Robinson.[26]

Robert Daniel, the brother of Thomas and William, was a tanner and a man of means. He and his wife Mary lived at Euxton House, the former home of James Foster the priest's father, where they had seven servants.[27] Robert died in 1778 and he left his Euxton property to his wife for her life and then to his cousin Robert Foster of Burton. In that same year James Foster left Hazlewood and became chaplain at Burton Constable where he remained for seven years.

In the meantime, Thomas and William's sister, Jane Daniel, together with the Daltons of Thurnham Hall, near Lancaster, endowed the Thurnham mission, with the stipulation that her cousin James Foster should be the first missioner.[28] James took up the post in 1785. He built the priest's house called Woodside in 1802 and the chapel in 1810. He would be able to ride over to Hornby, about fourteen miles to the north-east, to visit his friend John Lingard. James's portrait used to hang with those of the Daltons at Thurnham Hall.[29]

Thomas Daniel, a busy man of affairs, had the help of curates. One of his curates was his and Cecily Robinson's uncle William Foster, alias Charnock, about whom we must now hear more.[30] We shall also revisit Doctor Richard Challoner who has been referred to as the 'greatest leader' of the English Catholics through 'a time of acute pessimism and depression. The failure of the jacobite rebellion of 1715 had been the death-knell of catholic hopes; several staunch catholic families had given up the struggle and priests had deemed it prudent to go even further underground'.[31]

6. Descendants of Adam Daile and Sarah Richinson of Hutton, N. Yorkshire
showing Robinson and Dale relationships

Adam Daile of Hutton (- 1712) & Sarah Richinson (- 1716). In his will 20 Oct 1712, Adam uses the spelling 'Daile'; his son Robert, in his will of 7 Oct 1736, uses the spelling 'Dale'

- Robert Dale (c. 1678 - 1736) of Hutton Hall & Mary ? Tunstall ? Liddell (c. 1685 - 27 Dec 1777)
  - Lawrence Dale (c. 1707 - ?)
  - Adam Dale (c. 1713 - 13 Mar 1776) of Wycliffe Grange & Sarah ------ (c. 1712 - 8 May 1802)
    - Dorothy Dale of Wycliffe Grange (1737 - ?) & Ralph Robinson (c. 1709 - 1792) of Hutton Fields
      - Ralph Robinson (1763 - ?)
      - Anthony Robinson (1765 - ?) & Jane Barker (c. 1765 - ?)
      - John Robinson (1766 - ?)
      - Matthew Robinson (c. 1768 - c. 1795) of Hutton Fields, died in Jamaica
    - Robert Dale (c. 1740 - 2 Nov 1790) of Hutton Fields & Dorothy (c. 1748 - Mar 1815) dau. of Richard Brown of Aldbrough
      - Adam Dale (9 Mar 1773 - ?)
      - Robert Dale (22 Nov 1774 - 23 Nov 1849) of Scorton entered Douai Oct 1788, left 8 Jan 1793
      - Sarah Dale (1 Oct 1776 - ?)
      - Dorothy Dale (13 Jul 1778 - ?) & Joseph Clement m. 16 May 1810
      - Ann Dale (28 Dec 1779 - Sep 1821) & Cuthbert Watson (c. 1777 - 19 Feb 1850) of Ovington, his first wife, m. 13 May 1813
      - Francis Dale (9 Dec 1781 - 10 Feb 1795)
      - Mary Dale (9 Apr 1784 - ?)
      - Margaret Dale (13 Sep 1785 - ?) & Smith
      - William Dale (2 Apr 1789 - ?)
      - Teresa Ann Dale (7 May 1791 - ?) & John Middleton of Hutton Fields m. 26 May 18
    - Adam Dale (c. 1744 - ?) of Wycliffe Grange
    - Sarah Dale (c. 1746 - ?)
    - Ann Dale (c. 1748 - ?) & James Brown (c. 1746 - ?) of Aldbrough, son of Richard Brown of Aldbrough, m. 22 May 1777
      - A son d.s.p.
      - Sarah Brown (- 26 Jan 1853) & Thomas Robinson (30 Jul 1781 - 10 Feb 1868) of Hutton Hall
      - Ann Brown (c. 1786 - 18 Jan 1850) & Cuthbert Watson (c. 1777 - 19 Feb 1850) of Ovington, his second wife
    - Thomas Dale (c. 1751 - ?)
  - Robert Dale (2 Jul 1717 - 15 Jul 1722)
  - Elizabeth Dale (1719 - ?)
  - Mary Dale (1728 - ?)
  - Sarah Dale (1731 - ?)
- Elizabeth Daile & ------ Robinson m. c. 1712
  - Adam Robinson (c. 1713 - ?)
- Dorothy Daile (c. 1685 - ?) married a Robinson c. 1714 and had a son, Adam, by 1716; probably the parents of Adam and Robert as described
  - Adam Robinson (c. 1715 - 28 May 1800)
  - Robert Robinson (1721 - 27 Oct 1809) of Hutton Hall & Cecily Foster (1733- 1804) m. at Wycliffe 16 Jul 17
  - Tom
  - Ann
- Ann Daile
- Sarah Daile

CHAPTER VI

Charnock Richard to Cornamucklagh: a Bridge Across the Sea

*'The recognition of this cultural diversity
is the beginning of wisdom'.*
Michael Howard[1]

The Robinsons of Hutton Hall in North Yorkshire and the Robinsons of North Kildare had much in common: they were both Catholic families who resisted the Protestant Reformation; they were farmers; some of their children went abroad to become religious, or to train as priests, in order to return and keep the faith alive in their native lands; and their ardour for the old faith took its place with an enthusiasm for race horses! Did they know each other? The Venerable Richard Challoner certainly formed a bridge between two family members.[2]

Robert Witham, vicar-general to Bishop Giffard, left his ancestral home at Cliff Hall, which lies about six miles east of Hutton Magna, to become the twelfth president of his Alma Mater, the English College at Douai. The next year the hopes of Catholics were dashed by the collapse of the 'Fifteen' Jacobite Rebellion; but, at Douai, an era of renewal was to begin under this 'second founder'.

Richard Challoner was appointed vice-president and, also, professor of theology and prefect of studies, in 1720; the year in which William Foster entered the College as a boy of thirteen.[3] William took, as his alias, 'Charnock', the name of a family into which the Fosters married. William, as we have seen, was destined to become the uncle of my great-great-grandmother Cecily Robinson, née Foster, of Hutton Hall, whose ancestors came from Charnock Richard in Lancashire.[4]

William Foster's future patron, the young Robert Dalton of Thurnham Hall, in Lancashire, joined his brothers, John and William who were already students at Douai, in 1726. These boys would have enkindled the Jacobite spirit in the College. Their father John Hoghton (who had taken the name and arms of his mother Elizabeth Dalton) and his brother, Robert, were both out in the 'Fifteen'; the latter was convicted of high treason. Their paternal great-great-grandfather William Hoghton of Park Hall, Charnock Richard, a Catholic, zealously espoused the king's cause at the outbreak of the Civil War and was made a lieutenant-colonel. He fell at the first battle of Newbury in 1643. Their maternal great-great-grandfather Colonel Thomas Dalton of Thurnham Hall, a recusant like his ancestors, raised a Regiment of Horse at his own expense for the King. He died from wounds inflicted at the second battle of Newbury.[5]

William Foster studied under the guidance and tuition of the learned and pious Challoner, until he was ordained priest at Tournai in 1730; the year in which Challoner left for the English mission. William continued at Douai for a further six years. He taught rudiments and was prefect general and, later, he was prefect of the library and confessor ordinary.[6]

The Rev. William Foster, alias Charnock, left Douai for the English mission in 1736. In 1741 he was chaplain to his old schoolfellow, Robert Dalton, at Thurnham Hall. Robert had thirteen children. His third wife, Bridget, daughter of Thomas More of Barnborough Hall, was descended from Henry VIII's Lord High Chancellor whom he beheaded for his unwillingness to recognise the King as head of the English Church. The future of Thurnham Hall, this old catholic and royalist stronghold, seemed assured. However, 'After the Jacobite rising of 1745, Mr. Foster had to seek refuge elsewhere'. We have met him as a curate of Thomas Daniel in York; and there he died in 1754.[7]

The Rev. Gerard Shaw of Cornamucklagh, County Kildare, whose sister, Catherine, married Daniel McRobin of the same townland, was a student, not at Douai, but at the English College at Seville; nevertheless, he became Challoner's close friend. He, also, was acquainted with Lancashire Jacobites as is seen from the following quotation by his sister's great-great-great-great-great-grandson, James Robinson, in *The Robinsons of North Kildare:*

> The testator, Richard Richardson, of Poulton, Lancs, after a life of exile and ill fortune spent in the Jacobite cause, ended up in the remote town of Guadalcanal, in the Sierra Morena, between Seville and Badajoz. There, on the 6th of June 1730, fearing the approach of death, he dictated his last will and testament to a local notary, using Gerard Shaw [his executor] as interpreter. The fact that the old cavalry captain did not even have the ready money for his funeral did not prevent him making in imagination the bequests which, with better luck, he might have made in reality. The only tangible asset he had was an old fob watch which he hoped one of his creditors might accept in lieu of cash. His main hopes of a posthumous windfall rested with the ill-fated Mississippi Company which had crashed ten years earlier, and with the restoration of James III.[8]

Gerard Shaw served on the London Mission as priest at the Spanish Chapel for forty-eight years. One of the secret meeting places where Bishop Challoner carried out confirmations was referred to as 'Shaw's'. Challoner records how, 'The same mr Shaw gave also to me for the use of the clergy of the district a large handsome silver-gilt chalice and paten now in my possession'. Challoner remembered him in his will, 'As also that every one of my brother bishops would accept of one guinea each. As likewise my good friends,... Mr. Ger. Shaw,...'. Gerard never received his guinea; he died in 1780, three months before the Gordon Riots. Six months after that horrific event, the good bishop, still in harness in his ninetieth year, also went to his reward.[9] And now for more about the 'Jacobites'.

CHAPTER VII

The End of an Era: Demise of the Stuarts and Deaths at Wycliffe and in Lancashire

'It is observed both by historians and moralists, that there seldom happened any considerable alteration either in the management of public affairs or private life, without some previous matters which disposed mankind, and made them susceptible of such impressions'.
Hugh Tootell alias Charles Dodd, 1671-1743 [1]

Adam Daile of Manfield and later of Hutton, on the Wycliffe estate, North Yorkshire, my great-times-five-grandfather, had been presented before the Court of Correction as a recusant and for refusing to pay the parish clerk his 'Xmas dues' in 1705.[2] On 20th October 1712 he signed his will: 'first I bequeath my soul into the hands of my saviour Jesus Christ thro the merits of whose bitter passion I hope for salvation and my body to be buried at ye discretion of my executors hereafter named forbidding all unnecessary expences'. That year, he died. His name was honoured by his son, Robert Dale of Girlington, who called his own second son Adam, later to become Adam Dale of Wycliffe Grange, and also by his daughters Elizabeth Robinson and Dorothy Robinson each of whom called her first-born Adam.

Bishop James Smith, Vicar Apostolic of the Northern District, had died on 13th May the previous year at his residence at Wycliffe Hall; he was sixty-six. He had been ill for ten months following an exhausting tour of the East Riding the previous summer. On his death Robert Witham of Cliff Hall was made Vicar-General of the Northern District.[3]

Francis Tunstall himself, Lord of Wycliffe, now aged seventy-six, died the year after Adam Daile.

The following year, 1714, saw the demise of the Stuart monarchy, in England, with the death of Queen Anne. She was the younger daughter of James II by his first wife, Ann Hyde, whose daughters were brought up as Protestants; though she herself eventually became a Catholic. The Duke of Marlborough, who had fallen from Queen Anne's favour, now returned to England to ensure the Protestant succession.

In Lancashire, John Foster of Charnock Richard, tanner, the great-grandfather of my great-great-grandmother, Cecily Robinson of Hutton Hall, had made his will on 28th July 1709. He left: 'a penny dole to all such poor as shall resort and come to my ffuneral...to the poor of Charnock Richard aforesaid ten pounds...that the profit thereof be annually laid out in lynnen cloth for Winter shifts for the poor... Also to all shoemakers, leather cutters and others my constant customers whose names are in my trade book I give every one of them a pair of black gloves not exceeding one shilling price...I give and bequeath Margaret Tootell my Grandaughter fifteen pounds charged and chargeable to a certain parcell of land called Netherwood lying in Euxton'.

Margaret's father, William Tootell, and his brother, Hugh, were confirmed by Bishop Leyburn at Euxton in 1687. Her uncle, Hugh Tootell, alias Charles Dodd, the future church historian, entered the English College at Douai on 23rd July 1688 when he was aged seventeen.[4] Hugh was ordained in 1698 and returned to Lancashire where he worked with his uncle, Christopher Tootell, who had trained at the English College at Lisbon and who was the priest at Lady Well, Fernyhalgh, near Preston.

Alice Harrison was a well educated girl whose reading led her into the Catholic Church, much to the consternation of her parents. Christopher Tootell supported 'Dame Alice' in founding her school at Fernyhalgh for between one and two hundred boys and girls who boarded with her or in the neighbourhood. 'Every day she took the Catholic children (for she had some Protestant pupils) to Mass at Lady Well, lingering a few moments to offer up a prayer as she passed our Lady's Well in front of the ancient chantry..., this famous school was in reality nothing less than a nursery for the English colleges abroad'.

Among Dame Alice's pupils were Alban Butler, author of *Lives of the Saints,* and most of the Daniels, including John Daniel, President of Douai. 'The Daniels of Durton, Alston, Whittingham, and Catteralls, were one of those good old Lancashire families from which the Church obtained a fruitful supply of missioners during the days of persecution'.[5]

John Foster also stated in his will: 'to William Hoghton of Park Hall Esq. and Robert my son I give ten pounds to be by them disburst'. John Foster and his wife had been recorded in the Return of Papists for the Diocese of Chester, in 1705, under Charnock Richard, together with their son, Robert Foster, farmer, and his wife and two children, and also with William Hoghton Esq. and three children.

There is an old stone and red brick house in Charnock Richard called 'Tanhouse Farm' with this inscription carved in stone on the gable-end of the newer part:

F
R E
1695

Robert Foster, whose family had lived at Charnock Richard in Lancashire since the 16th century, was described as 'a well-to-do tanner connected with Tootells, Daniels, and other good Catholic families'. Robert's wife was Elizabeth Parker; and their eldest daughter, Helen, who married Thomas Daniel of Whittingham, was born in 1691.[6] Robert Foster died in 1719.

In penal times, the local Catholics attended Mass at Park Hall, in Charnock Richard. Edward Booth, alias Barlow, also died in 1719. He was aged 80, and he died at Park Hall where he had been chaplain to the Hoghton family for 47 years. Edward was the godson of Saint Ambrose Barlow OSB by whom he had been baptised on 15th December 1639; and he studied for the priesthood in Lisbon. He wrote: *Meteorological essays concerning the origin of springs, generation of rain and production of wind* which appeared, anonymously, in 1715, with a dedication to Robert, Earl of Oxford and Mortimer. Godfrey Anstruther says about Booth, 'he is chiefly remembered for his inventions for the improvement of clocks and watches which were appreciated in his own day in spite of religious prejudices. Thus in 1677 he served as steward of the Clockmakers' Company... In 1695 a patent for 14 years was granted to Edward Booth (under his true name), William Houghton and Thomas Tompion for a new sort of watch or clock which they had invented'.[7]

On the death of Queen Anne, George, Elector of Hanover, a great-grandson of James I and a Protestant, acceded to the British throne in accordance with the Act of Settlement. George I restored Marlborough to his old posts; and the general made preparation to resist the Jacobites who favoured Prince James Edward, the son of James II by his second wife, Mary of Modena.

The following year, in September, the Earl of Mar ushered in the 1715 Jacobite Rebellion by raising the standard of James Edward, Chevalier de St George, on the Braes of Mar; though the Chevalier himself was still in France.

In October, James Radcliffe 3rd Earl of Derwentwater recruited a small group of Jacobites in the north-east of England. He was aged 26 and happily married with one little boy at this time. James Radcliffe's mother, Lady Mary Tudor, was a natural daughter of Charles II; and James had pledged his loyalty to his cousin, James Edward, when they were boys together in the Court of St Germain.[8]

William Tunstall of Wycliffe, a wealthy Catholic who was advanced in years, and who was a first cousin of James Radcliffe's father, Edward, the 2nd Earl, joined the insurgents as Paymaster and Quartermaster-General.[9] Marmaduke Cuthbert Tunstall, the naturalist

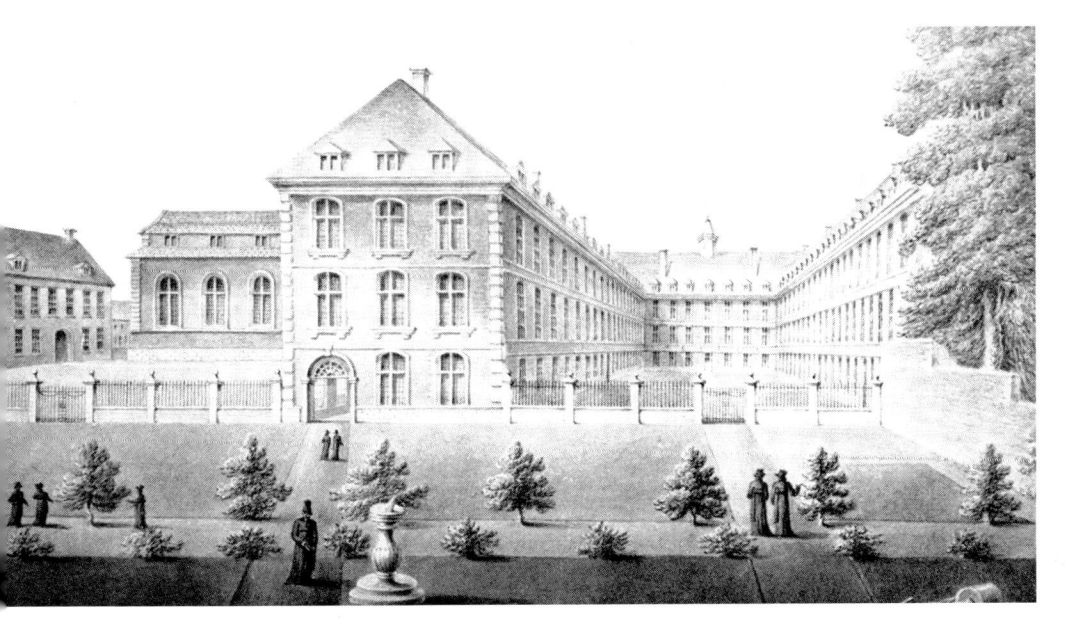

The English College at Douai in the eighteenth century. *(From a drawing at Ushaw).*

36 John Lingard (1771-1851). When he was a student at Douai, Lingard narrowly escaped being murdered by a revolutionary mob, in 1790. He escaped to England in February 1793: ordained at the Bar Convent by Bishop William Gibson, 18th April 1795; Vice-President at Crook Hall and Ushaw; priest at Hornby Castle where he wrote his famous History of England; friend of my great-great-grandmother's half-brother, James Foster who was also a Douai priest. *(From a print which hangs in St Mary's Catholic Church, Hornby; the original painting is at Ushaw College).* Photograph kindly given to me by Fr McArdle, the Parish Priest.

37 Rev. James Foster, son of James Foster and Emerentia Heys, he was a half-brother of my great-great-grandmother Cecily Robinson née Foster of Hutton Hall: born Ashton Hall, Lancaster, 14th February 1747; schooling at Fernyhalgh and Douai; ordained priest at Arras 1775; chaplain at Hazlewood Castle; at Burton Constable 1778-85; went to Thurnham 1785 where he remained until his death, 17th February 1824; his friend Dr John Lingard of Hornby Castle was his executor. *(Portrait in the possession of the Parish Priest, St Thomas and St Elizabeth, Thurnham). Fr Bernard Shuttleworth kindly allowed me to take this photograph.*

38 Ashton Hall, Lancaster: where my great-great-great-grandfather James Foster lived, with his second wife Emerentia Heys, as a tenant farmer under the Duke of Hamilton and Brandon. Years later his son Rev. James Foster was often a guest of the Duke of Hamilton and used to sleep in the room where he was born. The picture is of the Green Court as it would have been in James Foster's day. *(From: A History of Lancaster Golf Club, by J. H. Shennan, p. 50). Reproduced with the kind permission of Mr P. J. Irvine, Secretary/Manager of the Lancaster Golf Club Ltd., Ashton Hall, Ashton-with-Stodday, Lancaster.*

The Rt Revd RICHARD CHALLONER, BISHOP of DEBORA

Dr Richard Challoner (1691-1781) from an engraving by Symms and Mitchell, 1781. Challoner was appointed Vice-President, Professor of Theology, and Prefect of Studies, at the English College at Douai, in 1720 – the year in which William Foster of Charnock Richard entered the College as a student aged 13. William was Cecily Robinson of Hutton Hall's uncle. Challoner left for the English mission in 1730 and from 1758 was Vicar-Apostolic of the London District. His learning, piety, and devotion to his flock, during a century of great discouragement for English Catholics, earned him the title 'The Venerable'.

40 Cuthbert Tunstall (c.1680-1747) and his second wife, Elizabeth Heneage, in a painting by Peter van Bleeck. Cuthbert was the second son of Francis Tunstall of Wycliffe and Cecily, daughter of John Constable, 2nd Viscount Dunbar, of Burton Constable, East Yorkshire: student at Douai; qualified as Doctor of Medicine at Montpellier University; had to change his name to Constable when he inherited Burton Constable on the death of his uncle, William Constable, in 1718; patron of the arts. *Reproduced with kind permission from Dr David Connell, Director, Burton Constable Foundation. Photograph: Photographic Survey, Courtauld Institute of Art.*

41 Dr James Smith (1645-1711), 17th century French School: President of Douai, 1682-1688; in 1688, Vicar-Apostolic of the Northern District which he visited and administered from Wycliffe Hall where he lived, in relative obscurity to avoid persecution, in the home of his friend Francis Tunstall. He resisted King James II's desire to have him made a cardinal. James Smith died at Wycliffe. Francis Hodgson, a Douai priest, who died at Hutton Hall in 1726, was one of his three trustees. The man standing behind James Smith is probably Francis Tunstall. *(From a portrait on loan to Ushaw by the Diocese of Middlesbrough). Reproduced with kind permission from Rt. Rev. John P. Crowley, Bishop of Middlesbrough; attribution kindly supplied by Dr A. J. MacGregor, Librarian, Ushaw College.*

William Tunstall, 'the first to shoot flying'. My contention is:
t this William was a son of William Tunstall of Scargill Castle &
cliffe and his wife, Mary, daughter of Sir Edward Radcliffe of
ston & Derwentwater, Bart.; and that he is to be identified with
 'William Tunstall, Esq., of a Yorkshire Roman Catholic family'
o served as Paymaster and Quartermaster-General, under James
dcliffe, 3rd Earl of Derwentwater (who would have been his first
sin once removed), in the 1715 Jacobite Rebellion; and,
thermore, that he inspired Macaulay's poem 'A Jacobite's
itaph'. *Reproduced with kind permission from Dr David Connell, Director, Burton
stable Foundation. Photograph: Photographic Survey, Courtauld Institute of Art.*

Accounts of raids and searches at Fernyhalgh, near Preston.
e search: 'made in the night-time, for apprehending Persons
oxious to the Government, on account not only of the
urrection but also of Priesthood: and amongst other reputed
ests C. T. [Christopher Tootell] & E. M. [Edward Melling, his
hew] were particularly sought for, on the 5th January 1715'.
Fe 2/1 *Held at Lancashire Record Office, Bow Lane, Preston PR1 2RE.
roduced with kind permission of the Parish Priest, Fernyhalgh, St Mary Roman
holic Church.*

AND SEARCHES AT FERYHALGH, LANCA

After Plundering was over, fresh Troubles and Distresses were occasion'd by General and special Searches made in the Night-time, for apprehending Persons obnoxious to the Government, on account not only of the Insurrection but also of Priesthood: and amongst other reputed Priests C.T. & E. M. were particularly sought for, on ye 5th of Jany 1715: at Midnight: when C.T. had (in all likelyhood) been taken Napping, but that (upon accidental or rather providential Notice of the Danger) he lay nine Hours that Night, on a Hay-mow, in a lonesome Barn; where the fear of being found out, the coldness of the Weather, the rustling and squeaking of Mice within and ye screeching of Owles without, disturbed his Rest and kept him Waking all that Time.

Playing at Bob-peep was all that Winter's Pastime: but the Seekers advantage over the Hiders, spoil'd our Sport, ye long Frost and Snow then on the Ground, being ...

Mem.olim

1715.
On monday June ye last, the two Chappels at Holy-Well were visited by 20 Soldiers, sent from Preston by ye Commissioners, mounted upon hired Horses, and conducted by Mr Hitchmough: the value of their Booty is variously reported, not much less considerable than at first it was said to be; as not exceeding 100li

Chr: Tutell

44 Tanhouse Farm in Charnock Richard. The stone plaque, below the top window on the gable end of the newer part of the house, bears the letters F (for Foster), R (for Robert), and E (for Elizabeth), and the date 1695. No doubt, my ancestor Robert Foster, described as 'a well-to-do tanner connected with Tootells, Daniel and other good Catholic families', moved there soon after he married Elizabeth Parker. Perhaps, his father, John, also a tanner, had occupied the older part of the house. *Photograph by J. R. Robinson.*

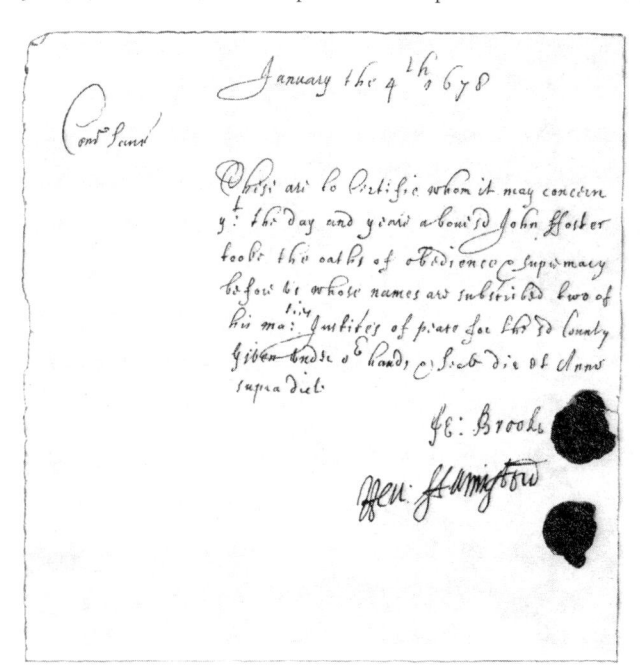

45 John Foster takes the Oaths of Obedience and Supremacy on 4th January 1678. QSP 493/18 *Reproduced with the permission of the County Archivist, Lancashire Record Office, Bow Lane, Preston PR1 2RE.*

46 John Foster and Ellen, his wife, and James Charnock of Charnock Richard, have attended Divine Service in the parish church of Standish and have received the Sacrament of the Lords Supper in both kinds according to the Liturgy of the Church of England. *QSP 493/1 Reproduced with the permission of the County Archivist, Lancashire Record Office, Bow Lane, Preston PR1 2RE.*

Euxton House, Euxton: home of [Ja]mes Foster and his first wife, [Eli]zabeth, only child of Robert Holden [of] Leagram, Lancashire; married c. 1724. [Th]is Elizabethan house had been [un]occupied for some time and was [res]tored by James Foster. The [ph]otograph was taken by the present [ow]ner, Sam Watkinson in the summer of [the] year 2000, to capture the return of [Ja]mes and Elizabeth's great-great-great-[gra]ndson nearly three hundred years [lat]er! No doubt, James could have told [me] about the religious difficulties of his [gra]ndparents, John and Ellen Foster, in [16]78 – a time of increasing anti-Catholic [pr]ejudice culminating in the 'Popish Plot' [of] Titus Oates, in that same year. [Ot]herwise, James might have referred me [to] his brother William, the Douai priest. [Ph]otograph by Sam Watkinson.

48 Robert Charnock (1604-1653), 'One Eye Charnock', of Astley Hall. Captain Robert Charnock was a Royalist and he was involved in both sieges of Lathom House. Robert and my ancestor John Foster had a great-aunt and a great-uncle in common: James Charnock of Astley Hall, Chorley, married Margaret Foster of Greenehurst, Charnock Richard, on 22nd January 1592. *(From a portrait at Astley Hall). Reproduced with kind permission of the Curator, Astley Hall.*

49 Astley Hall, Chorley, Lancashire, from a sketch by Herbert Cescinsky: as it would have appeared in the time of Captain Robert Charnock. *Reproduced with kind permission of the Curator, Astley Hall.*

50 The Battle of Brill, 1646 – a re-enactment. During the English Civil War (1642-1649), Henry Holden of Crawshaw served as an officer in the Royal Army under Colonel Thomas Dalton. In 1649 Henry entered Douai; and, as a priest, he served the Dalton family at Thurnham Hall until his death there in 1688. Three centuries later, Shaun and Nicola, Henry Holden's second cousins eight times removed, are serving under me, in somewhat more auspicious, though rather wet circumstances, at Brill! My ancestor Thomas Holden of Greengore was a younger brother of Henry Holden's grandfather, Richard Holden of Chaigley Hall, who was born around 1565. *Photograph by J. R. Robinson.*

51 My journey of exploration has led me, under the guidance of Tom Holden of Yew Tree Farm, to Greengore Farm, and to a warm welcome by David and Mary Kay the present owners. This fifteenth century house was the home of Thomas Holden, my great-times-seven-grandfather. Greengore in Bailey had come into the Holden family by 1388 and remained in their possession until 1618. Thomas' elder brother, Richard, lived at Chaigley Hall which the Holdens acquired 1330, the fifth year of the reign of Edward III. *Photograph by David Kay.*

52 Mary Ann (1800-1883): daughter of Rob[ert]
and Sarah Wright of Fitling in East Yorksh[ire],
my great-grandmother, through whom we c[laim]
relationship to John and Christopher Wrigh[t,]
the Gunpowder Plotters, of Ploughland Ha[ll].

53 Mary Ward (1585-1645): foundress of the Institute of the Blessed Virgin Mary, a religious community far ahead of its time. She was a niece of John and Christopher Wright. Her grandmother, Ursula Wright, spent fourteen years in prison rather than give up her Catholic faith. Ursula's cousin Francis Ingleby was condemned for his priesthood and hanged drawn and quartered at York, the year after Mary was born. *(The portrait represents a detail from one of the 50 pictures of the 'Painted Life' preserved in the IVBM Convent at Augsburg)*

...ristopher and John Wright with the other Gunpowder Plotters. *(Engraving in the Bodleian Library).*

...by St Ledgers: the gate-house, at the home of Robert Catesby's mother, where the Gunpowder Plot is
... have been planned. *Photograph by J. R. Robinson.*

56 Ripley Castle: in North Yorkshire where Francis Ingleby, the son of Sir William Ingleby and Ann Malle[ry] was born in 1550. Francis was educated at Brasenose College, Oxford, and at the Inner Temple, London. [In] 1582 he joined the English College at Douai, which had been evacuated to Rheims; and, in the following [year] he was ordained priest and returned to England. He was arrested in York, condemned for his priesthood, [and] he was hanged, drawn, and quartered there on 3rd June 1586. His martyrdom occurred less than three mo[nths] after that of his friend Margaret Clitheroe, also in York. *Photograph by J. R. Robinson.*

57 Francis Ingleby (also spelt Ingilby): 'He was a short man but well made, and seemed a man of 35 years of age or thereabouts. He was of a light complexion, wore a chestnut beard and had a slight cast in his eyes. In mind he was quick and piercing, ready and facile in speech, of aspect grave and austere and earnest and assiduous in action'. (Pollen, Acts, 259), quoted from Anstruther, I, pp. 181-2. *(From a portrait in the Knight's Chamber, Ripley Castle). Reproduced with the kind permission of Sir Thomas Ingilby, Bt., ARICS, FAAV, of Ripley Castle, Harrogate, North Yorkshire, HG3 3AY.*

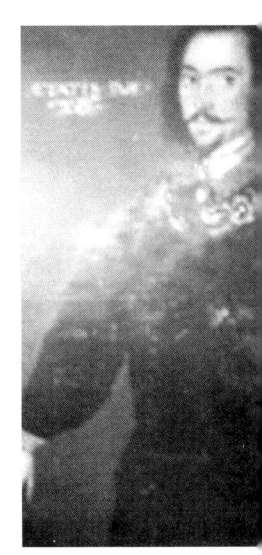

58 William Allen (1532-1594), 16th century Roman School: Allan came from Rossall in Lancashire, was educated at Oriel College, and became the Principal of St Mary's Hall, Oxford. Unable, in conscience, to accept the new religion, he joined the exiled Catholics in Louvain. On his return to Lancashire he was shocked to see Catholics falling away for lack of leadership. He was ordained priest at Malines in 1567. In 1568 he founded the English College at Douai for the higher education of English Catholics, both clerical and lay. The first Douai priest to be martyred on the English mission was Cuthbert Mayne, on 30th November 1577. Before Queen Elizabeth died, in 1603, four hundred and fifty Douai priests had returned to keep the faith alive in their native land; 120 of them met the fate of Cuthbert Mayne. *(From a painting at Ushaw). Reproduced with the kind permission of the President of Ushaw, Rev. James O'Keefe; attribution kindly supplied by Dr A. J. MacGregor, Librarian, Ushaw College.*

English College on a Plan of Douai in 1627.

60 Brasenose College, Oxford, where four Douai priests who appear in this account were contemporaries 1560s: Lawrence Johnson (Douai 1573) and Thomas Cottam (Douai 1577) who were martyred together at Tyburn, 30th May 1582; Francis Ingleby (Douai 1582) who was martyred at York 3rd June 1586; Thomas Worthington (Douai 1573) who became President of Douai from 1599 to 1613. Thomas Cottam's brother John, who became William Shakespeare's master at Stratford-on-Avon Grammar School, was also contemp with these four men at Brasenose. *Photograph by J. R. Robinson.*

61 Hoghton Tower: family seat of the de Hog – one of the most powerful families in Lanca Sir Richard de Hoghton's illegitimate son, Ric Hoghton, was settled at Park Hall, in Charnoc Richard, in 1572; and he acquired it in 1606. Richard Hoghton founded a Catholic branch the family at Park Hall; and Lawrence Johnso was chaplain there in about 1580. Local Cath attended Mass in secret at Park Hall. William Shakespeare was introduced into the family o Alexander Hoghton, at Hoghton Tower, by J Cottam, his schoolmaster at Stratford Gramm School, in about 1680 – according to recent scholarship. In that same year, Edmund Cam the Jesuit martyr, was a guest of Alexander Hoghton. *Reproduced with the kind permission of the T of the Hoghton Tower Preservation Trust and Sir Bernard Hoghton, Bt., DL.*

Thomas More by Hans Holbein the
ger: born in London in 1477; educated at
d, and at New Inn and Lincoln's Inn;
nt humanist scholar and Catholic reformer;
Chancellor in 1529; on 16th May 1532 the
accepted More's resignation; committed to
wer in 1534 for refusing, on grounds of
ence, to take the Oath of Succession
was based on an Act which also
ated the power of the Pope; executed for
th, by beheading, 6th July 1535. *The Royal
n © 2003, Her Majesty Queen Elizabeth II.*

63 Cuthbert Tunstall (1474-1559): educated at Oxford (where he was a contemporary of his close friend Thomas More), at Cambridge, and at Padua; in 1516 became Master of the Rolls and Vice-Chancellor; appointed Bishop of London in 1522 (his close friend John Fisher assisted at his consecration); translated to the Prince Bishopric of Durham in 1530 and he was also President of the Council of the North. Unlike More and Fisher, Tunstall took the Oath of Succession in 1534 and recognised King Henry as Supreme Head on Earth of the Church of England, but he tried to steer the King towards orthodoxy. He was imprisoned in the reign of Edward VI and decided to 'come boldly forward at whatever cost in defence of his faith now so heavily beset'. He was fully reinstated under Queen Mary. On Elizabeth's accession, he came to London to meet her and tried, unsuccessfully, to persuade her to modify her reforms and return to Catholicism. He was imprisoned in Lambeth Palace, where every attempt was make to win him over, 'But Tunstall had done with compromise'; and there he died, a Catholic, at the age of 85.

wsholme Hall in the Forest of Bowland:
me of my great-times-eight-grandmother,
arker, who married Richard Holden of
y Hall. *Photograph by J. R. Robinson with kind
n from Mrs Parker.*

65 Cardinal John Fisher by Holbein: born a[t] Beverley, East Yorkshire, in 1469; humanist scholar, eminent theologian, and Catholic reformer; Chancellor of Cambridge Universi[ty]; Bishop of Rochester; refused to recognise K[ing] Henry VIII as Supreme Head on Earth of [the] Church of England; executed for his faith, [by] beheading, 22nd June 1535. *The Royal Collectio[n] 2003, Her Majesty Queen Elizabeth II.*

66 St Mary's, Cricklade, where the Rector, between 1510 and 1514, was the Dominica[n] John Holden: a younger son of John Hold[en of] Chaigley Hall and Mary Lowde; born in 14[58]; ordained subdeacon, 1499, York; B.Th., 15[07,] Oxford; D.Th. 1510, when he was Prior of [the] Blackfriars, Oxford; incorporated at Cambr[idge] 1514, when John Fisher, Bishop of Roches[ter,] was Chancellor of the University; Prior of L[ondon] Blackfriars in 1522; Bishop of Sodor and M[an,] 1523; aged 80, in 1538, when he wrote to T[homas] Cromwell. John Holden was eleven years o[lder] than John Fisher. What was the old man's religious position three years after his fello[w] bishop's heroic death? *Photograph by J. R. Rob[...].*

and Fellow of the Royal Society, referring to his great-uncle, William, wrote 'One of my name, a distant relation, who did not die above fifty years ago, is said to be the first good shooter flying in these northern parts. Almost wish the art had remained in oblivion!'.

As we have seen, William Hoghton's son, John, who had taken the name and arms of his mother, Elizabeth Dalton of Thurnham Hall, and John's brother, Robert, were both out in the '15'; as was their cousin Thomas Riddell.

Robert Foster of Charnock Richard was steward to John Dalton of Thurnham for his Park Hall estate. When John Dalton's estates were forfeited after the defeat of the Jacobites their computed yearly value was returned, in 1716, as £1,300.[10]

The Jacobites were defeated at Preston on 14th November. Derwentwater was imprisoned in the Tower of London. He rejected the offer of a reprieve, if he renounced his Catholic religion, as 'inconsistent with honour and conscience'. He was beheaded on Tower Hill on 24th February 1716.

William Tunstall was tried together with John Dalton and both were found guilty; but their lives were spared. William Tunstall had 'amused his tedious prison hours with writing poetry'. And, in the poetry of another, history recalls his 'broken heart':

> To my true king I offer'd free from stain
> Courage and faith; vain faith, and courage vain.
> For him I threw lands, honours, wealth, away,
> And one dear hope, that was more prized than they.
> For him I languish'd in a foreign clime,
> Gray-hair'd with sorrow in my manhood's prime;
> Heard on Lavernia Scargill's whispering trees,
> And pined by Arno for my lovelier Tees;
> Beheld each night my home in fever'd sleep,
> Each morning started from the dream to weep;
> Till God, who saw me tried too sorely, gave
> The resting-place I ask'd, an early grave.
> O thou, whom chance leads to this nameless stone,
> From that proud country which was once mine own,
> By those white cliffs I never more must see,
> By that dear language which I spake like thee,
> Forget all feuds, and shed one English tear
> O'er English dust. A broken heart lies here.[11]

Meanwhile Robert and Mary Dale of Girlington had taken

responsibility for Hutton Hall, the largest farm on the Wycliffe estate, for which Robert made his first payment in 1715: '£55-10 in full of his last March rent'. Mary may well have been a member of the Tunstall family.[12]

After the defeat of the Jacobites, 'a serious effort was made to destroy parish mass-houses and confiscate any property left to superstitious uses... The chapel at Lady Well was destroyed during these anxious days and [Christopher] Tootell had to go into hiding. On one occasion he "lay nine hours on a hay mow in a lonesome barn" '. Tootell returned and rebuilt the chapel. He died there on 18th November 1727. Edward Melling, a Douai priest, Christopher Tootell's nephew and assistant, who succeeded him at Fernyhalgh described him thus:

> Yesterday it pleased Almighty God to call to his mercy my dear uncle mr Christopher Tootell after a laborious and painful life upon the mission for above forty years wherein his patience under a complication of distempers for a long time, and particularly in his last tedious sickness was remarkable. Indefatigable he was in study, a vigilant pastor, a zealous preacher, a constant catechizer, in visiting the sick forward, resigned under afflictions, whose function was his business and his business his diversion... I have lost a near relative, an able director and my best friend.[13]

At Hutton Hall, another faithful priest was a guest during his last days. Francis Hodgson was educated at the English College at Douai where he was a professor in 1676. He left for England on 26th April 1677 when he was aged twenty-seven. He was with the Withams at Cliff Hall and worked in Cleveland and on the Yorkshire moors. Here, and in his devotion to the poor, Francis Hodgson followed in the footsteps of his fellow Douai priest, 'the apostle of the northern moors', the Venerable Nicholas Postgate.[14]

The year after Francis Hodgson arrived in England, the same year in which Robert Dale was born, 1678, Titus Oates, who had inflamed anti-Catholic prejudice, 'discovered' his fabricated Popish Plot to murder Charles II and put his Catholic brother, James, on the throne. The major panic which ensued led to the execution of about thirty-five Catholics including: Oliver Plunkett, Primate of Ireland; Sir William Howard, Viscount Stafford; and eighty one year old Nicholas Postgate.

Nicholas Postgate was arrested, on 8th December 1678, at Redbarns, the home of Matthew Lyth, near Littlebeck; he had come there to baptise a baby. He was committed to York gaol where, during the winter, in preparation for his coming ordeal, he composed a hymn which became much loved and widely used. On 16th March 1679 he stood trial. The charge against him was his priesthood; by a statute of 27 Elizabeth it was Treason to be ordained overseas. On August 7th, Nicholas Postgate was drawn on a sledge to the gallows at Knavesmire.

> Bodily weakness prevented his making more than a brief speech stating he died for religion, not for complicity in the Oates Plot; that he forgave all who had part in bringing him to his death; that he prayed for the King; and sought forgiveness of all whom he might have offended. Then he suffered the barbarous hanging, drawing, and quartering which the law inflicted on priests.

Mr Tunstall of Wycliffe had sent an agent to discover what he could about Mr Postgate's death, a Mr Garlick, who was present at the event and managed to dip a cloth in the martyr's blood.[15]

King Charles II was reconciled to the Catholic Church on the eve of his death, 5th February 1685, by his friend John Huddleston, a Benedictine priest. Huddleston had saved Charles' life by sheltering him after his defeat at Worcester; a debt which the King never forgot. John Huddleston was installed at Somerset House as chaplain to the Queen Dowager and 'He was excepted by name in proclamations against priests and even during the Oates plot was not molested'.

James II succeeded his brother on 6th February 1685. Fresh hope dawned for English Catholics. James had become a Catholic in about 1670.

John Leyburn had been president of the English College at Douai from 1670 to 1676 after which he became secretary to Cardinal Howard. He was consecrated bishop on 9th September 1685 and arrived in England as Vicar Apostolic in October.

James Smith, the president of Douai, was nominated Vicar Apostolic by James II in 1687. On 13th May, the following year, he was consecrated in the chapel of the Queen Dowager at Somerset House and took charge of the Northern District.

King James had proved a brave soldier and a fearless horseman, but he lacked diplomacy. His tendency to promote Catholics to positions of power threatened vested interests. The birth of his son, Prince James Edward, in 1688, with the prospect of a Catholic succession, raised Protestant anxieties and led to an invitation to William of Orange and his wife Mary to claim the throne of England. Each was a grandchild of Charles I; Mary was James II's first daughter by Ann Hyde.

The King seemed to be deserted by everybody, including the Duke of Marlborough who owed his brilliant military career to James's patronage. He fled to France. James II's attempt to recover his throne was defeated decisively by William of Orange at the battle of the Boyne in 1690.

Bishop James Smith took refuge, from the Williamite persecution of Catholics, with his old friend Francis Tunstall in the relative remoteness of Wycliffe Hall from which he continued to labour among his flock in secret. He was the only one of the four Vicars Apostolic to escape imprisonment. Bishop Smith died on the twenty third anniversary of his consecration. Francis Hodgson was one of his trustees.

Francis Hodgson also witnessed the will of Robert Dale's mother Sarah, on 10th November 1716. Within two months she had died.

Ten years later, the memory of these events would begin to fade with the death, on 24th May, at Hutton Hall, of Francis himself. But the spirit of the Venerable Nicholas Postgate still quickens the hearts and minds of moorland folk and of people far beyond.

CHAPTER VIII

Recusants of Lancashire and Loyalty to the King

'Certainties come, certainties go; history alone remains, because history changes with the events it records. So we can look back at this brilliant, bewildering century of change and try to assess "what happened", where contemporaries saw only events governed by fortune'.
Christopher Hill [1]

Robert Foster of Charnock Richard my great-times-four-grandfather appeared before the Quarter Sessions Court at Wigan, on 13th February 1679, for refusing to attend the services of the Established Church. Among others, also appearing, was John Hoghton, gentleman, of Mawdsley.[2] Robert was a Catholic; as were many of his descendants and his ancestors.

The Titus Oates Popish Plot had raised the Government's anxiety and suspicion and this led to stricter reinforcement of an Act which had been laid down in 1606, after the Gunpowder Plot: 'for the better discouraging and repressing of popish recusants'. Church wardens and constables had to bring before the justices, each year, those people who had not attended the Church of England services for a month; and they were fined £20 for every month of their non attendance.[3]

Robert Foster, who was a farmer, was also a tanner like his father, John Foster, and, despite such fines, he participated in the rising wealth of the merchant classes. John Foster, however, experienced difficulties.

In March 1672, King Charles II had issued a declaration suspending the penal laws but the Commons insisted that only parliament could grant such a suspension. In March the following year they passed the Test Act making the taking of the sacrament obligatory for all holders of office; and, for loyal Catholics, the impossibility of taking the oath of supremacy was reinforced by the addition: 'I do declare that I do believe that there is not any transubstantiation in the sacrament of the Lord's Supper'.[4]

On 4th January 1678, John Foster took the oath of obedience and supremacy. Moreover, on January 20th, Will Haydock, Rector of Standish, certified that John Foster and Ellen his wife, together with James Charnock, had, for several Sundays, attended the parish church and received the sacrament of the Lord's Supper in both kinds in accordance with the Liturgy of the Church of England.[5] Perhaps John Foster had to become a Church Papist to hold off poverty? It will be seen how in more auspicious times he was confirmed as a Catholic.

John Foster's godmother was his father's cousin, Jane Foster of Charnock Richard; she never married. Jane's will, of 25th August 1694, introduces relevant members of her family; and Bishop Leyburn's confirmation register tells of their religious persuasions.

Jane left £10 to the poor of Charnock Richard and five shillings to John Foster. The largest of several specific bequests was that of £11 to her niece Cecily Houghton. Jane left the residue of her estate to the children of her niece Alice Gerard of Euxton and to the children of her nephew James Parker. James Parker was a yeoman of Charnock Richard; his daughter, Elizabeth, married John Foster's only son, Robert, her third cousin. Jane's inventory was appraised the following year by Robert Foster and by her godson, Cecily Houghton's nephew William Roscoe, at £35-17-0.

During the next reign, that of Charles' Catholic brother James II, Bishop John Leyburn, the Vicar Apostolic to England and Wales, undertook to administer the sacrament of confirmation to his flock; and he visited the Charnock Richard area in September 1687. Catholics in Lancashire had not received confirmation since the Reformation because of having no bishop; hence many adults as well as children presented themselves.[6]

On 13th September John Foster was confirmed at Euxton, two miles north of Charnock Richard, together with: Elizabeth Parker, the future wife of John's son Robert, and her sisters Ann and Cecily; William Roscoe; John Houghton and other members of his family from Park Hall; Andertons from Euxton Hall; and many local people among whom were the names of John Foster's relatives and friends.

Jane Foster and her sister Ellen appear in the confirmation register on 16th September, under Lostock, eight miles south-east of Charnock. Robert Foster, his sister Cecily, his future brother-in-law Richard Parker, and his father's second cousin Cecily Houghton, appear on 14th September, under Wrightington, two miles south-west of Charnock.

Cecily Houghton was the daughter of Jane Foster's sister Gennett who had married Edward Houghton of Euxton on 12th September 1623.[7]

Among 'Papists' of Charnock Richard who registered their estates in 1717 were Robert Foster, Richard Parker, and John Charnock.[8] The reign of King Charles I echoes the names Charnock and Houghton, as we shall see.

King Charles I's queen, Henrietta Maria, whom he had married in 1625, the year he succeeded his father James I, was the daughter of Henry IV of France. She was a Catholic, which gained some sympathy at court for her English co-religionists but which also prompted Protestant anxieties. The King was 'a gracious sovereign, who abhorred the shedding of blood under the pretext of religion, and in whose reign no-one had yet suffered [until 28th August 1628] on that account'.[9]

Charles was an exponent of the Divine Right of Kings. He tended to call Parliament only when he needed money; but the Parliamentarians wanted a greater say in the government and policies of their country. This tension between King and Parliament culminated in Charles' raising his standard at Nottingham on 22nd August 1642; and England was plunged into Civil War.

Captain Robert Charnock of Astley Hall, which lies about two miles north-east of Charnock Richard, was a Royalist. He was referred to as 'One Eye Charnock'; doubtless he lost the other eye in battle. John Foster, my ancestor, and Robert Charnock had a great-aunt and a great-uncle in common: Margaret Foster and James Charnock, who married on 22nd January 1592. Margaret was the eldest sister of John's grandfather, also John Foster, of Charnock Richard; and James was a younger brother of Robert's grandfather, also Robert Charnock, of Astley Hall.[10]

Captain Charnock was involved in both sieges of Lathom House.[11] Charlotte de la Tremouill, the formidable Countess of Derby, while her husband the Earl was absent, took command of this Royalist, fortified stronghold; the centre of operations which terrorised the surrounding country. Captain Charnock, whose first wife Ann Lougher had died, married, during the war, Alice, the daughter of Colonel William Farington of Worden, the Countess' military advisor during the first siege.

Prince Rupert, a nephew of Charles I, was the courageous commander of the Royalist cavalry; Charlotte was a first cousin of his father. When Rupert arrived at Lathom House, the Parliamentary besiegers, who had been held at bay for two months, had dispersed; and the Countess 'clasped the all-victorious Prince to her ample bosom'.[12]

Lathom House finally capitulated on 5th December 1645. Robert Charnock's estates were sequestered by Parliament but were returned to him for a fine of £266 in 1646.

The Hoghtons of Park Hall in Charnock Richard were Catholics and Royalists as were the Daltons of Thurnham Hall near Lancaster. As we have seen, Lieutenant Colonel William Hoghton, the father of John Hoghton, was killed in the first Battle of Newbury; and Colonel Thomas Dalton died of wounds after the second Battle of Newbury. The grandchildren and heirs of these two colonels, William Hoghton and Elizabeth Dalton, united the estates by their marriage in 1683.[13]

The Holdens of Chaigley Hall, from whom our family descended, also feature in these turbulent times. We have already met Elizabeth, the daughter of Robert Holden of Leagram, near Chipping in Lancashire, who was the first wife of James Foster of Euxton House – the mother and father of my great-great-grandmother Cecily Robinson of Hutton Hall. Robert Holden of Leagram's great-great-grandparents were Richard Holden of Chaigley Hall and Jane, daughter of Robert Parker of Browsholme.

Robert Holden of Leagram registered his estate as a 'Papist' in 1717.[14] Robert had been registered as a recusant, together with his father and mother, John and Elizabeth Holden of Townleys, Leagram, in 1679; and in 1715 he had been registered as a Catholic non-juror.[15]

Robert Holden was a tenant of Mary, Duchess of Norfolk, to whom he was distantly related. Robert's great-aunt, Ann, daughter of Thomas Holden of Greengore in Bailey, was the third wife of Richard Shirburne of Stonyhurst. Richard was the great-great-grandfather (by his first wife Catherine, daughter of Charles Lord Stourton and Lady Ann Stanley, daughter of Edward 3rd Earl of Derby) of Mary Shirburne who married Thomas Howard, 8th Duke of Norfolk, in 1709. Mary was a Catholic and a staunch Jacobite.[16]

The chapel at Leagram Hall served Catholics in the district from the 17th century. In Robert's day the priest was Dr Penketh 'a keen sportsman, and his name as a leading member of the Stonyhurst Hunt is celebrated in verses by the local poet Cottam'.[17]

Henry Holden, son of Richard and Margaret Holden of Crawshaw, and second cousin of Robert's father, John Holden of Townleys, fought for the King in the Civil War. Henry's brother George, a Captain in the Royal Army, was slain at Usk.[18]

Henry put up his sword; and, on 1st January 1649, he entered the English College at Douai; he was aged about twenty-seven. Twenty-nine days later the King of England was beheaded by the Parliamentarians.

Henry Holden received minor orders on 7th June 1653. He had held his commission under Colonel Thomas Dalton and, in 1655, the Colonel's son Robert entered Douai as a lay student. In 1676, Henry Holden became chaplain to Robert Dalton at Thurnham Hall and he remained there until his death in 1688.

The Jacobite flame was kept alive at Thurnham. Three of Robert's grandsons fought for Charles I's grandson, James Edward, in 1715: John Hoghton, who took his mother's name of Dalton, and his brother Robert, both of whom we met earlier; and Thomas, the son of their aunt Dorothy Dalton and Edward Riddell of Swinburne Castle.

Doctor Henry Holden, an uncle of the previous Henry Holden, was the second son of Richard Holden of Chaigley Hall and his wife Eleanor, daughter of Miles Gerard of Ince. Chaigley Hall is about five miles west of Leagram. Henry was born in 1597, entered Douai 17th September 1618 and was ordained 26th March 1622. He then proceeded to Arras College, Paris, and, in due course, graduated DD of the Sorbonne. Doctor Holden was a friend and disciple of Thomas White and shared his hopes of coming to terms with Cromwell.

During the Protectorate of Cromwell: 'Jane Foster, widow, William Crichlow, Elizabeth Parker as recusants asked to be allowed to compound for their estates in 1653-4'. William Crichlow, alias John Foster, the son of Ralph Crichlow and Katherine, daughter of Oliver and Elizabeth Tootell of Chorley, had entered the Venerable English College in Rome in 1627 and was ordained on 26th October 1631. He was in Preston in 1639 and became Rural Dean of Amounderness. He witnessed the will of James Foster of Charnock Richard on 3rd June 1622. Elizabeth Parker was the sister of Jane Foster, spinster, of Charnock Richard, and the grandmother of Elizabeth Parker who married Robert Foster.[19]

The Holdens of Chaigley remained loyal Catholics. It was not so with the Holdens of Holden in Haslingden; from whom the Chaigley family may have become detached many centuries before.

Dr Henry Holden of Chaigley had entered Douai six years after the ordination of one of the College's most famous sons, Edmund Arrowsmith, saint and martyr, who was betrayed by Robert Holden of Holden in 1628.

'The circumstances of the quarrel, which ultimately led to the zealous missionary's arrest and execution, are thus related by a contemporary:-'

> Two in Lancashire had married together; the woman was not a Catholic, the man was. There was somewhat in the marriage for which they stood in need of a dispensation. Mr. Arrowsmith was employed in obtaining it. In the meantime the woman became Catholic. When the dispensation came Mr. Arrowsmith would not make use of it before the parties had separated for the space of fourteen days; which thing incensed them much against him, so that knowing the time when he was to return to their father's house where they lived, they secretly sent word to one Rawstorne, a justice of the peace, to come and apprehend a priest. The justice, not willing to bring his neighbour into danger, sent him word that he was to search his house; that by this means having intelligence he might convey away the priest. Which being done, the searchers according to custom busied themselves in looking, but could find nobody, so returned home... On their way back the party arrested Fr. Arrowsmith...the relationship

which required the dispensation, [was] that of first cousins... Ralph Holden married Mary daughter of William Chorley of Chorley, his son Robert married Mary daughter of Alexander son of the same William Chorley;...[20]

On 28th August 1628, Edmund Arrowsmith was taken from his cell in Lancaster Castle and, as he was carried through the yard, his fellow priest and prisoner, John Southworth, appeared at a window. At a prearranged sign from Edmund, John Southworth gave him absolution and sped him on his way with the Sign of the Cross. He was then bound to a hurdle, his head towards the horse's tail, and dragged a quarter of a mile to the site of execution.

Father Arrowsmith resisted all attempts to convert him in return for his life. He sought the prayers of Catholics in the crowd and 'he prayed for his Majesty, recommended to Almighty God the state of this Kingdom and in a particular manner his persecutors, whom he freely forgave, desiring also forgiveness of whomsoever he had offended'. Nobody had been willing to carry out the butchery until, 'finally, a deserter, under sentence of death for leaving his colours, for forty shillings, the prisoner's clothes and his liberty, offered to be the vile instrument of this inhuman murder'.

> Fr. Arrowsmith now composed himself for his last act. He again covered his eyes, and fixed in ardent prayer, contemplated with lively faith Him whom he was immediately to possess for eternity. His lips were seen to move and Bone Jesu, Good Jesus, were the last words that immediately preceded his being thrown off the ladder and suffered to hang until his soul was admitted to the crown of justice which is laid up for God's faithful servants. The rest of the cruel sentence was immediately executed. He was cut down, dismembered, bowelled and quartered. His heart was torn out. His head was cut off and his quarters boiled in the cauldron. The blood, scraped up with sand and earth, was cast into the fire. Lastly his head was set upon a pole among the pinnacles of the castle and his quarters hung on the four quarters of it.[21]

Robert Holden's father, Ralph Holden was a 'Recusant' in 1629; he was unable to divert Holden and Duckworth from his son but gave Kelke to charitable uses, presumably because of his displeasure at his son's treacherous behaviour. Ralph's father, Robert Holden, was described as a 'Papist'; he is also referred to as Robert Elston because his father's marriage to Elizabeth Elston was regarded as bigamous and null, since it occurred before Elizabeth's childhood marriage to James Anderton of Euxton was dissolved in 1561.

After his betrayal of Edmund Arrowsmith, Robert Holden of Holden's descendants appear to have given up the Catholic faith; the old faith, to which the Holdens of Chaigley and their Leagram branch held firm. Let us return to Yorkshire and hear tales of intrigue and of heroism.

7. Descendants of Richard Holden of Chaigley Hall and Jane Parker of Browsholme down Cecily Robinson of Hutton Hall

Richard Holden (c. 1535 - ?) of Chaigley Hall & Jane, dau. of Robert Parker of Browsholme, relict of Thomas Shirburne of Ribbleton and mother of John Shirburne of Ribbleton

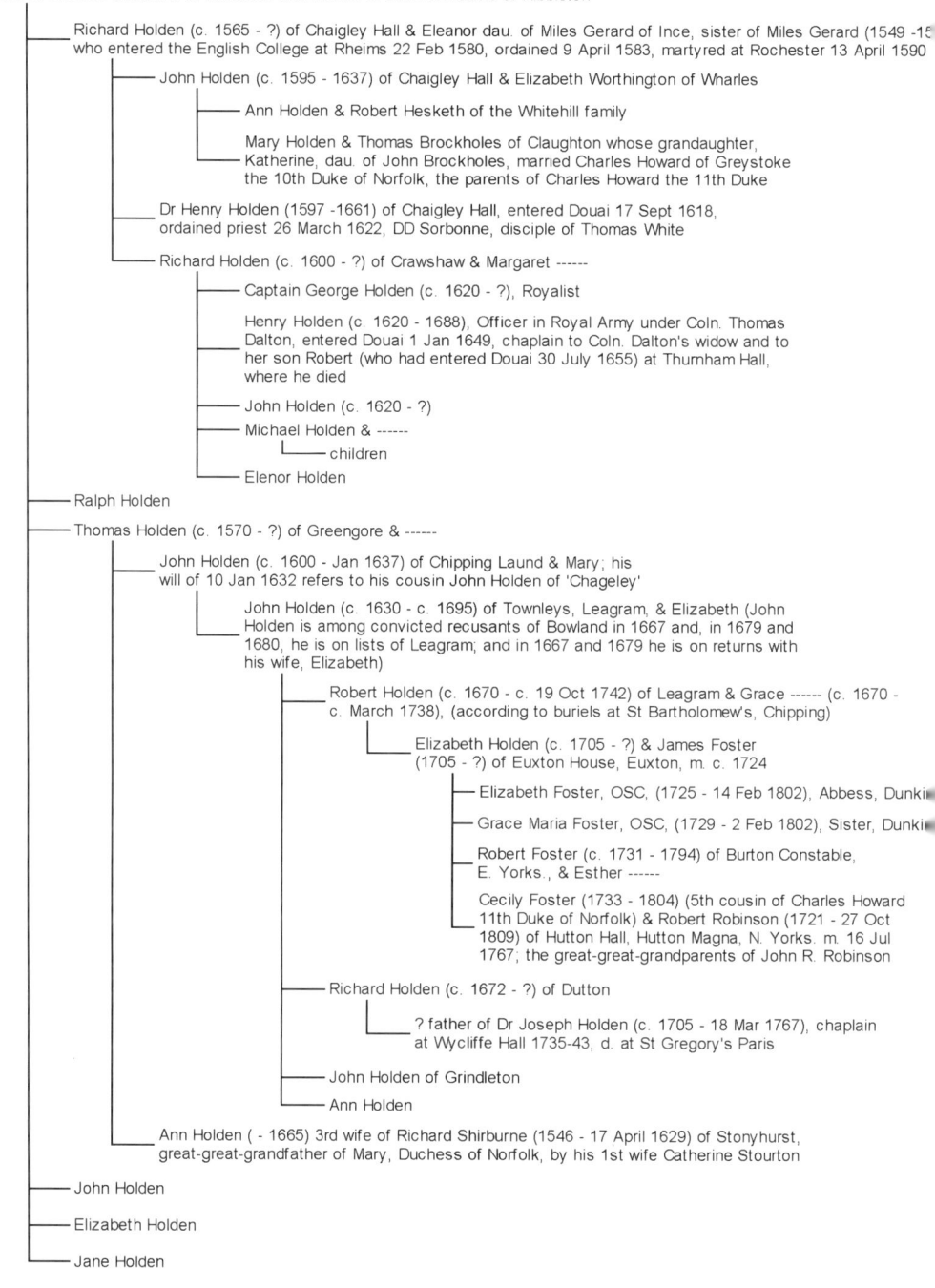

- Richard Holden (c. 1565 - ?) of Chaigley Hall & Eleanor dau. of Miles Gerard of Ince, sister of Miles Gerard (1549 -1⸺ who entered the English College at Rheims 22 Feb 1580, ordained 9 April 1583, martyred at Rochester 13 April 1590
  - John Holden (c. 1595 - 1637) of Chaigley Hall & Elizabeth Worthington of Wharles
    - Ann Holden & Robert Hesketh of the Whitehill family
    - Mary Holden & Thomas Brockholes of Claughton whose granddaughter, Katherine, dau. of John Brockholes, married Charles Howard of Greystoke the 10th Duke of Norfolk, the parents of Charles Howard the 11th Duke
  - Dr Henry Holden (1597 -1661) of Chaigley Hall, entered Douai 17 Sept 1618, ordained priest 26 March 1622, DD Sorbonne, disciple of Thomas White
  - Richard Holden (c. 1600 - ?) of Crawshaw & Margaret ------
    - Captain George Holden (c. 1620 - ?), Royalist
    - Henry Holden (c. 1620 - 1688), Officer in Royal Army under Coln. Thomas Dalton, entered Douai 1 Jan 1649, chaplain to Coln. Dalton's widow and to her son Robert (who had entered Douai 30 July 1655) at Thurnham Hall, where he died
    - John Holden (c. 1620 - ?)
    - Michael Holden & ------
      - children
    - Elenor Holden
- Ralph Holden
- Thomas Holden (c. 1570 - ?) of Greengore & ------
  - John Holden (c. 1600 - Jan 1637) of Chipping Laund & Mary; his will of 10 Jan 1632 refers to his cousin John Holden of 'Chageley'
    - John Holden (c. 1630 - c. 1695) of Townleys, Leagram, & Elizabeth (John Holden is among convicted recusants of Bowland in 1667 and, in 1679 and 1680, he is on lists of Leagram; and in 1667 and 1679 he is on returns with his wife, Elizabeth)
      - Robert Holden (c. 1670 - c. 19 Oct 1742) of Leagram & Grace ------ (c. 1670 - c. March 1738), (according to burials at St Bartholomew's, Chipping)
        - Elizabeth Holden (c. 1705 - ?) & James Foster (1705 - ?) of Euxton House, Euxton, m. c. 1724
          - Elizabeth Foster, OSC, (1725 - 14 Feb 1802), Abbess, Dunki⸺
          - Grace Maria Foster, OSC, (1729 - 2 Feb 1802), Sister, Dunki⸺
          - Robert Foster (c. 1731 - 1794) of Burton Constable, E. Yorks., & Esther ------
          - Cecily Foster (1733 - 1804) (5th cousin of Charles Howard 11th Duke of Norfolk) & Robert Robinson (1721 - 27 Oct 1809) of Hutton Hall, Hutton Magna, N. Yorks. m. 16 Jul 1767; the great-great-grandparents of John R. Robinson
      - Richard Holden (c. 1672 - ?) of Dutton
        - ? father of Dr Joseph Holden (c. 1705 - 18 Mar 1767), chaplain at Wycliffe Hall 1735-43, d. at St Gregory's Paris
    - John Holden of Grindleton
    - Ann Holden
  - Ann Holden (- 1665) 3rd wife of Richard Shirburne (1546 - 17 April 1629) of Stonyhurst, great-great-grandfather of Mary, Duchess of Norfolk, by his 1st wife Catherine Stourton
- John Holden
- Elizabeth Holden
- Jane Holden

108

8. Descendants of Robert Foster of Charnock Richard and Jenett
down to John Foster (c. 1640 - 1710) of Charnock Richard

Robert Foster (c. 1540 -1613) of Charnock Richard & Jenett. ('Greenehurst' tenanted by 1. 1562, James Foster, ? father or brother of Robert; 2. 1586, Robert & Jenett his wife; 3. 1618, James Foster & Cecily his wife; 4. 1623, Cecily Foster, widow, Jenett her daughter & Edward Houghton husband to Jenett)

- Margaret Foster (c. 1567 - bur. 18 Feb 1640) & James Charnock (c. 1547 - 20 May 1633), (brother of Robert C. the father Thomas C. the father of Cpt. Robert C.), m. 22 Jan 1592. Will of Robert Foster, 1613, refers to his son-in-law James Charnock; will of Richard Parker, 1623, refers to James Charnock the elder and and James' wife Foster
  - Robert Charnock
  - Paul Charnock
  - Jane Charnock
- James Foster (c. 1568 - 1622) of Charnock Richard & Cislie
  - Genett Foster (c. 1601 - ?) & Edward Houghton of Euxton (c. 1600 - ?) m. 12 Sep 1623
    - Richard Houghton (c. 1625 - 1689) of Charnock Richard, yeoman. His will, 22 March 1688: refers to his property in Charnock Richard bought from James Anderton of Clayton; executors are William Anderton of Euxton, Cecily Houghton his sister, and Robert Foster son of John Foster his kinsman
    - Cecily Houghton (c. 1630 - 1717) of Charnock Richard, spinster
    - James Houghton of Euxton & Ellen (- 1692). Will of Ellen, 1691, refers to Mr Houghton of Park Hall, trusted friend (either John H., aged 62, son of Coln. William H., or John's son William, aged 32, who married Elizabeth Dalton of Thurnham Hall); witnesses: Robert Ffoster; Cisli Hoghton; James Parker
    - ------ Houghton & ------ Roscoe, parents of Cecily Houghton's nephew William Roscoe of Charnock Richard
  - Elizabeth Foster (c. 1603 - ?) & James Parker
    - James Parker (- 1698) & Margaret ------, parents of Elizabeth Parker (c. 1665 - ?) who married Robert (- 1719) son of John Foster of Charnock Richard
  - Margaret Foster (c. 1605 - ?) & ? John Low m. 26 Nov 1627
  - Elline Foster (16 Jun 1607 - ?)
  - Jane Foster (12 Sep 1612 - 1695) of Charnock Richard, spinster. Her will of 25 Aug 1694 mentions nephews and nieces and godson John Foster
  - Ann Foster of Euxton & -------- Hodson
- John Foster (c. 1570 - May 1622) of Charnock Richard & Jenet --------
  - James Foster (30 Oct 1605 - c. 1633) & ? Jane, widow in 1653
  - Seth Foster (31 Mar 1609 - ?)
  - Elizabeth Foster (18 Nov 1611 - ?)
  - William Foster (24 Feb 1614 - ?) & ? Alice Buckley m. 1636 at Standish, appears to be the most likely candidate to be John Foster's father
    - John Foster (c. 1640 - 1710) of Charnock Richard & Ellen ------; John's will of 1709 refers to only son Robert who married Elizabeth Parker, great-great-great-great-grandparents of John R. Robinson
- William Foster (c. 1573 - ?) ? of Greenfields in 1626 & Ann, or ? & Margaret Nightgall m. 20 May 1604 at Standish
  - a daughter Foster
- -------- Foster & Thomas Waring
- Richard Foster (c. 1675 - ?) & ------
  - children Foster
- Elizabeth Foster (c. 1577- ?)

109

CHAPTER IX

Oral Tradition and the Wrights of Ploughland Hall

'In history, what you see depends on where you sit'.
John Guy[1]

Sarah Wright, the baby girl who was destined to become my grandmother, was baptised in the parish of Burton Pidsea on Sunday 4th March 1827. No doubt she was christened Sarah after her grandmother and Wright to remind her, and those who were to follow her, of the family tradition that she was descended from the Wrights of Ploughland Hall in East Yorkshire. Her father was Thomas Ford of Burton Pidsea, a farmer, and her mother was Mary Ann daughter of Robert Wright of Fitling, also a farmer, and his wife Sarah.[2]

The Tunstalls of Wycliffe in North Yorkshire and the Constables of Burton Constable in East Yorkshire intermarried and, as we have seen, the Robinsons were closely involved with both these families who were powerful Catholic landowners. Moreover, as we shall see later, another branch of the Constables was related to the Wrights.

Nicholas Postgate, of Ugglesbarnby, was three years junior to my ancestor John Holden's cousin Dr Henry Holden at the English College at Douai; he entered on 4th July 1621, eight months before Henry was ordained.[3] Nicholas, the future apostle of the North York Moors and martyr, was ordained on 20th March 1628. In 1642 he became chaplain to Lady Dunbar, the widow of Sir Henry Constable of Burton Constable, at Halsham, in Holderness, the residence of the Constables since the twelfth century.[4] Lady Dunbar's granddaughter Cecily Constable was the wife of Francis Tunstall of Wycliffe who sent an agent to discover what he could about Nicholas Postgate's execution in 1679. We may recall that, one hundred and seventy-three years later, when Sir Thomas Aston Clifford Constable was Lord of Burton Constable, my grandfather Thomas Robinson, who was farming at Nuthill on the Burton Constable estate, married Sarah Wright Ford who lived in the neighbouring village of Burton Pidsea. Ploughland, Fitling, Halsham, Burton Pidsea, Nuthill, and Burton Constable, are all situated within a twelve mile radius of each other.

We must now leave the more familiar family members, to recapture an event involving more tenuous members and then to touch on the struggles of their remarkable niece. But look out for William Robinson and John Thompson!

John Wright, the founder of the Wright family of Ploughland Hall had been Seneschal to Henry VIII; and he came up to Holderness from Kent in 1542. John's wife Alice was a great-granddaughter of Sir William Ryther, High Sheriff of Yorkshire in 1427.[5]

John and Alice's son Robert Wright was first married to Ann, daughter of Thomas Grimston of Grimston Garth; and this is probably the branch of the family from which we descended.

Robert Wright's second wife was Ursula, daughter of Nicholas Rudston of Hayton by his second wife, Jane, daughter of Sir William Mallory of Studley Castle. When, early in the Reformation, government agents had come to desecrate his village church, Ursula's grandfather Sir William drew his sword and sent them packing.[6] Ursula spent fourteen years in prison rather than give up her Catholic faith. Her two sons took a more aggressive and reckless initiative which only brought down trouble on their fellow Catholics.

Christopher was the second son of Robert and Ursula Wright of Ploughland Hall; he was born in 1570. In 1602, Christopher Wright and Guy Fawkes were in the house of the Jesuit, Father Creswell, in Madrid and, there, they met Thomas Wintour. Christopher Wright was described as 'one of the leading swordsmen of the day'. Guy Fawkes served with distinction under Sir William Stanley, commander of the English Catholic troops in the Netherlands. Thomas Wintour, who was related to Christopher Wright by marriage, had a good knowledge of languages and acted as secretary to Lord Monteagle who had funded Wintour's present mission.[7]

Thomas Wintour had gone to Spain with the Jesuit, Father Oswald Tesimond, as agents, it is said, of Father Henry Garnet SJ, Robert Catesby, and Francis Tresham. Their aim was to persuade Philip III of Spain to support an invasion of England by Stanley's regiment. The invasion would coincide with an internal rising in support of the Catholic cause. When he lay dying in the Tower, 'On his salvation, Tresham, in the last letter of his life, protested that he had wronged Garnet by stating that he was privy to it'. Queen Elizabeth died in March 1603; and Philip preferred to pursue a more peaceful course with James VI of Scotland and I of England.[8]

This endeavour, like the Gunpowder Plot, was largely a family matter. Catesby, Tresham, and Wintour, were all great grandchildren of Sir George Throckmorton of Coughton Court and his wife Catherine, daughter of Lord Vaux of Harrowden; and Lord Monteagle was married to Francis Tresham's sister Elizabeth. Guy Fawkes and Christopher Wright were contemporaries at St Peter's School in York where the head master, John Pullen, was later suspect of being a Jesuit. Among their schoolfellows were: Christopher's elder brother, John Wright; Oswald Tesimond; and Edward Oldcorne, who also became a Jesuit priest. John and Christopher's sister, Martha Wright, was married to Thomas Percy, constable of Alnwick Castle, the principal seat, in Northumberland, of his cousin the Earl. Thomas Wintour's sister, Dorothy, was married to John Grant of Norbrook. The two Wrights, Catesby, Tresham, Thomas Wintour, Grant, and Monteagle, had all been involved in the Earl of Essex's rebellious and futile attempt to seize control of Queen Elizabeth.

King James, at first, seemed better disposed towards English Catholics than had been Queen Elizabeth. The Earl of Northumberland had sent Thomas Percy to Edinburgh to discern James's attitude to Catholics, should he become King of England on the impending death of Elizabeth; and James had written to Thomas: 'As for the Catholics I will neither persecute any that will be quiet and give but an outward obedience to the law; neither will I spare to advance any of them that will by good service worthily deserve it'. After all, they had favoured his Catholic mother, Mary Queen of Scots. Some of them considered that, as a great niece of Henry VIII, Mary had a better claim to the throne than Henry's illegitimate daughter by Ann Boleyn.

James, on his way to London to be crowned, paused in York where Thomas Gerard, brother of the Jesuit John Gerard, was among the Catholic gentlemen who welcomed him and testified their loyalty to the Crown. The King expressed his gratitude to Thomas for his family's loyalty to his mother: 'I am particularly bound to love your blood on account of the persecution you have borne for me'.[9]

However, hopeful expectations were dashed by the reinforcement of the penal laws against Catholics early in James's reign. The disappointment proved too much for these high spirited young men.

Robert Catesby, a born leader, focused their frustration and energy, under an oath of secrecy, towards a plan to blow up Parliament and, at the same time, to effect a Catholic rising in the Midlands – and this, despite wise counsel in confession to a priest. The story is well known; though Government complicity in the Plot is still debated.

Guy Fawkes was discovered; and there was practically no Catholic support for the rising. The remaining handful of conspirators were overcome at Holbeach, the house of Stephen Littleton, by the Sheriff of Worcester Sir Richard Walsh, on the morning of the 8th of

November 1605. Robert Catesby was killed in the fighting and John and Christopher Wright and Thomas Percy were mortally wounded. Thomas Wintour was wounded but recovered to undergo questioning and trial.[10]

On the 17th November the exhumation and quartering of those slain at Holbeach was ordered; and the heads of Catesby and Percy were exhibited in London on the scene of their intended crime.

Francis Tresham died of a strangury while a prisoner in the Tower.[11] A traitor's death, to be hung drawn and quartered, awaited the rest. Thomas' brother Robert Wintour, John Grant, Sir Everard Digby, and Thomas Bates, were thus executed in St Paul's Churchyard on 29th January. The next day, Guy Fawkes, Thomas Wintour, Robert Keyes, and Ambrose Rookwood, met a similar fate in Old Palace Yard, Westminster.

'The plot enabled Robert Cecil, heir of his father's hostility to Catholics, to procure further legislation against them'. Among other penalties, 'The treason of reconciling a convert, or of being reconciled, could now be committed abroad. Householders were made responsible for the recusancy of a guest or servant'.[12] Francis Tunstall Esq. of Barningham, the great-grandfather of Francis who sent a witness to Nicholas Postgate's execution, was fined £300 in 1624, at Richmond Quarter Sessions, for harbouring catholic servants, one of whom was a yeoman, William Robinson.[13]

Perhaps, John and Christopher Wright would not have taken up the sword and perished by the sword had not their mother, Ursula, been away in prison for her faith during so many of their formative years. It was otherwise with John and Christopher's niece, the daughter of their sister Ursula and her second husband Marmaduke Ward of Mulwith.

Mary Ward was born on 23rd January 1585. Her family was heavily involved in the Catholic cause. The year after Mary was born, her grandmother Ursula's cousin Francis Ingleby, was condemned for his priesthood and hanged drawn and quartered at York. Francis was the son of Ann Mallory and Sir William Ingleby of Ripley. Jane Ingleby, the sister of Sir William's grandfather, John Ingleby, was the wife of Sir Robert Constable of Flamborough who was a leader in the Pilgrimage of Grace and who was attainted in 1537.[14] Sir Robert's brother Sir William Constable and his wife Maude, heiress of Hatfield, were the great-grandparents of John Constable of Hatfield, eldest son and heir of his father Hilary.

John Constable was the first husband of Mary Ward's mother, Ursula, who was about sixteen years younger than him, by a childhood betrothal.[15] John was called before the Ecclesiastical Commission of the

North in 1580 when he 'appeared and confessed that he neither resorted to the church, or doth communicate, nor hath done these five year last past'. He refused to hear sermons preached by the Lord Archbishop and his chaplain and so was imprisoned in York Castle. A fellow prisoner said of him 'So sober, so constant, and so godly a youth maketh me ashamed of my former days'. John developed a 'grievous sickness' and died in 1581; he was aged 27.[16] When Mary Ward was five years old she went to live at Ploughland Hall where the piety of her grandmother made a lasting impression on her.[17]

Mary, who was of joyful temperament, grew into a beautiful, intelligent, and well educated girl. She spoke several languages including Latin. Edmund Neville, heir to the Earldom of Westmorland, sought her hand in marriage. She confided to him her strong calling to the religious life. Edmund became a Jesuit and died, at the age of eighty-five, ' "a noble confessor of Christ", after an illness resulting from nine months of chains, cold and hunger in a foul prison'.[18]

Mary was induced to become a lay sister with the Poor Clares in St Omer, in 1606; and she went on to found a Poor Clare convent for English girls, at Gravelines; but this was not her vocation. In consultation with her Jesuit confessor Father Roger Lee she decided to return to England in search of her calling to help, in some way, her persecuted fellow Catholics.

Mary became inspired to found an Institute along Jesuit lines. It was not to be under the jurisdiction of the local bishop, nor subject to a male order, but under the rule of a woman and answerable to the Pope. It was not to be enclosed but was to have freedom to open schools, to work amongst the poor, and to meet whatever was the greatest need. Such an innovation was completely opposed to Catholic thinking in the seventeenth century and met with corresponding resistance.

Despite prejudice against them, Mary and her 'English Ladies' founded highly successful schools for the education of future wives and mothers who would keep the faith alive in England. She educated, not only the rich, but also the local poor. 'Her tenderness towards those who looked to her as a leader was one of the most loveable traits of a loveable character'.[19]

Mary tramped across Europe, again and again, with a small band of companions, including Father Lee's nephew, Father Henry Lee her chaplain, and her cousin Robert Wright. Robert's father had been killed at Holbeach. He devoted his life to serving the Institute. They covered the fifteen hundred miles to Rome in two months, on foot, crossing the Alps in the winter of 1621. But, despite her entreaties before Cardinals and Popes, she remained unable to secure recognition of her Institute.

Mary's enemies seemed to prevail. On 13th January 1631, Pope Urban VIII signed a Bull of Suppression of her Institute. The Inquisition had Mary imprisoned as a heretic in the Poor Clare convent in Anger. On hearing of her plight, Urban ordered Mary's immediate release. But the Suppression broke up the lives of nearly three hundred religious, living in ten houses of the Institute.

Once again Mary tramped to Rome. 'Kneeling before the Pope, she said, "Holy Father, I neither am, nor ever have been, a heretic" '. Urban VIII replied, 'We believe it; we believe it'.[20] The Pope received her kindly and enabled her to re-establish the remnants of her community in Rome, under his protection; and, modelled on their original simplicity, a new start was made.

Through all her endeavours, plagued by prejudice, malicious gossip, and personal illness, Mary unfailingly submitted humbly to the Will of God and the authority of the Pope; and she enjoined her sisters to do likewise. 'Love, whether of God or her neighbour, was the secret of Mary's power'.[21] John Gerard the Jesuit, who escaped from the Tower, where he had been tortured, stood out among Mary's many friends for his constant support and encouragement. While on the English mission Gerard had seen what initiative, steadfastness, and heights of heroism, Catholic women could achieve.

Mary returned to England in 1639. With the threat of Civil War, in 1642, she left London for her native Yorkshire. After a spell at Hutton Rudby, she established her community at Hewarth. She died on 30th January 1645.

Mary Ward 'followed the principle of not attacking the beliefs of others, however false, but of offering them something better, so they abandoned their errors of their own accord. This explains the remarkable fact that the whole Protestant population of Hewarth, near York, when she died, with the exception of one enraged no-Popery man, attended her funeral'.[22]

Frances Bedingfield had been one of the ten English girls to enter the noviciate in Munich in 1629. It was Frances Bedingfield who, in 1686, founded the Bar Convent in York, where John Thompson, Thomas Robinson of Nuthill's cousin, following the noble tradition of Father Henry Lee, served as Chaplain for forty-three years.[23] When Canon Thompson died, in 1884, 'on behalf of the community an entry in the convent annals strikes a note, muted but sincere, of real grief. "We could not believe we had lost him whose name seemed inseparable from the old house, him on whom we had leant trustfully so many years" '.[24]

In the words of Urban VIII, Mary Ward, a pioneer of the Catholic

Reformation, was 'a woman of great prudence and of extraordinary courage and powers of mind, but, what is much more ... a holy and great servant of God'. She was three hundred years ahead of her time.[25] A time which was fashioned in Tudor days.

9. Descendants of John Wright of Ploughland Hall, E. Yorkshire, and Alice Ryther
simplified, with some relevant relationships

John Wright of Ploughland Hall, Seneschal to Henry VIII, left Kent in 1541, & Alice dau. and co-heir of John Ryther, Esq.

- Robert Wright, Esq., of Ploughland Hall, bur. at Welwick 18 July 1594, & (1) Ann dau. of Thomas Grimston, Esq., of Grimston Garth

    - William Wright, Esq., (- 23 Aug 1621) of Ploughland Hall & Ann (- 28 Dec 1618), dau. of Robert Thornton, Esq., of E. Newton, bur. together at the east end of the north aisle of Welwick church

        - William Wright, Esq., bur. at Welwick 18 Dec 1648, & Ann, dau. of William Mills of Westmoreland, bur. at Welwick 14 July 1640

            - Francis Wright. Possible ancestor of Robert Wright of Fitling, great-great-grandfather of John R. Robinson

        - Nicholas Wright, Esq., bur. at Welwick 22 May 1648 & ------

            - Francis Wright, Esq., (c. 1610 - ?) & Margaret (1 July 1628 - ?), dau. of Gregory Creyke of Marton and Ursula dau. of Sir John Legard of Ganton, Knt. Margaret m. (2) Hugh Chomley, Esq., at Welwick on 31 May 1664. Francis is also a possible ancestor of Robert Wright of Fitling

- Robert Wright of Ploughland Hall & (2) Ursula, dau. of Niclolas Rudston of Hayton and Jane, dau. of Sir William Mallory of Studley and Jane, dau. of Sir John Norton. Jane Rudston's sister, Ann Mallory, married Sir William Ingleby (1518 - 1578) of Ripley and their son, Francis, a Douai priest, was martyred at York 3rd June 1586; and their dau., Jane, m. George Wintour

    - John 'Jack' Wright (1568 - 8 Nov 1605), Gunpowder Plotter, & Dorothy. Robert and Thomas Wintour, both Gunpowder Plotters, and their sister Dorothy, who married John Grant, Gunpowder Plotter, were Jack's second cousins, children of Jane and George Wintour (see above)

    - Christopher Wright (1570 - 8 Nov 1608) of Ploughland Hall, Gunpowder Plotter, & Margaret

    - Ursula Wright & (1) John Constable (1554 - 1581), gt-grandson of Sir William Constable and Maud Hatfield. Sir William's brother, Sir Robert Constable of Flamborough (of Pilgrimage of Grace), m. Jane Ingleby whose brother, Sir John Ingleby, m. Sir Robert's sister Eleanor. Sir John and Eleanor were gt-grandparents of Francis the martyr

        - Ursula Wright of Ploughland Hall & (2) Marmaduke Ward (c. 1552 - ?) of Mulwith

            - Mary Ward (23 Jan 1585 - 30 Jan 1645), founder of the Institute of the Blessed Virgin Mary (IBVM)

            - David Ward (c. 1587 - ?)

            - Frances Ward (1590 - 11 Apr 1649), a Carmelite nun, buried in Antwerp

            - Elizabeth Ward, IBVM, (30 Apr 1591 - ?)

            - Barbara Ward, IBVM, (21 Nov 1592 - 25 Jan 1623), buried in Rome

            - George Ward, SJ, (18 May 1595 - 21 Jun 1654), died in London

    - Alice Wright of Ploughland Hall

    - Martha Wright of Ploughland Hall & Thomas Percy (- 8 Nov 1605), Gunpowder Plotter

CHAPTER X

Foster alias Charnock

'In condemning us you condemn all your own ancestors – all the ancient priests, bishops and kings – all that was once the glory of England, the island of saints, and the most devoted child of the See of Peter'.
Edmund Campion at his trial [1]

'He had been a good soldier and a tall fellow... He was a proper man in his apparel, somewhat tall, and very strong, his visage somewhat wan and pale'.

On 21st September 1586, John Charnock, with his six companions, was dragged through the London streets from the Tower to the gallows in the fields near St Giles.

> When he came to the ladder he began the Ave Maria and asked all Catholics to pray for him, and again said the Paternoster and Ave Maria. He confessed he had concealed the treason when he knew of it, and begged the queen's pardon. He paid little attention to the well-meant offices of the Protestant minister, and saying 'O Jesu, esto mihi Jesus,' was thrown off the ladder.

The crowd had been so horrified by the brutality of the seven executions the previous day that he was allowed to hang until he was dead before being cut down to be drawn and quartered.[2]

John Charnock of Astley Hall, near Chorley in Lancashire, was executed as a traitor for his part in the ill-conceived Babington Plot: 'a plot involving along with Anthony Babington a number of young romantic Catholic gentlemen to rescue Mary Queen of Scots then a prisoner in England, but it was infiltrated by government agents who sprung it in July 1586, presenting it as an attempt to assassinate Queen Elizabeth'. Robert Southwell, Jesuit and poet, in his work *An Humble Supplication,* exposed the conspiracy as fictitious.[3]

Was James Charnock mingling in the crowd to catch sight of his youngest brother's last moments?

Robert Foster, my great-times-eight-grandfather, lived at Greenehurst in Charnock Richard which lay two miles south of Astley Hall. Did Robert Foster ride to London with James, his future son-in-law? Were any of Robert's family there, especially his daughter Margaret who, five years hence, was to marry James Charnock, or perhaps his son John, my ancestor?[4]

Queen Elizabeth reluctantly signed her cousin's death warrant; and Mary Queen of Scots was beheaded at Fotheringay Castle on 8th February 1587.

Philip II of Spain, when he was married to Mary daughter of Henry VIII and Catherine of Aragon, liked to consider himself King of England. In 1588 his Spanish Armada was defeated by the small English fleet off Gravelines. A faction, including Cardinal Allen who was getting out of touch with the mood at home, had favoured Philip's invasion as a way of sparing Catholics persecution in England and of restoring the old faith. However, the answer which Robert Southwell gave to the 'bloody question' spoke for most Catholics, despite the penal laws, 'We assure your Majesty that what army soever should come against you, we will rather yield our hearts to be broached by our enemies' swords than we our swords to the effusion of our country's blood'.[5]

Robert Charnock of Old Hall, who descended from the Leyland branch of the Lords of Astley and Charnock, was a secular priest. He was one of the thirteen Appellants who, in January 1603, signed the Protestation of Allegiance to Queen Elizabeth in civil but not in spiritual matters. They were prepared to die in her defence but also in defence of the legitimate authority of the Catholic Church.[6]

The Appellants tended to identify with the more old fashioned gentry and with the traditional English Church rather than with the innovative and missionary attitude of priests who were products of Elizabethan Oxford and the English College at Douai, or of its collegiate foundations abroad; several of whose famous sons joined the Jesuits. Robert Southwell had been at Douai as a boy before he became a Jesuit.[7]

Southwell had returned to England at the time of the Babington Plot when the persecution of Catholics was at a peak. Seven Douai priests had been executed in the first six months of 1586. An Act of Parliament of March the previous year:

> '…aimed at the "utter extirpation of Popery" in England. The Act had not only made it treason for any priest, born in England and ordained overseas, to return to the country, but extended the same penalty of death by hanging, disembowelling and quartering to all men and women who gave shelter to any such priests'.[8]

Robert Southwell was betrayed; and he was captured by the notorious Richard Topcliffe in the spring of 1590. Topcliffe had special permission to torture prisoners in his own house; and that is where he set to work on Robert, torturing him almost to the point of death. Robert divulged nothing. He was thrown into gaol and later he was transferred to the Tower. At his trial in February 1595 he stated, 'I confess that I am a Catholic priest, and thank God for it, but no traitor; neither can any law make it treason to be a priest'.[9]

Robert presented such a gentle and dignified appearance on the scaffold that he won the hearts of the crowd and Lord Mountjoy, who held back those who would have cut him down while still alive, exclaimed, 'I cannot answer for his religion, but I wish to God that my soul may be with his'. In his last moments, Southwell protested that he never intended harm against the Queen for whom he prayed that 'she may so use those gifts and graces which God, nature and fortune hath bestowed on her that with them she may both please and glorify God, advance the happiness of our country and purchase to herself the preservation and salvation of her body and soul'.[10]

The Queen, as Princess Elizabeth, was well educated, especially in languages. She was a child of Protestant humanism. She was astute, having learnt to survive the unpredictable attitudes of her father in the turbulent politics of her childhood. At her accession to the throne, on 17th November 1558, she was immensely popular.[11] This was partly because Mary, though also popular at her accession in 1553, had become unpopular: through her marriage to Philip II of Spain; because she allowed the burning of some three hundred heretics, even though such execution for heresy was the cruel custom of the day and although she was, otherwise, pious and kind to the poor; and because she lost Calais, the last English foothold on French soil. Furthermore, Mary had failed to produce a son; who might have continued her attempts to re-establish the Catholic Faith in England.[12]

Elizabeth had practised as a Catholic during Mary's reign but, 'After her coronation she entirely threw off the mask ... she substituted the Anglican Establishment for the Catholic Church'. Her Parliament of January 1559 passed the Act of Supremacy, making the Queen supreme governor over her realm in spiritual as well as temporal matters; so that Catholics could never take the Oath of Supremacy without apostasy. The same Parliament also passed the Act of Uniformity, whereby only the established liturgy, that is, the Book of Common Prayer, might be used, thus abolishing the Holy Sacrifice of the Mass: ' "under penalty of loss of goods for the first offence, of a year's imprisonment for the second, and of imprisonment for life for the third;" a fine, moreover, of one shilling being imposed "on all who should absent themselves from church on Sundays and holidays" '.[13]

All the bishops except Kitchen of Llandaff now stood firm and refused to conform; though some of them had conformed under Henry VIII or Edward VI and had later been reconciled to the Church. Eleven of them died in prison. Cardinal Allen wrote, 'They have pined and smothered in their filthy prisons above thirty famous Prelates [Deans and Archdeacons are included with the Bishops]; above forty excellent learned men; of nobles, gentlemen, and matrons, a number; whose martyrdom is before God as glorious as if they had by a speedy violent death been despatched'.[14]

Cuthbert Tunstall was the illegitimate son of Thomas Tunstall of Thurland Castle, in Lancashire, whose descendants became Lords of Scargill, Wycliffe, and Hutton Magna, in North Yorkshire; the Tunstalls with whom our family of Robinsons and Dales were to become so intimately involved.[15]

Cuthbert Tunstall had been delayed in the North because Mary and then Elizabeth had appointed him to negotiate with the Scots. But now, in July 1559, aged 85, the venerable and scholarly Prince Bishop of Durham was travelling to London. He had asked for a meeting with Queen Elizabeth.

> The permission was granted and on 20 July Tunstal arrived in London accompanied, as befitted his princely status, with sixty horsemen. His audience with Elizabeth took place about a fortnight later. Probably the Queen thought that she could play on memories of his half-century of service to her family to win him over. Instead, Tunstal almost turned the tables.
>
> Tunstal had been Henry VIII's theological adviser during the crucial summer progress of 1538 when the King, who had toyed with Lutheranism in the wake of the Boleyn Marriage, had turned decisively against it. We know Tunstal and Henry wrote joint papers and it seems that Tunstal had kept one. For he now confronted Elizabeth with evidence in the King's own hand that her father had rejected the views of the Eucharist which she had just legislated. Dramatically, according to Feria, Tunstal exhorted the Queen 'at least to respect the will of her father, if she did not conform to the decrees of the church'. They also discussed the deprived bishops. 'I am grieved for York and Ely,' Elizabeth remarked. Brutally, Tunstal pointed out the obvious: 'How can you grieve when you have the remedy in your own hands? If you are willing to be a Catholic you can have not only those two among your councillors, but many others beside'.[16]

Cuthbert Tunstall, as a prisoner in Lambeth Palace, died on the 18th November, 'after he had atoned for his earlier weakness by brave upholding of the faith under Elizabeth, and by the endurance for nearly two months of imprisonment, subjected to continual questionings', aimed at winning him over.[17]

The existing Hierarchy was extinguished; and the Bishops were replaced by 'men whose teaching even upon the most sacred subjects was opposed diametrically to that of their predecessors'.

> We must not think of these first intruders into the Catholic Sees of England as if they were modern Anglican Bishops, gentlemen of refinement and of enlarged and liberal minds, who, if we could imagine them in the positions of unwilling jailers to Catholic Bishops, would seek by every means to alleviate their lot. The first Protestant Bishops were, almost without exception, the bitterest of Puritan fanatics, and they were under the express orders of the Council to seek by every means to bring their prisoners to conformity.[18]

Another view is that:

> ... the exiles who arrived in time to enter or influence the Parliament of 1559 can no longer be regarded as radical or rebellious exponents of Puritanism. However dramatic their postures on the Continent, once returned to England they became anxious to dissociate themselves from the revolutionary treatises of Goodman and Knox. Indeed, no integrated Puritan faction opposing Elizabeth's government can be discerned much before the 1570s. While at one time or another former exiles are to be found occupying no less than seventeen English bishoprics, they and their lay associates emerge as moderate 'Establishment men' who loyally supported the government in 1559 and thereafter aided it to complete and maintain the Settlement propounded in that crucial year.[19]

The newly Established Church retained the semblance of the old faith in that it kept the ancient sees and such of the medieval churches as had not been destroyed or left to fall into decay; but the ruins of the great Abbeys and the exiled monks and nuns told a different tale.

Elizabeth was not concerned with her subjects consciences provided they obeyed her laws.[20] The hope of the Queen, of her Secretary of State William Cecil, and of her Council, was that, without the leadership of the Catholic bishops and as the Marian priests died off, the Catholic Faith would expire.

William Allen, Principal of St Mary's Hall, Oxford, was unable, in conscience, to accept the new religion and, in 1561, he joined the increasing number of English Catholic exiles in Louvain. On his return to England for health reasons, in 1563, he was shocked to find his fellow Catholics in Lancashire falling away from the faith for lack of leadership. In 1568 he founded the English College at Douai, in the Spanish Netherlands where a new university had recently also been created, to train men who would normally have gone to the universities in England if they had not had to take the Oaths of Supremacy and of Uniformity.

In England things moved apace. In 1568, Mary the Catholic Queen of Scots, who had been imprisoned in her own country, escaped and sought the hospitality of her cousin Queen Elizabeth, much to the latter's embarrassment. In 1569, the Northern Earls rose, unsuccessfully, in the Catholic cause. In 1570, Pope Pius V, in his Bull *Regnans in Excelsis,* excommunicated Queen Elizabeth and absolved her subjects from obedience to her, thus increasing their considerable difficulties even further. They could now, very easily, be dubbed traitors. Other anti-Catholic Acts followed making it high treason: to call the Queen a heretic, in 1571; to bring papal bulls into England, also in 1571; and 'to persuade to popery', that is, to be reconciled or to reconcile others or induce them to be reconciled to the Catholic Church, in 1581.

The Douai priests began to return to England. The enthusiastic missionary spirit of these young men, trained to defend the Catholic Faith and to expose the faulty thinking of its opponents, threatened the Government's hopes for a Catholic decline. Cuthbert Mayne became the first Douai martyr, on 30th November 1577. When, in 1580, at Allen's request, the Jesuits began to join the secular priests in their missionary endeavour, the Government became even more alarmed. 'Until 1582, Elizabeth had been afraid to persecute Catholics: thereafter, she was afraid not to'.[21] And now we return to Allen's native Lancashire.

William Allen's childhood friend Thomas Hoghton of Hoghton Tower, High Sheriff, refused to conform to the new religion and went into exile for 'Blessed Conscience sake'. He was a generous benefactor of Douai College to which, after his death in 1580, his body was eventually translated. His son Thomas became a priest and served in Lancashire prior to his imprisonment and death in 1584.[22]

When he left England, the Right Worshipful Thomas Hoghton entrusted the administration of his estate to his half brother Richard Hoghton of Park Hall, in Charnock Richard, about nine miles south-west of Hoghton Tower.[23]

Robert Foster, his family, and his Catholic friends, would have attended Mass at Park Hall where Richard Hoghton kept a priest and a recusant schoolmaster. The priest in 1580 was Lawrence Johnson.[24]

Four contemporaries at Brasenose College, Oxford, in the late 1560s were: Lawrence Johnson and Thomas Worthington, both of whom proceeded to the English College at Douai in 1573; Thomas Cottam, who went to Douai in 1577, the year in which the former two were ordained; and Thomas' brother John Cottam who became William Shakespeare's master at Stratford-on-Avon Grammar School.[25] Also at Oxford at that time, but at St John's College, was Edmund Campion who was Proctor and Public Orator of the University. Campion went to Douai College in 1572 and left the next year to join the Jesuits. He was ordained in 1578.

In 1580, Edmund Campion returned to England with his fellow Jesuit Robert Persons.

He left Persons in the South and he, himself, travelled North disguised as a gentleman of moderate means; he was mounted and accompanied by a servant. Campion had been one of Oxford's brightest scholars and was a man of great personal charm. He went into Lancashire where the old faith was still so strong in order to obtain recruits for the newly founded colleges abroad.

Thomas Worthington was in England when Campion went to stay with his eldest brother, Richard Worthington, at Blainscough Hall, Coppul, which is about a mile south of Charnock Richard. Richard's wife, Dorothy, was a sister of James and John Charnock. This was eleven years before Robert Foster's eldest daughter, Margaret, married James Charnock.

The Government was alert to the presence of the Jesuits and they were being hotly pursued. The story is told about the maidservant at Blainscough who, when she spotted a pursuivant trailing Campion, had the presence of mind to pretend that a retainer had offended her and she pushed Campion into a nearby pond. The pursuivant laughed at this indignity and moved on in search of his quarry![26]

Richard and Dorothy Worthington suffered fines of at least £600 for their recusancy. Richard ended his life as a prisoner in Lancaster Castle because of his refusal to conform to the new religion; and he died there on 25th September 1590 at the age of 53.[27] His son Thomas Worthington who was married to the daughter and heiress of Gabriel Allen of Rossall, Poulton-le-Fylde – William Allen's elder brother – succeeded to Blainscough Hall.

Edmund Campion also stayed with Thomas Hoghton's younger brother Alexander at Hoghton Tower. At the same time, William

Shakespeare, under the local name of Shakeshafte, was among the troop of players employed by Alexander Hoghton.

Shakespeare's parents were both Catholics. Indeed, his mother, Mary Arden, was related, through her kinsman Edward Arden's marriage with Mary Throckmorton, to the great-great-grandchildren of Sir George Throckmorton, among whom were the gunpowder plotters: Catesby; Tresham; and the Wintours, who, in turn, were related by marriage to the Wrights of Ploughland Hall.

John Cottam had introduced Shakespeare to Alexander Hoghton, his patron. Perhaps the young actor received a few tips from Oxford's Public Orator.[28]

Robert Foster and his family would have been among those who, behind closed doors, attended Mass and heard the famous Jesuit preach, either at Blainscough Hall, or Hoghton Tower, or even at Park Hall. Perhaps they saw Shakespeare act.

In his will of 3rd August 1581, Alexander Hoghton desired that, if his half brother Thomas, 'will not keep and maintain players', then his musical instruments and costumes were to go to Sir Thomas Hesketh of Rufford Old Hall, who was also enjoined to befriend William Shakeshafte and take him into his service, or find him some good master. Thus was Shakespeare introduced to Lord Strange son of the fourth Earl of Derby, a friend of the Hoghtons.[29]

Edmund Campion was captured at Lyford Grange in Oxfordshire on 17th August 1581. He was imprisoned in the Tower and was confined in 'Little Ease'. The Queen offered him his life and honours if he would conform. When persuasion failed he was tortured and racked.

Campion was tried, on 20th November, together with Lawrence Johnson who had been captured in Lancashire, and Thomas Cottam. Thomas, after he was captured, had been entrusted as a prisoner to his friend Humphrey Ely, who was not suspected; and Ely had set him free. However, Thomas then gave himself up lest Ely should suffer for failing to hand him over to the Governor of the Cinque Ports.

On December 1st, Edmund Campion, bound to a hurdle, was dragged behind a horse through the rain and the mud up Cheapside and along Holborn and, at Tyburn, he was hung drawn and quartered.

Lawrence Johnson and Thomas Cottam were executed at Tyburn the following year, on 30th May.

Alison Plowden comments:

> The execution of Edmund Campion is generally accepted today as an act of judicial murder. Certainly there can be little doubt that Campion and the thirteen others arraigned with him in Westminster Hall were not guilty

as charged and that their trial was rigged as ruthlessly as in any modern purge,...[30]

Four of the sons of Campion's hosts Richard and Dorothy Worthington became Jesuits.[31]

The urgent need for priests on the English mission was such that dispensations were granted from previous obstacles to ordination. For instance, Miles Gerard had lost an eye in childhood.

Miles was the brother of Eleanor, wife of Richard Holden of Chaigley Hall which lies about twenty-four miles north-east of Charnock Richard. Richard, in turn, was the eldest brother of Thomas Holden of Greengore, near Stonyhurst. Thomas Holden was the great-great-grandfather of Elizabeth Holden of Leagram who married James Foster of Euxton House, the parents of Cecily Robinson of Hutton Hall, my great-great-grandmother.[32]

Miles was thirty-one when he became a student at Rheims, to which the English College at Douai had been evacuated in 1578 because of political troubles in Flanders. After his ordination, three years later, he remained teaching for six years.

On sailing back to England in November 1589, Miles and his companion Francis Dickinson were caught in a terrible storm and shipwrecked off the coast of Dover. The two priests were captured and were required to swear acknowledgement of the Queen as head of the church. Miles was imprisoned first in the Bridewell and then in the Gatehouse. On 3rd December he was examined before Topcliffe and the 'Bloody Question' was put to him.

Since 1585 it had been treason for a priest to land in England; and as a priest Miles Gerard was condemned. He was hung drawn and quartered at Rochester on 30th April 1590.[33]

In the next generation, William, Oliver, and Richard, the sons of Ralph Crichlow and Katherine Tootell of Clayton-le-Woods, four miles north of Charnock Richard, trained for the priesthood at the Venerable English College in Rome. They were the grandchildren of Oliver Tootell of Chorley and his wife Elizabeth. Each took as his alias 'Foster': William as John Foster; Oliver as John Foster or John Gerard; and Richard as Christopher Foster. Elizabeth, their grandmother, may well have been a sister of Robert Foster of Charnock Richard.[34]

How did such division come to torture the Catholic Church in England?

10. Foster, Charnock, Crichlow, relationships

James Foster (c. 1510 - ?) tenanted Greenehurst in 1562, he was probably the father of Robert Foster since three subsequent generations of the family were tenants at Greenehurst, & ------

- Robert Foster (c. 1540 - 1613) of Greenehurst, Charnock Richard & Jenett ------
  - Margaret Foster (c. 1567 - bur. 18 Feb 1640) & James Charnock (c. 1547- 20 May 1633) m. 22 Jan 1592. (Will of Robert Foster, 1613; will of Richard Parker, 1623). James' sister, Dorothy Charnock, married Richard Worthington of Blainscough Hall 17 June 1566; their brother, John Charnock, b. 1566, was executed 21 Sept 1586
    - Robert Charnock
    - Paul Charnock
    - Jane Charnock
  - James Foster of Charnock Richard (c. 1568 - 1622) & Cislie
    - Genett Foster (c. 1601 - ?) & Edward Houghton (c. 1600 - ?) of Euxton m. 12 Sep 1623
    - Elizabeth Foster (c. 1603 - ?) & James Parker, son of Richard Parker of Charnock Richard and Gennet
    - Margaret Foster (c. 1605 - ?) & ? John Low m. 26 Nov 1627
    - Elline Foster (16 Jun 1607 - ?)
    - Jane Foster (12 Sept 1612 - 1695) of Charnock Richard, spinster
    - Ann Foster of Euxton & -------- Hodson
  - John Foster (c. 1570 - May 1622) of Charnock Richard & Jenet --------
    - James Foster (30 Oct 1605 - 1633) & ? Jane who was a widow in 1653
    - Seth Foster (31 Mar 1609 - ?)
    - Elizabeth Foster (18 Nov 1611 - ?)
    - William Foster (24 Feb 1614 - ?) & ? Alice Buckley m. 1636 at Standish,
  - William Foster (c. 1573 - ?) ? of Greenfields in 1626 & Ann, or ? & Margaret Nightgall m. 20 May 1604 at Standish
    - a daughter
  - -------- Foster & Thomas Waring
  - Richard Foster (c. 1575 - ?) & ------
    - children
  - Elizabeth Foster (c. 1577 - ?)

? Elizabeth, wife of Oliver Tootell of Chorley (c. 1540 - ?). The fact that their three grandsons, who were priests, all took as an alias the name 'Foster' is suggestive that their grandmother was a Foster; if so, she could have been a sister of Robert Foster as shown

- Christopher Tootell (- 1623) of Clayton bur. at Chorley near his father and mother (will 16 Aug 1623)
- William Tootell of Healey (- 1638) & Elizabeth Gillibrand
- Hugh Tootell of Healey & ------
  - children
- Katherine Tootell & Ralph Crichlow (c. 1570 - ?)
  - Rev. William Crichlow alias John Foster (c. 1600 - 1669)
  - Alice Crichlow
  - Ralph Crichlow
  - Rev. Oliver Crichlow alias John Foster and also alias John Gerard (1607 - 1671)
  - Rev. Richard Crichlow alias Christopher Foster (c. 1610 - ?)
- Alice Tootell & William Farington
  - 3 daughters
- Jane Tootell & ------ Walles
  - children

CHAPTER XI

Severed from the Unity of Christendom: a People Confused

'Had the solution of the crisis rested with men of Tunstall's type, the transition to the modern world and the reform of the Church might have followed less tragic lines'.
Charles Sturge [1]

John Holden of Chaigley Hall in Lancashire, my great-times-nine-grandfather, arranged the marriage of his son Richard. It was 1561. [2] Elizabeth I had been Queen of England for three years. The old Catholic Hierarchy had been extinguished. The Anglican Church was being firmly established. Elizabeth's half-sister Mary, during her five year reign, had been unable to restore Catholicism. Elizabeth and Mary's half-brother Edward VI, the boy king, had developed strong Evangelical attitudes under the influence of his tutors and of the Protector, his uncle, Edward Seymour, Duke of Somerset. At Seymour's fall from power in 1549, this Evangelical influence continued under John Dudley, Earl of Warwick and self-appointed Duke of Northumberland. King Edward had even overruled his father's will for the succession. He gave preference, over Mary and Elizabeth, to the Protestant, Lady Jane Grey, to whom Dudley had married his eldest son.

Edward VI reigned for only six years; he died of tuberculosis at fifteen. In that short time Protestantism had taken root in the ground prepared for it, perhaps unwittingly, by his father. Henry VIII had severed the English Church from the unity of Christendom centred on the See of Rome; and, by making himself its Supreme Head, he had exposed it to the unpredictable attitudes of his successors and their advisors.

Henry, at his accession on 23rd April 1509, had promised well for Church and State. 'There had come to the throne the very perfection of Christian kingship – gracious, gifted and enlightened – and with his coming it seemed, bleak days must give way to bounteous prosperity'. [3] The seventeen year old King was tall, well built, and an athlete of great physical endurance. 'He knew Latin, French, and some Italian'; he had a good grasp of Theology and was a gifted musician. He frequently consulted Thomas More on intellectual and other matters.

This formidable king kept a magnificent court. The task of his seneschal John Wright, tentative ancestor of my great-great-grandfather Robert Wright of Fitling in East Yorkshire and grandfather of the gunpowder plotters John and Christopher Wright of Ploughland Hall, must have been an exacting one.

Pope Julius II had granted a dispensation for Henry to marry his brother Arthur's widow, Catherine of Aragon 'who, though five years his senior, was probably still beautiful and certainly of a quality of mind and life which few queens have seriously rivalled'.[4] Henry and Catherine were married on 11th June in the Franciscan church at Greenwich.

The general optimism was, no doubt, shared by John Holden's parents Ralph Holden and Elizabeth daughter of Richard Hancocke of Lower Higham in Pendle Forest. Ralph inherited Chaigley Hall. The heir of Ralph's elder brother Thomas, in 1512, was, in fact, their brother John. But John was a priest and Rector of St Mary's Church at Cricklade in Wiltshire; he granted lands to Ralph.[5]

John, Ralph's brother, was a contemporary of the great Catholic humanists who were intent on reforming the Church from within. He was born in 1458, that is: two years before Thomas Linacre; eight before John Colet and Erasmus; eleven before John Fisher; sixteen before Cuthbert Tunstall; and twenty years before Thomas More.

John Holden joined the Dominicans and he was at the Black Friars Convent in York when, at the age of 41, he was ordained subdeacon on 25th May 1499.[6] This was the year in which Erasmus and Thomas More met the eight year old future King Henry at Eltham; and the year in which Thomas Linacre returned from Padua and Venice to England where he, also, met Erasmus.

John was at the Oxford Convent in 1508 when, 'After 12 years study in Logic, Philosophy and Theology', he obtained his B.Th. on 17th October. He obtained his D.Th. in 1510; and in that year he was Prior of the Oxford Convent. John was Rector of St Mary's from 1510 until 1514 in which year he was incorporated at Cambridge where John Fisher, now Bishop of Rochester, was Chancellor.[7]

In the summer of 1513, Henry VIII, as a member of the Holy League in alliance with Pope Julius II against Louis XII, was with his army in France. He had left Catherine as 'governor of the realm and captain-general of the forces' at home. Henry had 'led England to war, fulminating against the "great sin of the king of France" and against those who "lacerate the seamless garment of Christ", who "would wantonly destroy the unity of the Church", who are guilty of "the most pernicious schism" '.[8]

The Scots, taking advantage of Henry's absence, invaded England. But the Earl of Surrey devastated their army, at Flodden. James IV, King of Scotland and the husband of Henry's sister Margaret, was killed in battle together with many of his nobles. Surrey was restored to his former Dukedom of Norfolk.

Surrey's son Thomas Howard, the 3rd Duke, and John Holden, the Dominican's father, were both to become great-times-seven-grandfathers of Charles Howard, the 11th Duke, to whom my great-great-grandmother Cecily Robinson (née Foster), of Hutton Hall on the Wycliffe estate in North Yorkshire, was, thus, a 5th cousin.[9]

The Tunstalls of Wycliffe and Burton Constable, to whom our family was related through the Dales and William Liddell of Wycliffe, if not more intimately, and with whom we became so closely involved, acquired the manor of Hutton Magna in 1614 when Nicholas Girlington sold it to Francis Tunstall. Francis' son Marmaduke came into Wycliffe when he married Katherine daughter and heiress of William Wycliffe, in 1606.

Cuthbert Tunstall was a son – alleged to be illegitimate – of Thomas Tunstall of Thurland in Lancashire, by a daughter, whom Thomas subsequently married, of Sir John Conyers of Hornby Castle. Cuthbert was educated at Oxford, where he was a contemporary of Thomas More, and at Cambridge and Padua. He was ordained subdeacon in 1508 and he became Chancellor to Archbishop Warham of Canterbury.[10]

But now, in 1514, Thomas Wolsey helped Cuthbert Tunstall 'to obtain the lands, wardship, and marriage of his nephew Marmaduke Tunstall' of Thurland Castle. Marmaduke married Alice, daughter and co-heiress of Sir Robert Scargill of Scargill in Yorkshire. Marmaduke and Alice were the grandparents of Francis who left Thurland and acquired Hutton. Marmaduke's father, Cuthbert's half brother Sir Brian Tunstall, had been slain at Flodden.[11]

Cuthbert Tunstall accompanied the Emperor Charles V to the city of Worms, in readiness to attend the meeting of the Diet of the Empire on 6th January 1521, and he was 'in a position to view at close quarters a momentous stage of the Lutheran controversy'.[12] Dr Martin Luther, professor of theology at the University of Wittenburg, had nailed his paper of Ninety-five theses to the door of the Castle church on 31st October 1517. He proceeded, increasingly, to attack Catholic doctrine and practice. His teaching of justification by faith alone: indicated the equality of all people before God; dispensed with priestly intermediaries; and it encouraged marriage of the clergy, communion under both kinds for the laity, and translation of the

Scriptures. The Diet, which was presided over by Charles, denounced Lutheran heresy; and Luther himself was outlawed by both spiritual and temporal powers.[13]

Luther's writing against the Sacraments led Henry VIII to publish his 'A Defence of the Seven Sacraments', with which he had been helped by John Fisher and Thomas More; and for which he received the title 'Defender of the Faith' from Pope Leo X.

Tunstall was a close friend of Fisher whom he encouraged to write against Luther; and Fisher sought Tunstall's critical opinion on his writings; he dedicated his *Sacri Sacerdotii* to Tunstall.[14]

The following year, 1522, Cuthbert Tunstall was appointed Bishop of London and Fisher assisted at his consecration. Archbishop Warham wrote to Wolsey, 'In my poor opinion Your Grace could not have owed your favour in that behalf more honorably and laudably than to the said Master Tunstall'.[15] It is highly likely that Cuthbert Tunstall and John Holden OP, who had become Prior of Black Friars in London, would have known each other at this time, if not before. And in 1523, the second year of the pontificate of Pope Clement VII, John Holden OP became Bishop of Sodor and Man.[16]

Queen Catherine, in 1527, was 41; her only living child was Mary. It seemed unlikely that she would produce a male heir. Henry had increasing doubts about the validity of his marriage because, surely, Julius II could not have dispensed from the law in Leviticus which forbade marriage with a brother's widow? The King asked Cardinal Wolsey, his Lord Chancellor, to obtain an annulment; but, here there was a problem. Pope Clement VII was compromised by being in the pocket of Catherine's nephew Charles V; and Wolsey, in turn, was dependant on the Pope.

When Charles' soldiers sacked Rome, Wolsey made an alliance with France against the Emperor. The Pope was eventually prevailed upon to commission Wolsey and Campeggio to try the case in London. By June 1528 Wolsey had to abandon the war for economic reasons. By September the French had capitulated. In May 1529, King Henry was summoned to the Legatine Court in his own capital by a foreign power. In June, the Pope, and in August, Francis, made peace with Charles. By 22nd July the Pope had revoked the suit to Rome and Campeggio adjourned the Court until October.

On 9th October Wolsey was indicted in the Court of King's Bench under Statute of Praemunire for alleged misdeeds in his legatine capacity.

On 25th October Sir Thomas More was appointed Lord Chancellor. 'More had so far refused his support for the divorce; that is he had refused to speak either for or against it'. The King said he would use

More 'otherwise' and 'never with that matter molest his conscience'. More 'should look first unto God, and after God unto him'.[17]

Wolsey travelled North to his Province. On the eve of his enthronement as Archbishop of York he was arrested. He died at Leicester Abbey on his way to London.

Henry, conscious that he was an anointed King, was reflecting on the status of kingship in the Old Testament and upon the imperialism of Constantine – who summoned the bishops to the Council of Nicaea which opened in the year 325. And the King was developing an increasing sense of his own spiritual, as well as temporal, jurisdiction over all his subjects, clergy and laity alike. Such aspirations and his need for the annulment were mutually reinforcing.[18]

Sir Thomas More opened the Reformation Parliament on 3rd November 1529. By its means, Henry managed to overawe the clergy into agreeing to his demands and, also, to amass lay support; but he did not manage to intimidate the Pope as he had hoped. Tunstall was translated from London to Durham early in 1530 and he was also President of the Council of the North; so that he was absent from London.[19]

In January 1531 the two Convocations of Clergy faced the threat of praemunire against their whole body for recognising Wolsey's legatine authority. Canterbury paid £100,000 and York £19,000 to obtain the King's pardon.

When, in February 1531, the King required the Convocation of Canterbury to grant him the title 'Supreme Head of the English Church' they did so only with the proviso 'as far as the law of Christ allows'. Tunstall considered this title ambiguous and open to abuse. He suggested 'Only and Supreme Lord, after Christ in Temporal Matters'. However, Tunstall's correspondence with Henry led the Bishop to examine the historical evidence for Papal primacy; and he found it lacking. Thomas More's thinking, from being somewhat sceptical about Papal primacy, moved in the opposite direction.

By the Act of Annates, in March 1532, the commission fees to Rome were reduced from 100 per cent of the first year's income from ecclesiastical preferments to 5 per cent. Its enforcement was postponed for a year while Henry sought an arrangement with the Pope.

Sir Thomas More, sensing the coming storm, resigned on 16th May. In the same year the Bishop of Sodor is mentioned as signing an agreement between the clergy and laity.[20]

Thomas Cromwell, protégé of Wolsey, now rose to be chief minister and presided over Henry's break with Rome.

The death, in August, of Warham, Archbishop of Canterbury,

removed an obstacle to the plans of Henry and Ann Boleyn. Ann was a niece of Thomas Howard 3rd Duke of Norfolk. Ann, for several years, had refused to become the mistress of the infatuated King; she insisted that he marry her first. But, by December, Ann was pregnant, perhaps with Henry's longed for son and heir. Henry and Ann were secretly married in January 1533. The King prevailed upon the Pope to appoint Thomas Cranmer to the see of Canterbury; and in March he was consecrated.

Legislation reinforcing the independence of the English Church proceeded rapidly. In April the Act of Restraint of Appeals forbad taking appeals in church cases to Rome. In May Cranmer declared Catherine's marriage to be null and void and recognised Henry's marriage to Ann Boleyn. Ann was crowned on June 1st. Tunstall attended the coronation and tried to persuade his friend Thomas More to do so. But More refused; he warned Tunstall that it would be very difficult to stop at this concession.[21] On July 9th Clement VII provisionally excommunicated both Henry and Cranmer unless Henry put away Ann by the end of September.[22]

In December 1533, the King issued his Nine Articles in which he attacked the Pope's character and denounced his authority. Tunstall warned Henry of the danger of schism; and he reminded the King that, because Louis XII had promoted schism, he, Henry, had joined the Holy League against Louis.

Henry did not trust Tunstall. He summoned him to London, in March 1534, so that he would be unable to attend the Convocation at York which, on May 5th, 'assented unanimously to the proposition that the Pope had no more authority in England than any other foreign bishop'. Two days after Tunstall left, his three houses in his Bishopric were searched for incriminating evidence.[23]

'Arrived in London, Tunstall came face to face with the king and was probably told to choose between him and the Tower. Under this pressure, the bishop snapped... For the rest of Henry's time Tunstal would be a king's man, serving a Royal Supremacy which he at one time so obstinately repudiated'.[24]

Two weeks after his arrival, Tunstall, one of Catherine's best friends, confronted her with his changed attitude to the validity of her marriage because 'divers other questions had risen', which he listed.[25]

The Act of Succession of March 1534 declared Ann Boleyn's child Elizabeth heir to the throne. Both Fisher and More refused to take the Oath of Succession because it asserted that Henry's marriage to Catherine was invalid. On 17th April, More and Fisher were imprisoned in the Tower. Tunstall took the Oath.

A member of Tunstall's household named Burton visited More in the Tower. 'Will not your master come to us, be as we are?' asked the prisoner. Burton replied that he did not know Tunstall's intentions. Then said More, 'If he do, no force, for if he live he may do more good than to die with us.' A touching and characteristic glimpse. We see More longing for his friend, yet ready to subordinate his own feelings to the welfare of the cause for which he died, and to put the best possible construction on Tunstall's absence.[26]

More and Tunstall were the closest of friends. In 1516, the year in which Tunstall became Master of the Rolls and Vice-Chancellor, he had been on embassy in the Netherlands with More who wrote of him to Erasmus:

> But yet certain things on that mission of mine pleased me very much. The first of these was that Tunstall dwelt with me for such a long time continuously, for while no one is better versed in all good literature, no one more strict in life and behaviour, yet no one whatever is a more delightful companion.[27]

Erasmus shared More's sentiments and, in writing to the great classical scholar William Budé, 'He named in particular Tunstall's quite exceptional scholarship and keen critical faculty combined with unusual modesty and manners humorous and charming yet always dignified, and congratulated himself on his good fortune in sharing his table'.[28]

At this stage Henry's intentions were not clear; and religious issues were confused. 'In confession at Syon Abbey Sir George Throckmorton was counselled to oppose to the death the anti-papal legislation, or "he should stand in a very heavy case at the Day of Judgement" '.[29] 'What distinguished men like Fisher and More was their courage and foresight, and when, in later years, John Stokesley, bishop of London, was reported to have exclaimed that he wished he had followed their example, he may have spoken for many who awoke too late'.[30]

The Act of Supremacy of 1534 declared Henry 'the only Supreme Head on Earth of the Church of England'. 'Some priests of Syon Priory were banned from hearing confessions in 1534 because of reports that they used its secrecy to undermine the royal supremacy'.[31] The Treasons Act was passed in the same year.

> More, together with Bishop Fisher of Rochester, and the London Carthusians, the most ascetic and honourable custodians of papal primacy and the legitimacy of the Aragonese marriage, were tried for "denying"

Henry's supremacy under the terms of the Treason's Act... The victims of the Act, who were in reality martyrs to Henry's vindictiveness, were cruelly executed in the summer of 1535.

The Act against the Pope's Authority of 1536 'removed the last vestiges of papal power in England'.[32]

King Henry had the last word in his theological declarations; but Tunstall was influential in steering him towards orthodoxy. Tunstall, however, had little part in drawing up the 'Ten Articles', of July 1536, which, among the seven Sacraments, mentioned only Baptism, Penance, and the Eucharist; though they insisted on the Real Presence. At this time, the King came under threat from Paul III who was seeking alliance with Charles and Francis against Henry, so shocked was Catholic Christendom by the martyrdoms. Henry sought allies among the Lutheran princes. But the death of Queen Catherine, that year, renewed the possibility of alliance with Charles.[33]

In the same year, Thomas Cromwell, having conducted an ecclesiastical census, proceeded with the dissolution of the smaller monasteries.

This desecration led to the Pilgrimage of Grace, a northern rising so strong that it could probably have overthrown the regime. However, the leaders were loyal to the King whom they considered had been misled by his Councillors and in whose promises they trusted. The followers were dispersed. Henry, then, broke his promises; and the Duke of Norfolk crushed the rebellion and hanged representative rebels, without trial, under Martial Law.

The Cistercian Abbey of Whalley, where John Holden OP's uncle Ralph Holden had been Abbott from 1471 to his death in 1480, was dissolved in 1537. The Abbott, John Paslew, was executed on 10th March that year. Other larger religious houses were ransacked in 1538.[34]

In that same year, the Dominican bishop wrote to Thomas Cromwell:

> I received the King's command under the seal your Lordship uses in causes ecclesiastical the Tuesday in Rogation week, and perceive his Grace is informed I have given orders to persons not able in learning to receive the same. I have never given orders but to those I thought sufficiently learned, and who had "letters dimissaries" from the bp. of their diocese. What restraint is made by the King and his Council with the consent of the Bishops was and is unknown to me; but now that I have the King's command I shall minister only to able persons within my own diocese. I beg to be excused from appearing in person; I am fourscore years of age,

have been sick and cannot labour so far. Please remember your favour to me when I was prior of the Black Friars in London.
Ormyskyrke, Lancashire, 13 June,
Signed: Joh'es Sodorensis [35]

In relation to this favour, it may be relevant that a Parliament had been held at Black Friars in 1523, the year in which, on 19th June, the Prior, John Holden OP, was provided Bishop of Sodor and Man.[36] Black Friars in London was dissolved on 12th November 1538.[37] On the Isle of Man the Reformation was a more gradual process than in England.[38]

Henry's 'iconoclasm, like his supremacy, was justified by an appeal to the word of God' and the translated scriptures would promote his subject's understanding of his claims and their obedience. Cromwell ordered every parish priest to buy an English Bible by 1st August 1537. But, 'Henry's Reformation had eroded too many old mental landmarks by trespassing on the ancient liberties of the church, by breaking the taboo of sacrilege that protected ecclesiastical property, and by condemning traditional pieties as idolatry and superstition. Opening the Bible to a people thus disorientated was an invitation to dissent which was readily accepted in many quarters'.[39]

The booty acquired from the monasteries and from the robbing of shrines, such as that of St Thomas, at Canterbury, was largely squandered on Henry's wars and on consolidating political support for his Reformation. 'Not the commonwealth, but the king, peers, and landowners were the true beneficiaries of the dissolution'.[40]

Cromwell had served his King well; but, when Henry became aware of his radical religious views, he left him to the mercy of his enemies, such as the Duke of Norfolk. Cromwell was condemned without trial; the bill of attainder charged him with heresy and treason. He was executed on 28th July 1540.[41]

Henry played a major part in the production of the King's Book of 1543 about which Chapuys, the Imperial Ambassador, wrote 'the accustomed ceremonies and ritual of the Christian religion have been restored to their first state, save in what relates to the authority of the Apostolic See'. During its production Tunstall did not dispute 'that circumstances might arise which would justify a layman making priests or in administering sacraments'; but, 'He was firm in denying that royal appointment, without consecration, could create a bishop, or that a layman might excommunicate'.[42]

However, on 22nd January 1546, sometime after the death of John Holden OP, 'The King appears to claim Pontifical power, for he creates his chaplain [Henry Man] a bishop [of Sodor] and invests him with spiritual rights:- "And we appoint and depute the same Henry Man to be Bishop of the Bishopric of that name, with all and every benefit, right and emolument whatsoever of the said Bishopric, both spiritual and temporal' ". He was consecrated on 14th February.[43]

Henry VIII died on 28th January the following year. He was fifty-five. Tunstall walked beside the new king, Henry's nine year old son, Edward, in the coronation procession.

The child's Protector, Edward Seymour, and Tunstall, though differing in religion, were on friendly terms. Seymour presided over the composition of the English Prayer Book of 1549 when Tunstall insisted on the literal truth of the words 'This is my body' and 'This is my blood' since, 'God hath spoken it, which is able to do it… As able is he to make his body as when he said *'Fiat Lux'*. Tunstall voted against the Prayer Book, the use of which was enforced throughout the realm by the Act of Uniformity.[44]

John Dudley, who supplanted Somerset in 1549, had also been on friendly terms with Tunstall but 'he was not the man to let personal feelings stand in the way of his ambitions'. Dudley coveted control of the Palatinate of Durham and his opportunity had arrived.[45]

It seems that Tunstall refused 'to sign certain ordinances made here respecting religion'. He was also suspected of withholding knowledge of a plot, possibly in favour of Somerset.[46]

Tunstall was deprived of his diocese. During his three years in prison, first, in his own house and, later, in the Tower, he 'decided that he could no longer find refuge in silence, since self-respect and duty alike required that he come boldly forward at whatever cost in defence of his faith now so heavily beset'.[47]

Mary acceded to the throne on 3rd August 1553. Three days later Tunstall was released. He attended her coronation in his role of Bishop of Durham. On 14th August he was a member of her Council. Early next year Tunstall was fully reinstated.

Cardinal Pole arrived in London as Legate on November 24th 1554 and, when Tunstall accompanied him up river from Gravesend, 'The memory of their old controversy over the Supremacy must have been in the minds of both'.[48]

Tunstall abhorred the corrosive effects of heresy, as did most of his contemporaries both Catholic and Protestant; but he shrank from the dreadful punishment incurred and strove to find points of agreement with the accused.[49]

In the next reign, as we have seen, Tunstall confronted Queen Elizabeth with 'documents in the handwriting of King Henry against the heresies now received, and especially as regards the sacraments, and begged her at least to respect the will of her father, if she did not conform to the decrees of the Church'. But Elizabeth was not to be persuaded.[50]

In a letter to Sir Thomas Parry in which he seeks a second interview with the Queen, Tunstall expresses his faith 'my conscience will not suffer me to receive and allow any doctrine in my diocese other than Catholic'.[51]

Every attempt was made to win over Tunstall, a bishop, consecrated before Henry's break with Rome, and one, so highly esteemed, who had shown moderation in his views. 'But Tunstall had done with compromise'.[52] He refused to take part in the consecration of Matthew Parker. He refused to take the Oath of Supremacy. On 28th September 1559 he was deprived of his bishopric. Tunstall was confined in Lambeth Palace, in the keeping of Parker, where efforts to convert him continued, but without success. And there he died, suddenly, on 18th November. He was eighty-five.

Tunstall, if he died in London, wished to be buried beside the tomb of 'my old friend Thomas Linacre the physician'. He was, in fact, honourably interred at Parker's expense in Lambeth parish church. Walter Haddon, a Protestant, composed an epitaph at Parker's request, referring to the 'golden old man'. And Alexander Nowell, also a Protestant, in his funeral sermon, is recorded, by a third Protestant, as delivering 'such liberal and singular commendation of this man for his virtuous life, learning, gravity, and good service done to many princes of England that more could not be of any man, being spoken truly'; and the recorder comments, 'Such force hath virtue that we ought to commend it even in our enemies'.[53]

Cuthbert Tunstall in his will regrets his waverings: 'I beseech thee, O just Judge, appear not as accuser against me thy runaway slave'.[54]

Richard Holden of Chaigley Hall, whose marriage had been arranged in 1561, had no issue by his first wife, Ann Nowell. His second wife, Jane, daughter of Robert Parker of Browsholme and widow of Thomas Shirburne of Ribbleton, was, as has been seen, my great-times-eight-grandmother. Much of this story has been about Richard and Jane Holden's descendants and their relatives and friends – lay-folk, priests, and religious – who strove, often with great courage and self-sacrifice, to keep the Faith alive in England.

This journey into history has, I think, provided some answers and hints of answers to my quest, perhaps enough to spur my fellow travellers upon their pilgrim way – such is my hope.

11. Descendants of Richard Holden of Chaigley Hall, Lancashire, and ? Margaret Loud
down to Richard Holden (c. 1535 - ?) of Chaigley Hall

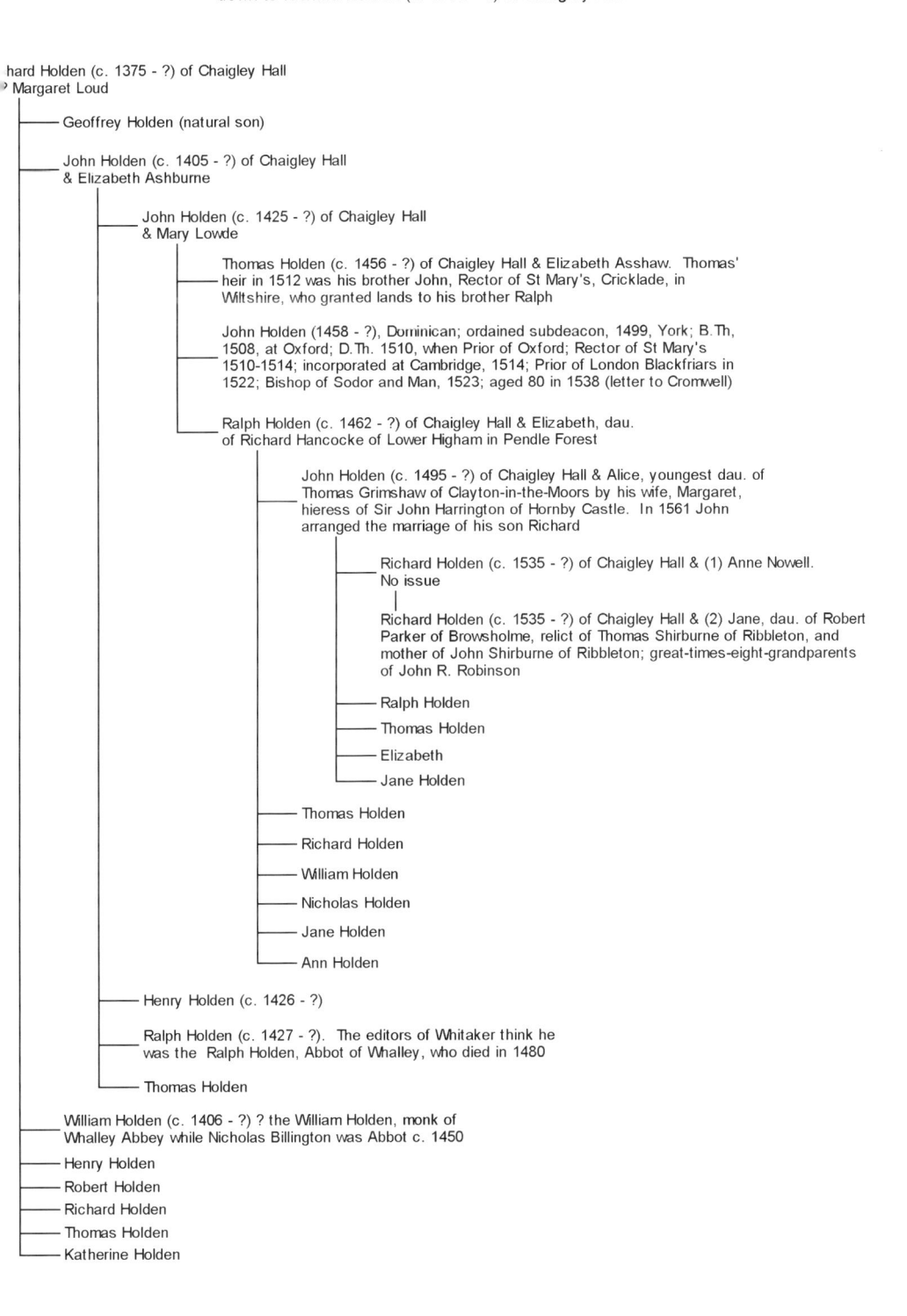

Richard Holden (c. 1375 - ?) of Chaigley Hall
& ? Margaret Loud
- Geoffrey Holden (natural son)
- John Holden (c. 1405 - ?) of Chaigley Hall & Elizabeth Ashburne
  - John Holden (c. 1425 - ?) of Chaigley Hall & Mary Lowde
    - Thomas Holden (c. 1456 - ?) of Chaigley Hall & Elizabeth Asshaw. Thomas' heir in 1512 was his brother John, Rector of St Mary's, Cricklade, in Wiltshire, who granted lands to his brother Ralph
    - John Holden (1458 - ?), Dominican; ordained subdeacon, 1499, York; B.Th, 1508, at Oxford; D.Th. 1510, when Prior of Oxford; Rector of St Mary's 1510-1514; incorporated at Cambridge, 1514; Prior of London Blackfriars in 1522; Bishop of Sodor and Man, 1523; aged 80 in 1538 (letter to Cromwell)
    - Ralph Holden (c. 1462 - ?) of Chaigley Hall & Elizabeth, dau. of Richard Hancocke of Lower Higham in Pendle Forest
      - John Holden (c. 1495 - ?) of Chaigley Hall & Alice, youngest dau. of Thomas Grimshaw of Clayton-in-the-Moors by his wife, Margaret, hieress of Sir John Harrington of Hornby Castle. In 1561 John arranged the marriage of his son Richard
        - Richard Holden (c. 1535 - ?) of Chaigley Hall & (1) Anne Nowell. No issue
        - Richard Holden (c. 1535 - ?) of Chaigley Hall & (2) Jane, dau. of Robert Parker of Browsholme, relict of Thomas Shirburne of Ribbleton, and mother of John Shirburne of Ribbleton; great-times-eight-grandparents of John R. Robinson
        - Ralph Holden
        - Thomas Holden
        - Elizabeth
        - Jane Holden
      - Thomas Holden
      - Richard Holden
      - William Holden
      - Nicholas Holden
      - Jane Holden
      - Ann Holden
  - Henry Holden (c. 1426 - ?)
  - Ralph Holden (c. 1427 - ?). The editors of Whitaker think he was the Ralph Holden, Abbot of Whalley, who died in 1480
  - Thomas Holden
- William Holden (c. 1406 - ?) ? the William Holden, monk of Whalley Abbey while Nicholas Billington was Abbot c. 1450
- Henry Holden
- Robert Holden
- Richard Holden
- Thomas Holden
- Katherine Holden

12. Descendants of Sir Thomas Tunstall, Knt., of Thurland, Lancashire, and Eleanor Fitzhugh
down to William Tunstall husband of Mary Radcliffe

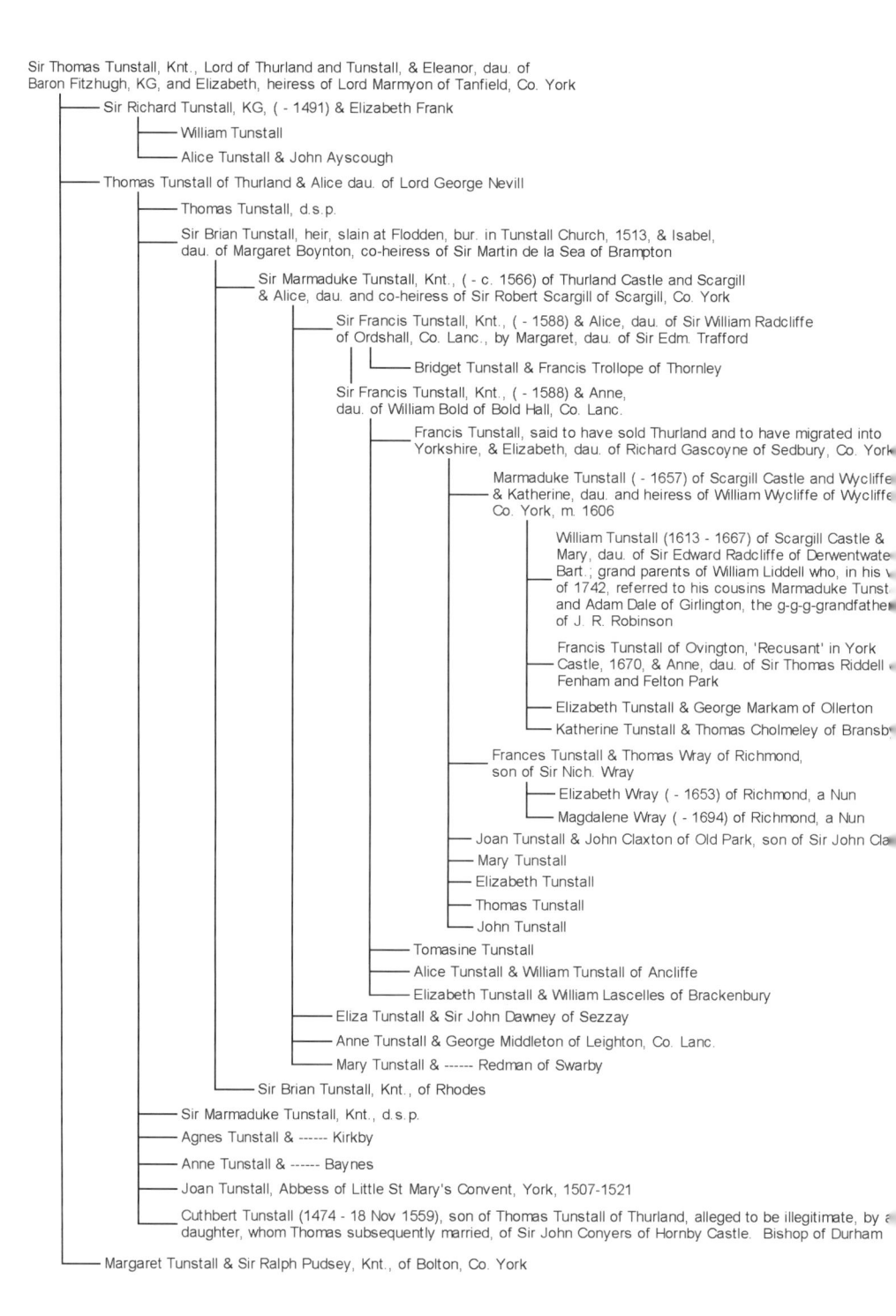

- Sir Thomas Tunstall, Knt., Lord of Thurland and Tunstall, & Eleanor, dau. of Baron Fitzhugh, KG, and Elizabeth, heiress of Lord Marmyon of Tanfield, Co. York
  - Sir Richard Tunstall, KG, (- 1491) & Elizabeth Frank
    - William Tunstall
    - Alice Tunstall & John Ayscough
  - Thomas Tunstall of Thurland & Alice dau. of Lord George Nevill
    - Thomas Tunstall, d.s.p.
    - Sir Brian Tunstall, heir, slain at Flodden, bur. in Tunstall Church, 1513, & Isabel, dau. of Margaret Boynton, co-heiress of Sir Martin de la Sea of Brampton
      - Sir Marmaduke Tunstall, Knt., (- c. 1566) of Thurland Castle and Scargill & Alice, dau. and co-heiress of Sir Robert Scargill of Scargill, Co. York
        - Sir Francis Tunstall, Knt., (- 1588) & Alice, dau. of Sir William Radcliffe of Ordshall, Co. Lanc., by Margaret, dau. of Sir Edm. Trafford
          - Bridget Tunstall & Francis Trollope of Thornley
        - Sir Francis Tunstall, Knt., (- 1588) & Anne, dau. of William Bold of Bold Hall, Co. Lanc.
          - Francis Tunstall, said to have sold Thurland and to have migrated into Yorkshire, & Elizabeth, dau. of Richard Gascoyne of Sedbury, Co. York
            - Marmaduke Tunstall (- 1657) of Scargill Castle and Wycliffe & Katherine, dau. and heiress of William Wycliffe of Wycliffe Co. York, m. 1606
              - William Tunstall (1613 - 1667) of Scargill Castle & Mary, dau. of Sir Edward Radcliffe of Derwentwater Bart.; grand parents of William Liddell who, in his w of 1742, referred to his cousins Marmaduke Tunst and Adam Dale of Girlington, the g-g-g-grandfather of J. R. Robinson
              - Francis Tunstall of Ovington, 'Recusant' in York Castle, 1670, & Anne, dau. of Sir Thomas Riddell Fenham and Felton Park
              - Elizabeth Tunstall & George Markam of Ollerton
              - Katherine Tunstall & Thomas Cholmeley of Bransb
            - Frances Tunstall & Thomas Wray of Richmond, son of Sir Nich. Wray
              - Elizabeth Wray (- 1653) of Richmond, a Nun
              - Magdalene Wray (- 1694) of Richmond, a Nun
            - Joan Tunstall & John Claxton of Old Park, son of Sir John Cla
            - Mary Tunstall
            - Elizabeth Tunstall
            - Thomas Tunstall
            - John Tunstall
        - Tomasine Tunstall
        - Alice Tunstall & William Tunstall of Ancliffe
        - Elizabeth Tunstall & William Lascelles of Brackenbury
      - Eliza Tunstall & Sir John Dawney of Sezzay
      - Anne Tunstall & George Middleton of Leighton, Co. Lanc.
      - Mary Tunstall & ------ Redman of Swarby
    - Sir Brian Tunstall, Knt., of Rhodes
    - Sir Marmaduke Tunstall, Knt., d.s.p.
    - Agnes Tunstall & ------ Kirkby
    - Anne Tunstall & ------ Baynes
    - Joan Tunstall, Abbess of Little St Mary's Convent, York, 1507-1521
    - Cuthbert Tunstall (1474 - 18 Nov 1559), son of Thomas Tunstall of Thurland, alleged to be illegitimate, by a daughter, whom Thomas subsequently married, of Sir John Conyers of Hornby Castle. Bishop of Durham
  - Margaret Tunstall & Sir Ralph Pudsey, Knt., of Bolton, Co. York

Epilogue

My researches have led me to reflect that accidental factors seem to play a big part in determining religious faith; or, perhaps more truly, the form that such faith takes. And, perhaps, these factors are not so accidental after all? As for me, I choose to identify with Pope John XXIII who shall have the last word:

> In the daily exercise of our pastoral office, we sometimes have to listen, much to our regret, to voices of persons who, though burning with zeal, are not endowed with too much sense of discretion or measure. In these modern times they can see nothing but prevarication and ruin. They say that our era, in comparison with past eras, is getting worse, and they behave as though they had learned nothing from history, which is, none the less, the teacher of life. They behave as though at the time of former councils everything was a full triumph for the Christian idea and life and for proper religious liberty.
>
> We feel we must disagree with those prophets of gloom, who are always forecasting disaster, as though the end of the world were at hand. In the present order of things, Divine Providence is leading us to a new order of human relations which, by men's own efforts and even beyond their very expectations, are directed toward the fulfilment of God's superior and inscrutable designs. And everything, even human differences, leads to the greater good of the Church.
>
> Pope John XXIII
> Opening speech to the Second Vatican Council 11th October 1962
> Quoted from *The Tablet* 12th October 2002 p. 32

APPENDIX

Robert Robinson of Hutton Hall, 1721-1809: in Search of His Origins

'There is nothing like certainty as an instrument for closing the mind'.
Conrad Pepler, OP[1]

The whereabouts of Robert Robinson my great-great-grandfather, prior to 1760 when he went to Hutton Hall, remains an enigma. Furthermore, although we have seen that his mother was almost certainly Dorothy, a daughter of Adam Daile of Hutton and Sarah Richinson, and a sister of Robert Dale of Hutton Hall who died in 1736, the identity of his father is a mystery.[2] We must now search for clues which might shed light on this problem.

Who occupied Hutton Hall between the death of Robert Dale in 1736 and the advent of Robert Robinson in 1760?

In his will of 1736 Robert Dale makes the following bequests: 'I give and bequeath unto my son Lawrence Dale the sum of two hundred pounds and all my stock of cattle corn hay and husbandry geer upon the ffarm whereon I live. I also give and bequeath unto my son Adam Dale the sum of two hundred pounds and all my stock of cattle corn hay household ffurniture and husbandry geer at Girlington where my said son Adam now lives'.

From these entries it would seem that Lawrence was set to continue at Hutton Hall. It would also appear that Robert Dale had furniture, as well as stock and farm equipment, at Girlington where his son Adam was living in 1736; and, perhaps, he himself lived and farmed there before coming to Hutton Hall. It is also of interest that the witnesses to Robert Dale's will were 'Thomas Robinson and Robart Robinson', both of whom were able to sign their names. It is tempting to think that these were Robert my great-great-grandfather and his brother Thomas; but Robert would only have been 15 years old. The administration of the will was carried out by Robert Dale's widow, Mary, and Thomas Robinson of Walworth in the parish of Heighington and his signature appears to be identical with that of Thomas the witness.

In the *Returns of Papists, 1767: Diocese of Chester,* under Wycliffe, the following entry appears: 'Adam Dale, a Farmer, (this being the second time of his living in this parish, after 10 years intermediate absence) aged 54 years, resident 22 years'.[3] The total of 32 years would mean that Adam Dale went to Girlington when he was 22 and spent 22 years between there and Wycliffe Grange and 10 years somewhere else.

The following summaries of findings in the Chichester-Constable catalogues are relevant:

DDCC (2) Box 20A	Rental 1734-37. No places specified except Hutton, but Robert Dale, Mrs. Mary Dale and Lawrence Dale, Matthew Robinson mentioned.
Box 23	North Riding Estate Rental Book 1746-52. "Mr. Lawrence Dale, tenant of Hutton Hall farm at £131-10/year left his farm Mayday 1750 and brother Adam Dale took part of it, £53-15 rent half yearly".
DDCC (2) 17/4	Account Book (on cover "Adam Dale's Accounts 1747") to include accounts made by AD for his and other's rents, payments etc. up to Pentecost 1750.
/3	Similar (on cover "Girlington and Ovington Accounts 1747") AD up to Pentecost 1750.
DDCC (2)	Rental (and accounts) 1746-51. Detail for Lawrence Dale and brother Adam Dale of Hutton Hall and Mathew Robinson of Field House Hutton.[4]

The Returns of Papists, 1767: Diocese of Chester, locates Robert Dale's widow, Mary, aged 80, in Coldwell, and also her son Lawrence, a labourer, aged 60, and her daughter Mary, all resident two years; and her daughter Elizabeth, a widow, resident one year.

It seems likely that following Robert Dale's death, in 1736, his widow, Mary, continued at Hutton Hall assisted by her sons Lawrence and Adam. Perhaps Adam had to be involved because Lawrence lacked competence; though, in 1779, 'Lawrence Dale' contributes £10 to the Yorkshire Brethren Fund.[5]

Mathew Robinson of Field House, Hutton: his identity

Mathew Robinson has already appeared in the Chichester-Constable catalogues under 'Rental (and accounts) 1746-51 … Mathew Robinson of Field House in Hutton'. The Matthew Robinson mentioned in relation to Hutton in the 'Rental 1734-37' is likely to be the same person, a variant of the spelling.

'Matthew Robinson' also appears together with 'Marm. Wilson' as a witness to the following deed, 8th May 1716:

> Bargain and Sale: Marmaduke Tunstall of Wycliffe esq. to Christopher Wilkinson of Thorpe gent. and Francis Hutton of Barnard Castle merchant: - - manors and property in Scargill, Hutton Long Villers and Wycliffe; titles of Hutton Long Villers - - : On trust to pay scheduled debts and annuities.

In 1712, 'Mar – Wilson' appears as a witness to the will of Adam Daile of Hutton.

An entry in the parish register of Hutton Magna records:

1720 4th Jul. John son of Matthew Robinson, born.

In 1765, Hugh Tootell makes the following registration: 'a messge. etc., let to Math. Robinson at £75'.[6]

Finally, the *Returns of Papists, 1767: Diocese of Chester* in the Chapelry of Gt. Hutton, lists: 'Matthew Robinson aged 79, resided 40 years, a Farmer'.

Matthew, then, was a recusant and was born in 1688. He had resided in Hutton since 1727. He would have been in his mid twenties when Elizabeth and Dorothy, daughters of Adam Daile of Hutton, each married a Robinson. Presuming that these 'Matthews' are one and the same person and that 'Field House Hutton' is also referred to as 'Hutton Fields',[7] Matthew Robinson was also a successful farmer, resident, for probably half his life, at Hutton Fields. Could he be the husband of Elizabeth Daile? No will has been found for this Matthew Robinson; he could have been an uncle of my great-great-grandfather Robert. Perhaps two brothers Robinson married two sisters Dale.

Robert Dale of Hutton Fields: ties of friendship

Robert Dale of Hutton Fields appears as the friend of:
a) Ralph Robinson of Hutton Fields.
b) Richard and Ruth Robinson of Pecknall House, Romaldkirk.
c) William and Mary Robinson 'Above Smallways.'
d) Robert and Cecily Robinson of Hutton Hall.

What significance did this common friendship have for the relationship between the families concerned? This question will now be explored.

ROBERT ROBINSON OF HUTTON HALL, 1721-1809:

a) Ralph Robinson of Hutton Fields

On 6th January 1795, 'Dorothy Robinson, widow' was required to 'swear that Matthew Robinson your late son deceased, made and left at the time of his Death, no last Will and Testament'. Matthew is described as 'formerly of Hutton Fields in the Chapelry of Hutton in the Province of York but dying in Jamaica Having in his lifetime and at his Death Bona Notabilia in divers Dioceses or peculiar Jurisdictions within the Province of York aforesaid/Gentleman a Bachelor'.

On 12th January 1795 there were bounden: 'Dorothy Robinson of Hutton Fields in the Chapelry of Hutton and County of York widow; James Collier of Wycliffe in the same County, Gentleman; and George Bell of East Middleton within the same County Gentleman'. All sign their names; Dorothy Robinson's signature is large and a little scratchy. Dorothy Robinson is further described as 'Mother only next of kin and Administratrix'. The document is 'Sealed and Delivered in the presence of "Dorothy Dale" ', who also signs her name.

Dorothy Robinson 'declares that to the best of her knowledge and belief the goods and chattles and credits of the said deceased would not amount to the sum of six hundred pounds'.

Dorothy Dale, née Brown, the widow of Robert Dale of Hutton Fields who had died on 2nd November 1790, signed as witness to the above quoted document.

Dorothy Dale's brother, James Brown, married Ann, the sister of Robert Dale of Hutton Fields, and James and Ann's daughter, Sarah Brown, married my great grandfather Thomas Robinson of Hutton Hall, 1781-1868.

Robert Dale of Hutton Fields, 1738-1790, inherited an estate at East Middleton from his father, Adam Dale of Wycliffe Grange, and it is of interest that George Bell, who, with Dorothy Robinson, was 'bounden' in the probate documents, was also of East Middleton.

Robert Dale, together with his sister Sarah, appear on the Chapelry of Gt. Hutton list of Papists in 1767, when our original Matthew Robinson was aged 79.

Dorothy Robinson, the mother of Matthew Robinson who died in Jamaica, was the widow of Ralph Robinson of Hutton Fields who died in 1792 and whose will is dated 5th May 1787; and she was a sister of Robert Dale of Hutton Fields.

In this will, Ralph Robinson refers to his wife, Dorothy, and to his children, Ralph, Anthony, and Matthew, and to his brother-in-law, Robert Dale of Hutton Fields. His marriage to Robert Dale's sister is suggestive that Ralph Robinson was a Catholic and this is confirmed by the *Returns of Papists, 1767: Diocese of Chester* where the following entry appears under Manfield:

> Ralph Robinson, Farmer, Aged 58. No entry for years of residence.
> Dorothy Robinson his Wife, Aged 30. Resident 8 years.
> Ralph Robinson his Son, Aged 4.
> Anthony Robinson, Do, Aged 2.
> John Robinson, Do, Aged 1.
> No entry for years of residence is given for the children.

This would mean that Ralph Robinson was born in 1709 and was aged 78 when he made his will and aged 83 when he died. Dorothy had been resident for eight years which suggests that she and Ralph were married in 1759 but the dates of birth of their children are suggestive of a later date, such as 1761. The dates of birth of their sons were: Ralph in 1763; Anthony in 1765; John in 1766; and Matthew would have been born after the date of the Returns, say in 1768. John does not appear in Ralph Robinson's will, but he may have died.

Matthew would have been aged about 27 when he died in Jamaica and his mother, Dorothy, would have been aged 58. These facts seem to fit, in which case, Ralph Robinson was a Catholic and he would have moved to Hutton Fields sometime after 1767. His religion, his location, and his relationship to Robert Dale of Hutton Fields are strongly suggestive that Ralph Robinson was related to Robert Robinson of Hutton Hall. It similarly suggests that there was a Manfield dimension to our family.

Another Ralph Robinson appears under Manfield in the same Returns, as follows:

> Ralph Robinson, Farmer, Aged 70. No entry for years of residence.
> Elizabeth Robinson, his Wife, Aged 63. No entry for years of residence.
> John Robinson, Grandson, Aged 14. Resident 5 years.
> Richard Robinson, Do, Aged 6.
> Dorothy Robinson, Do, Aged 2.
> No entry for years of residence is given for
> Richard and Dorothy.

It seems likely that this Ralph Robinson was related to Ralph Robinson of Hutton Fields, perhaps a cousin or even an uncle.

ROBERT ROBINSON OF HUTTON HALL, 1721-1809:

b) Richard and Ruth Robinson of Pecknall House, Romaldkirk

In his will of 19th September 1790, Richard Robinson, of Pecknall House in the parish of Romaldkirk, states: 'I give and bequeath unto my friend Robert Dale of Hutton Fields the sum of one hundred and fifty pounds in trust to place the same out at interest on good security and to pay the interest thereof from time to time arising unto my dear wife Ruth Robinson'. Richard Robinson makes his mark; and the will is witnessed by Richard Lamb, Surgeon, and by Joseph Atkinson.

There follows: 'An Inventory and Valuation of the Horses, Cattle, Implements of Husbandry and household Furniture taken at Pecknall on the 16th Day of November 1790, Belonging to the Late Richard Robinson Deceased... by me Joseph Atkinson'. The total value amounted to £100.

Richard Robinson could not have anticipated that his friend Robert Dale of Hutton Fields, himself, would die on 2nd November that year at the age of 52.

In the *Returns of Papists, 1767: Diocese of Chester* no Robinson is returned for the parish of Romaldkirk. However, there is the following interesting return for the parish of Brignall:

Mary Robinson Widow	resident in
Richard Robinson a Farmer	this Parish
Ruth Robinson his wife	5 years.

The children of the said Richard and Ruth Robinson:

Mary Robinson aged 4 years.
Jane Robinson aged 3 years.
Richard Robinson aged 2 years.

In his will of 1790, Richard Robinson refers to his children: Richard of Westend parish of Romaldkirk; his son-in-law, William Stephenson; Margaret Robinson; John Robinson; and his youngest son, George Robinson.

It seems very likely that the Richard and Ruth Robinson of Brignall are identical with those of Pecknall House, having moved or returned there at a later date. Mary and Jane are not mentioned in Richard Robinson's will of 1790; but, they may have died, or, they may have got married and have received their settlement; one of them may have been the wife of William Stephenson.

This theory is strengthened by an entry in the Catholic Register of

Lartington, in the parish of Romaldkirk, which began in 1769, and which records under Robinson:
> John, son of Richard and Ruth, baptised, 10th March 1770.
> George, son of Richard and Ruth, baptised, 27th February 1775.[8]

The Catholicism of the Brignall Richard and Ruth Robinson re-emerges in Romaldkirk, and the distribution of their children's ages fits. The common identity may be regarded as virtually certain.

c) William and Mary Robinson 'Above Smallways'

The Catholic Baptismal Register of Wycliffe Hall contains the following entries:

> William and George Robinson twins of William and Mary near the high street above Smallways. The first born William. Sponsors: Francis Malthouse junior, Helen Boldren. The second born George. Sponsors: Richard Robinson and Old Mary Robinson. November the 30th 1764.

It is tempting to think that this may refer to Richard Robinson of Brignall and 'Mary Robinson widow'.

> Richard the son of William and Mary Robinson above Smallways near Newsham. Sponsors: Sarah Jackson and Tom Wiseman for Mary Atkinson and Robert Dale. 17th March 1768 three or four days old.

Robert Dale would have been Robert Dale of Hutton Fields, 1738-1790.

> Frances Robinson above Smallways of William and Mary. Sponsors: Henry Thompson of Newsham and _____ of [?] "Barwick of Dollary." September the 22nd 1771, four or five days old.

The *Returns of Papists, 1767: Diocese of Chester* for Newsham: 'Henry Thompson, a Blacksmith aged 84 resided 50 years', and 'Henry Thompson the Son of a Farmer aged 45 born and lives here'.

> Rose Robinson of William and Mary above Smallways. Sponsors: William Clayton and Katherine Carter 4 days old 17th April 1775.

William and Mary had five children before Fr Thomas Penswick began the Wycliffe Register in 1762. For the Township of Dalton within the parish of Kirby Ravensworth the *Returns of Papists, 1767: Diocese of Chester* makes the following return:

William Robinson (a Farmer)	aged 53	
Mary his Wife	aged 40	
Jane their Daugt.	aged 14	have resided
Thos their Son	aged 11	here 6 years.
Mary their Daugt.	aged 9	
Ann a Daugt.	aged 7	
Eleanor	aged 5	born in the Parish
William and George Twins	aged 2	and live in it.

From these data it is seen that:
1) William and Mary and their 4 eldest children came to live above Smallways, in the Township of Dalton in 1761 (a year after Robert Robinson went to Hutton Hall).
2) They went to Wycliffe to have their children baptised, at any rate after they came to Smallways.
3) Robert Dale of Hutton Fields was a friend of theirs, as well as of Richard and Ruth Robinson.
4) 'Richard and Old Mary Robinson' may refer to Richard of Brignall and 'Mary Robinson Widow' who probably lived with him and his wife Ruth.

Could Ralph Robinson of Hutton Fields, Richard Robinson of Brignall and of Pecknall House, and William Robinson above Smallways be related?

The answer to this question may lie in the will made by James Robinson of Saddle Bow in the parish of Romaldkirk on 27th July 1753. In this will James Robinson refers to:

Ralph – his eldest son
Richard – his second son
John – his third son
William – presumably his youngest son
Margaret Pinkney – his daughter
Alice Tinkler – his daughter

James's father, Richard Robinson of Parkend in Crostwhaite, in the parish of Romaldkirk, in his will of 20th February 1714, the year in which he died, refers to: James his only son; and to James's children, Ralph, Margaret, and Alice; but not to Richard, John, and William.

Since Richard Robinson also refers to the children of his daughters, Margaret Dent and Elizabeth Emmerson, by name, we may assume that James's sons, Richard, John, and William, were born after the will was made and, probably, between 1714 and about 1725. The *Returns of Papists, 1767: Diocese of Chester* gives no age for Richard Robinson of Brignall, but it states that William Robinson of Dalton (above Smallways) was 53, so that he was born in 1714. It appears that the ages given in the Returns are not always accurate and his date of birth could have been a few years later.

From the above observations it seems virtually certain that Ralph Robinson of Hutton Fields, Richard Robinson of Brignall and later of Pecknall House, and William Robinson 'above Smallways' were brothers and were the sons of James Robinson of Saddle Bow.

James Robinson of Saddle Bow does not mention his wife in his will and so she was probably dead and would not have been 'Mary Robinson Widow', living with Richard Robinson of Brignall in 1767; of course, 'Mary Robinson Widow' may have been some other relative and probably 'Old Mary Robinson' who sponsored William and Mary's son, George, in 1764.

In his will of 1714, Richard Robinson refers to 'Elizabeth Dayles of Romaldkirk, my God Daughter'. Could this be another Dale connection of significance?

d) Robert and Cecily Robinson of Hutton Hall

It has already been recorded that Robert Dale of Hutton Fields acted as sponsor to Robert and Cecily's daughter, Ann, in 1771 and that his wife, Dorothy Dale, acted as sponsor to their daughter, Cecily, in 1779.

The relationship between Robert Robinson of Hutton Hall and Ralph, Richard and William, the sons of James Robinson of Saddle Bow in the parish of Romaldkirk is not known, other than that they were all Catholics and friends of Robert Dale of Hutton Fields. In addition, Robert Robinson and William Robinson 'above Smallways' had their common interest in the areas of Dalton and Newsham in the parish of Kirby Ravensworth.

The Parish of Kirby Ravensworth: Townships of Newsham and Dalton

The parish of Kirby Ravensworth adjoins the south border of Hutton Magna parish; and Hutton Magna itself is only two miles north-east of Newsham.

ROBERT ROBINSON OF HUTTON HALL, 1721-1809:

Robert Robinson's will, made 11th February 1805, is as follows:

In the name of God Amen I Robert Robinson of Hutton hall in the county of York yeoman do by this my will devise all my real estate whatsoever situate and being at Newsham or elsewhere unto and to the use of my two sons Robert and Thomas their Heirs Executors Administrators and Assigns as Tenants in Common share and share alike chargeable as hereinafter is expressed And whereas I have already given and delivered unto my son Robert Robinson all my late stocks of cattle, sheep and other stock and all my Furniture and Husbandry utensils carts carriages etc. which then were upon the Farms at Dalton fields in the said County of York, And to my son Thomas Robinson I have given all my late stock of cattle sheep and other stock and the Furniture and Husbandry utensils carts etc. which then were upon the Farm at Hutton hall aforesaid and upon my estate at Newsham the tenant right in which I have given to him.

A further entry, in the Probate document, reads: 'Richmond March 8th 1810 – Robert Robinson of Dalton Fields in the County of York Yeoman & Thomas Robinson of Hutton Hall in the said County Yeoman the sons and joint Executors… and also made oath that the whole of the personal estate & effects… do not amount to the sum of Fifteen Hundred Pounds'.

Robert Robinson of Hutton Hall appears to have owned or rented an estate at Newsham and one at Dalton Fields, which is half a mile south-east of Newsham.

Robert's son, Thomas Robinson of Newsham Grange (formerly of Hutton Hall) in his will of 5th July 1866, states: 'I give and devise my freehold messuage or dwellinghouse called Newsham Grange with the outbuildings yards gardens and the several closes or parcels of land timber and other trees sights and appurtenances thereto belonging situate in the parish of Kirby Ravensworth aforesaid and now in my occupation…'. Newsham Grange lies one mile north of Newsham and just over one mile south-west of Hutton Magna.

With regard to Dalton, Thomas Robinson's youngest son, William, writing to his cousin Canon Robert Thompson, 25th June 1867, states: 'I enclose your cheque for £10-16-4 for the Dalton rent after the property tax has been deducted'. Monsignor Edward Wilcock, who kindly gave me the letter in which this appears, states in his letter to me of 25th January 1993, 'Canon Thompson was a canon of Beverley Diocese for twenty five years, a post in which I succeeded him in 1950 and occupied for the next thirty five years. The "Dalton Rent" to which the letter refers was the ground rent on a piece of land at Dalton and the sum of £10-16-4 was still being paid to the diocese up to the time I left'. Canon Robert Thompson died 8th November 1875 aged 68.

Newsham Grange

Thomas Robinson clearly owned Newsham Grange and, no doubt, inherited it from his father, Robert Robinson of Hutton Hall. In her will of 13th March 1860, Thomas's sister, Cecily Robinson, who was two years and two months older than him, is also described as 'of Newsham Grange'. She died 13th April 1861.

In the Newsham Tithe Apportionment, 1840, Merryne Watson noted the following: 'Newsham Grange. Owner Mrs. Ann Chambers. Occupier: Mrs. Ann Chambers and William Thompson. The latter farmed the land, about 115 acres (46.5 ha)'.[9]

The Catholic Baptismal Register at Wycliffe has this entry about my grandfather Thomas Robinson of Nuthill: 'Thomas Robinson, baptised 23rd March 1823. Sponsors: Adam Dale and Ann Chambers'. Thomas's uncle, Robert Robinson, and his aunt, Dorothy Robinson, had sponsored his sister, Mary Ann, in 1819; and his aunt, Elizabeth Thompson, née Robinson, was to sponsor his younger brother, William, in 1824. Moreover, Ann Chambers appears as sponsor to Elizabeth Thompson's daughter, Ann, who was baptised 11th April 1812. Could Ann Chambers be Ann, the sister of Elizabeth and aunt of Thomas?

The International Genealogical Index has this entry: 'Ralph Chambers – Ann Robinson – Husband. Married 16th June 1809 Kirkby Ravensworth'. If this refers to Thomas's aunt, Ann, who was born 3rd March 1771, she would have been aged 38 when she married and 53 when he was baptised. In 1840, she would have been 69 and her husband would probably have died. William Thompson is likely to have been William, the third child of her sister Elizabeth. He was born in 1810 and would have been aged 30 when he was farming at Newsham Grange. In 1844 he married Maria Robinson of South Park. The theory seems to fit well.

Newsham House

Merryne Watson also found, in the Newsham Tithe Apportionment, 1840: 'Newsham House. Owner and occupier Robert Robinson. There were two small cottages (now derelict) included with the estate of some 57 acres (23 ha)'.

This would probably refer to Robert Robinson who was baptised at

Wycliffe on 4th April in what appears to be 1796 (the writing is not clear but the entries around it are 1796) and whose sponsors were John Rutter and Mary Rutter; he is likely to have been a grandson of William and Mary Robinson 'above Smallways'. Merryne Watson continues:

> These cottages were close to Smallways, now the A66 Motel and the Smallways Inn. In the deed of 1602, Small Ways became Small Waches. Ways, Waches, Worth, With are all derived from the Old Scandinavian meaning "ford". As a member of the Tees Greta Section of the Yorkshire Vernacular Building's Study Group we have recorded Newsham House; an imposing Georgian front wedded to an older farm house in the rear. I have heard it said (no written evidence) that a Robinson was responsible for the improvement of Newsham House. Apparently this was a tremendous drain on the Robinson finances and eventually the estate was sold to the Milbank (of Barningham) family... A final point: Newsham House does not appear on Thomas Jeffery's map of Yorkshire, 1775. At that time it may have been a small farm house in which case I doubt he would have included it. In its present imposing appearance, I suspect he would have certainly done so.

Merryne Watson, referring to 'above Smallways near Newsham' states: 'This exactly describes the position of Newsham House, its old drive leaving Smallways and arising up to Newsham House, about 600 m.'. Hence, this would have been where William and Mary Robinson were living when they were having their children baptised in the 1760s and 1770s.

The Catholic Baptismal Register of Wycliffe has an entry: 'William Robinson of George and Jane of Newsham. Sponsor Mary Peacock June 18th 1788 a day and a half old'. This George Robinson may well be George, one of the twins born to William and Mary, above Smallways, in 1764.

The Hutton Hall Robinsons and the Robinsons 'above Smallways' have been shown to have had a substantial presence in Newsham, but when did they first go there?

According to Yorkshire Pedigrees, William Robinson, son of Ralph Robinson, Citizen and Haberdasher of London seized of the lands in Carleton-juxta-Snaith, and his wife Agnes, daughter and coheir of James Phillippe of Barningham, purchased the manor of Brignall from Hen. Phillippe Esq. in 1601 and the manor of Rokeby from Sir Thomas Rokeby on 7th June 1611 and 'a great part' of the Mortham estate in 1616. He was a Protestant and died in service with the Parliamentary forces in 1643.

The question is, was this William Robinson, Parliamentarian, identical with William Robinson mentioned under Hutton Longvillers, in Yorkshire Deeds, by A. S. Ellis? The Deed entry: '20th May 1602. Grant by Thos. Rookeby of Mortham Yorks. esq. to Wm. Robinson of Brignall, Yorks. for 300l. of 3 enclosures called Hooton closes in *Hooten Longe Villers,* Yorks; the south side adjoining the King's highway called le Small Waches; now in the occupation of John Messinger'.

The name is the same but William Robinson was a common name in the area. William Robinson, Parliamentarian, was of Brignall Manor by 1602, but William Robinson of Hutton closes is only described as 'of Brignall'. No mention is made that William Robinson, Parliamentarian, owned Hutton closes, neither is this mentioned in his will August 1643. Hutton closes is to the east of the Rokeby and Mortham estates. Hutton closes is north of le Small Watches and by 1764 a catholic family, William and Mary Robinson, were 'above Smallways near Newsham'.

I propose that William Robinson of Hutton closes was a catholic and an ancestor of our family.

This theory might fit the oral tradition that our family, whose name was originally Vane, came up from Kendal; and that a protestant branch went to Rokeby and a catholic branch went to Hutton, were it not for the entry in William Robinson of Rokeby's pedigree that, although his grandfather William Robinson was of Kendal, this William's father came from Struan in Scotland. It is conceivable that the Struan entry is a mistake.

In 'An Armorial for Westmorland and Lonsdale' the following entry appears, 'William Robinson, of White Hall, Kendal, settled there in the reign of Henry VIII and was engaged in the staple trade of the Town (CW2 vi 171). His son, Ralph, removed to Yorkshire, and the latter's son, William (d. 1643), bought the manors of Brignall and Rokeby and was ancestor of Richard Robinson, M.A., D.D., 1st Lord Rokeby, Archbishop of Armagh (1709-94)'. This also fits the oral tradition that a protestant branch of our family went to Ireland. There is no mention of Struan.

However, the very next entry is of a 'leading Appleby family' called Robinson, of 'The White House', a member of which, John Robinson, MP, in 1784 'adopted a version of the arms of Robertson, of Struan, "in lieu of" the family arms'.[10]

There is early evidence that, as two catholic families, our fortunes were united with those of the Tunstalls: Francis Tunstall Esq. of Barningham was presented at Richmond Quarter Sessions, 5th October 1624, also 16th January 1627, for harbouring servants among whom was William Robinson, yeoman, possibly a son of William of Hooton closes; the total penalty was £300.[11] Perhaps this William, as a youth, was being trained in the Tunstall household. To quote Mgr. Edward Wilcock:

> There was a family of recusant Robinsons living at Caldwell, Stanwick early in the 17th century. Thomas and his wife Jennet appear in 1604 (Thomas as a recusant and Jennet as a non-communicant). They were presented at the Quarter Sessions held at Northallerton in 1610, Thirsk 1611, Helmsley 1611, Northallerton in 1612. They were presented by the churchwardens under Stanwick in 1617.
> Jennet Robinson, a spinster of Hutton Longvillers was convicted at Northallerton in 1617. William Robinson of Barningham was charged before the Courts of Correction in 1624. Frances the wife of John Robinson, a gardener of Hutton Longvillers was also presented at the Thirsk Q.S. in 1641 and Margaret the wife of William, a yeoman, was charged at the Richmond Q.S. in 1623. She also belonged to Caldwell.[12]

Because Robinson was such a common name and because Catholics were relatively numerous in the North of England it might be supposed that these Robinsons were not related to each other and to our family; but in the *Returns of Papists, 1767: Diocese of Chester* Hutton Magna and the surrounding district showed a larger cluster of catholic Robinsons than appeared elsewhere. I think it likely that these Robinsons were related to each other, though, perhaps distantly for some of them. Monsignor Edward Wilcock, referring to Robert Robinson who took the Oath of Allegiance (as drafted for Catholics) on 13th January 1792, is evidently sufficiently confident of the evidence to say 'Robert Robinson of Hutton Hall, whose family had been recusants since the early sixteenth century'.[13]

The Hearth Tax Returns of 1673 record no Robinson at Newsham, 'A township without any person of social standing',[14] nor any Robinson at Hutton Long Villers, nor at Brignall. Merryne Watson refers to 'Mr. Matthew Robinson', at Ravensworth, 'one hearth. The Mr. and one hearth turns up now and then. I suspect an old retired gentleman living in a two roomed cottage (possibly only one) single story, with help from the village. If there had been another Mr. Robinson living in a larger house, then I would have suspected Matthew was his father'. He also refers to 'Mrs. Robinson' at Kirby Hill, '10 hearths. Presumably a widow of importance', I suspect that both Mr Matthew Robinson and Mrs Robinson belonged to the family of Leonard Robynson of Kirkby Ravensworth which is not obviously related to our family.[15]

Whereabouts were our family of Robinsons living in 1673?

Romaldkirk origins and the candidature of William Robinson of Holwick

The case for the Romaldkirk origins of Robert Robinson of Hutton Hall is based on the following premises:
1. That, according to the oral tradition, our ancestors came up from Kendal to North Yorkshire in about the 16th century.[16]
2. That, according to the oral tradition received by me from my cousin Philip Wright Ford and, I believe, also, from Uncle Thomas, a branch of our family went to Virginia.
3. That the catholic contemporaries of Robert Robinson of Hutton Hall, the brothers: Ralph Robinson of Hutton Fields; Richard Robinson of Pecknell House, Romaldkirk; and William Robinson of 'above Smallways'; had their origins in Romaldkirk.
4. That Robert Robinson of Hutton Hall by virtue of name, religion and an ancestral branch which went to Virginia was almost certainly related to the family of Ralph, Richard and William.

For a catholic farming family migrating from Kendal to North Yorkshire, via, perhaps, Brough or Penrith and Culgaith, to the remote country of Romaldkirk at first and then, following the river Tees ten miles south-east to become tenant farmers of catholic landlords on better land, would be a natural progression.

Three plausible hypotheses of decent are considered:[17]

1) Ralph, Richard and William, sons of James Robinson of Saddle Bow, were probably descended from John Robinson and Agnes Savage of Crostwick as follows:

John Robinson of Crostwick, whose wife was 'Angnes', died in 1545. According to his will his eldest son was John and the College of Arms identifies him as John Robinson of Crostwick whose wife was Ann Dent; John died in 1569. John and Ann's second son was Richard Robinson of Crostwick. Richard's eldest son was William Robinson of Crostwick who was alive in 1634 and he may be identical with William Robinson of Saddle Bow whose wife was called Margaret and who died in 1693; the Saddle Bow connection suggests that this William may well be the father of Richard Robinson of Parkend, Crostwhaite, who died in 1714 and who was the father of James Robinson of Saddle Bow. William Robinson of Saddle Bow died without making a will but a Richard Robinson is one of the signatories of the inventory of his goods.

To return to John Robinson of Crostwick who died in 1569 and his wife Ann Dent, another of their sons was George Robinson of Cleasby who died before 1634 and whose wife was Frances Layton. Cleasby lies about twenty-two miles down the Tees from Crostwick and eight miles west of Hutton Magna. The third son of George and Frances was John Robinson of Cleasby who married Elizabeth Potter. The third son of John and Elizabeth was Christopher Robinson of Rappahannak in Middlesex County, Virginia — surely our ancestor about whom I was told as a boy.

Christopher Robinson was Secretary for the Colony of Virginia. He was born at Cleasby in the County of York in 1645 and he died at Hewick in Middlesex County Virginia in 1692. His will was dated 27th January 1692 and proved 6th March. Christopher's pedigree was recorded in 1712 by his younger brother John Robinson, Bishop of Bristol, a Church of England diocese, which indicates that his branch of the family was no longer catholic.[18]

This would mean that, somewhere in the descent, Ralph, Richard and William Robinson, sons of James Robinson of Saddle Bow, and Robert Robinson of Hutton Hall must have had a common ancestor. Richard Robinson, the son of John Robinson of Crostwick and his wife Ann Dent, could well have been their common great-great-grandfather provided that a Robert Robinson of Holwick, who died in 1682, was another son of Richard.

Robert Robinson of Holwick, in his will of 1682, the year in which he died, refers to his son John and to his daughter-in-law Elizabeth and his grandchildren William and George Robinson; he also refers to his wife, Elizabeth and to his daughter Eylnor and his son William. Robert's son, John Robinson of Holwick, in his will of 7th April 1724, the year in which he died, refers to his son William and to his son George; 'and five pounds at the end of the second year provided that my son Georg doo live as long... and to every one of my children...'. Perhaps this implies that George was not expected to live very long. When Robert Robinson made his will in 1682 his daughter was still Robinson and he mentions no wife or children of his son William, and so his grandsons William and George were probably still small boys, maybe born around 1675. The father of Robert Robinson of Hutton Hall would have been of William's generation and, indeed, William himself appears to be a strong candidate.

2) John Robinson of Crostwick who died in 1545 had a younger son 'Wyllm' for whom no will is available. It is possible that the descent of one or both the families in question was from Wyllm. William Robinson of Holwick, whose wife was called Sythe, and who died in 1591, may have been his son; and, in his will of 1591 William mentions his son Robert and 'a child' of Robert; and this child or a brother of his could have been Robert Robinson of Holwick who died

in 1682. William also mentions his son William, possibly the father of William Robinson of Sadle Bow. This hypothesis is more tenuous and the relationship to the branch which went to Virginia would have been more remote.

3) A friend of my late cousin Arthur Robinson, Mrs Harrison of Burton Pidsea, told me that Arthur would tell her to wave to his ancestors at Culgaith as she passed by on her way to Scotland. Here the most likely candidate would have been Robert, grandson of John Robinson of Culgaith who mentions him in his will of 10th September 1625. John leaves Robert land in the Culgaith area and also a lamb. John appoints his son Thomas to have use of the land 'for bringing to the childe til he be seaventeen years old…'. Robert may have been born about 1615 and he may have moved to Holwick and be identical with Robert who died in 1682, the father of John and grandfather of William and George. However, again, the connection with the branch of the family which went to Virginia would have been more remote.

The first hypothesis seems to be the most plausible; and, of course, it would be compatible with Culgaith origins in the time of John Robinson of Romaldkirk who died in 1545.

No catholic Robinsons were recorded under Romaldkirk in the Return of Papists, 1767, but by then James Robinson of Saddle Bow was dead and his sons Ralph, Richard and William had moved elsewhere. It is also of interest that Henry Machell who returned the list states, 'Mr. Gibson, the Day after your letter arrived, was obliged to go into Lancashire for a Week or Ten Days, and therefore ordered me to make out a List of the Papists resident in this Parish, and return it to your Lordship with as much Espedition as possible'.

In conclusion, I suggest that John and Elizabeth Robinson of Holwick's son William married Dorothy, daughter of Adam and Sarah Daile of Hutton, in 1713 when William was aged about 38 and Dorothy aged about 31. William and Dorothy's first son Adam, born in 1715 would have been named after his maternal grandfather and their second son Robert after his paternal great-grandfather, there is no obvious precedent for their son 'Tom', though the name does come up in the Dale family; their daughter Ann would have been named after Dorothy's sister Ann. Robert and Cecily of Hutton Hall's eldest daughter, Dorothy, would have been named after her grandmother and their eldest son, Robert, would have been named after his father; the name William reappears in the next three generations.

ROBERT ROBINSON OF HUTTON HALL, 1721-1809:

Conclusions so far – 22nd November 2002

1) Robert Robinson, 1721-1809, lived at Hutton Hall from 1760.
2) Robert Robinson inherited or acquired an estate at Newsham and had farming interests at Dalton.
3) An hypothesis that Robert Robinson's family came from Newsham or Dalton in the parish of Kirby Ravensworth is probably flawed by the absence of Robinsons there in 1673.
4) Robert Robinson's friendship with Robert Dale of Hutton Fields was shared by: Ralph Robinson of Hutton Fields; Richard Robinson of Brignall and of Pecknall House, Romaldkirk; and William Robinson who lived 'above Smallways' – sons of James Robinson of Saddle Bow; and these brothers, who were Catholics, almost certainly shared a common ancestor with Robert.
5) Ralph Robinson of Manfield who was aged 70 in 1767, and born in 1697, Mathew Robinson of Field House, Hutton, born in 1688, James Robinson of Saddle Bow, born about 1680, and the father of Robert Robinson of Hutton Hall, born about 1675, are all of the same generation, they are Catholics, and they are likely to have been related. Robert Robinson of Hutton Hall may possibly have originated in Manfield.
6) Robert Robinson's father is quite likely to have been William Robinson son of John and Elizabeth Robinson of Holwick.
7) Robert Robinson's mother is highly likely to have been Dorothy, daughter of Adam Daile of Hutton.
8) Mary, the wife of Robert Robinson's postulated uncle Robert Dale of Hutton Hall, may well have been a Tunstall.[19]

Robert Robinson has been identified in a context of places and relationships but the theory as to his origins requires proof.

A WORKING HYPOTHESIS

Adam Daile, a 'Recusant of Manfield' presented before the Courts of Correction in 1705, moved to Hutton Magna, possibly to Richardson's farm through his wife Sarah Richinson; and he died there in 1712.

Adam and Sarah Daile's son, Robert Dale, when aged about 32, married Mary, aged 25, in about 1710; he was farming at Girlington at the time. Mary was probably a Tunstall, possibly a daughter of Thomas Tunstall of Barningham. Or she may have been a daughter of one of the 'Others' among Francis and Thomas Tunstall's brothers and sisters on the Tunstall Pedigree, perhaps a daughter of William Tunstall 'the first good shooter flying' who, I suggest, was one of the 'Others'. This would fit the story told to me by my old uncle, Thomas Robinson (1861-1951) of Nuthill, on the Burton Constable estate, that our ancestors were involved in the Jacobite Rebellions. Robert and Mary's first son Lawrence was born in about 1711, and by 1716 their second son Adam, later of Girlington and Wycliffe Grange, was born.

Matthew Robinson, later of Field House Hutton, married Robert Dale's sister Elizabeth in about 1711. William Robinson of Holwick married Robert's sister Dorothy in about 1713, and their first son Adam, was born in 1715, and their son Robert, later of Hutton Hall, was born in 1721.

William Tunstall was at Hutton Hall in 1664 and Catherine Tunstall, his widowed mother, was at Wycliffe. William's brother, Francis, was at Ovington. William's eldest son, Francis, aged 27, was at Wycliffe. Francis and his wife Cecily Constable had their first son, Marmaduke, in 1672, when Francis was aged 35. Francis was possibly at Hutton Hall when he died in 1713 and his son Marmaduke, now a bachelor aged 41, was at Wycliffe. William's second son, Thomas Tunstall, lived in a house with thirteen hearths at Barningham in 1673 when he was aged 33.

In 1715 Robert Dale, through his Tunstall wife, Mary, took over Hutton Hall; and Rev. Francis Hodgson was staying with them when he died in 1726. When Robert Dale died in, 1736, his widow, Mary, and their son, Lawrence aged about 26, continued on at Hutton Hall; Robert and Mary's second son Adam was at Girlington. Lawrence Dale left Hutton Hall in 1750 and part of the farm was taken by his brother Adam. In 1760 Adam Dale moved to Wycliffe Grange and his mother's nephew by marriage Robert Robinson, an experienced farmer aged 39, took over Hutton Hall.

On 16th July 1767, Robert Robinson married Cecily Foster at Wycliffe and Rev. Thomas Penswick was probably the celebrant. Cecily was on the pay roll of Wycliffe Hall, perhaps as a housekeeper to Marmaduke Tunstall; her brother, Robert Foster was an agent of the Burton Constable estate and she was almost certainly related to Hugh Tootell, agent of the Wycliffe estate.

Both Adam Dale and his wife, Sarah, though Catholics, were buried in Wycliffe Parish Church; Adam died on the 17th March 1776 and Sarah on 8th May 1802.

Adam and Sarah's son, Adam, also of Wycliffe Grange, and Robert Robinson of Hutton Hall witnessed the will of Rev. Thomas Penswick on the 17th March 1791, the year in which he died.

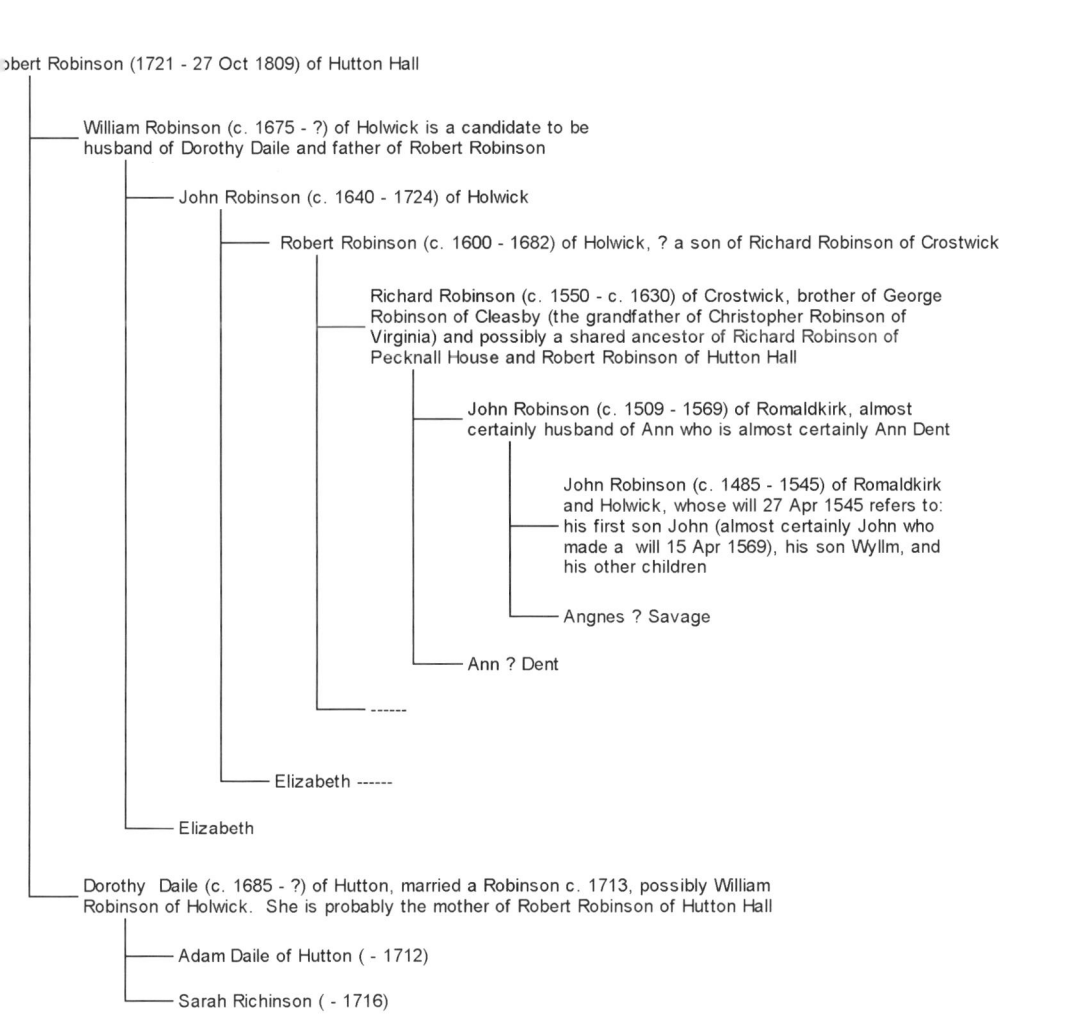

13. Pedigree of Robert Robinson (1721 - 1809) of Hutton Hall   Hypothesis 1

Robert Robinson (1721 - 27 Oct 1809) of Hutton Hall
- William Robinson (c. 1675 - ?) of Holwick is a candidate to be husband of Dorothy Daile and father of Robert Robinson
  - John Robinson (c. 1640 - 1724) of Holwick
    - Robert Robinson (c. 1600 - 1682) of Holwick, ? a son of Richard Robinson of Crostwick
      - Richard Robinson (c. 1550 - c. 1630) of Crostwick, brother of George Robinson of Cleasby (the grandfather of Christopher Robinson of Virginia) and possibly a shared ancestor of Richard Robinson of Pecknall House and Robert Robinson of Hutton Hall
        - John Robinson (c. 1509 - 1569) of Romaldkirk, almost certainly husband of Ann who is almost certainly Ann Dent
          - John Robinson (c. 1485 - 1545) of Romaldkirk and Holwick, whose will 27 Apr 1545 refers to: his first son John (almost certainly John who made a will 15 Apr 1569), his son Wyllm, and his other children
          - Angnes ? Savage
        - Ann ? Dent
      - ------
    - Elizabeth ------
  - Elizabeth
- Dorothy Daile (c. 1685 - ?) of Hutton, married a Robinson c. 1713, possibly William Robinson of Holwick. She is probably the mother of Robert Robinson of Hutton Hall
  - Adam Daile of Hutton (- 1712)
  - Sarah Richinson (- 1716)

14. Pedigree of Robert Robinson (1721 - 1809) of Hutton Hall Hypothesis 2

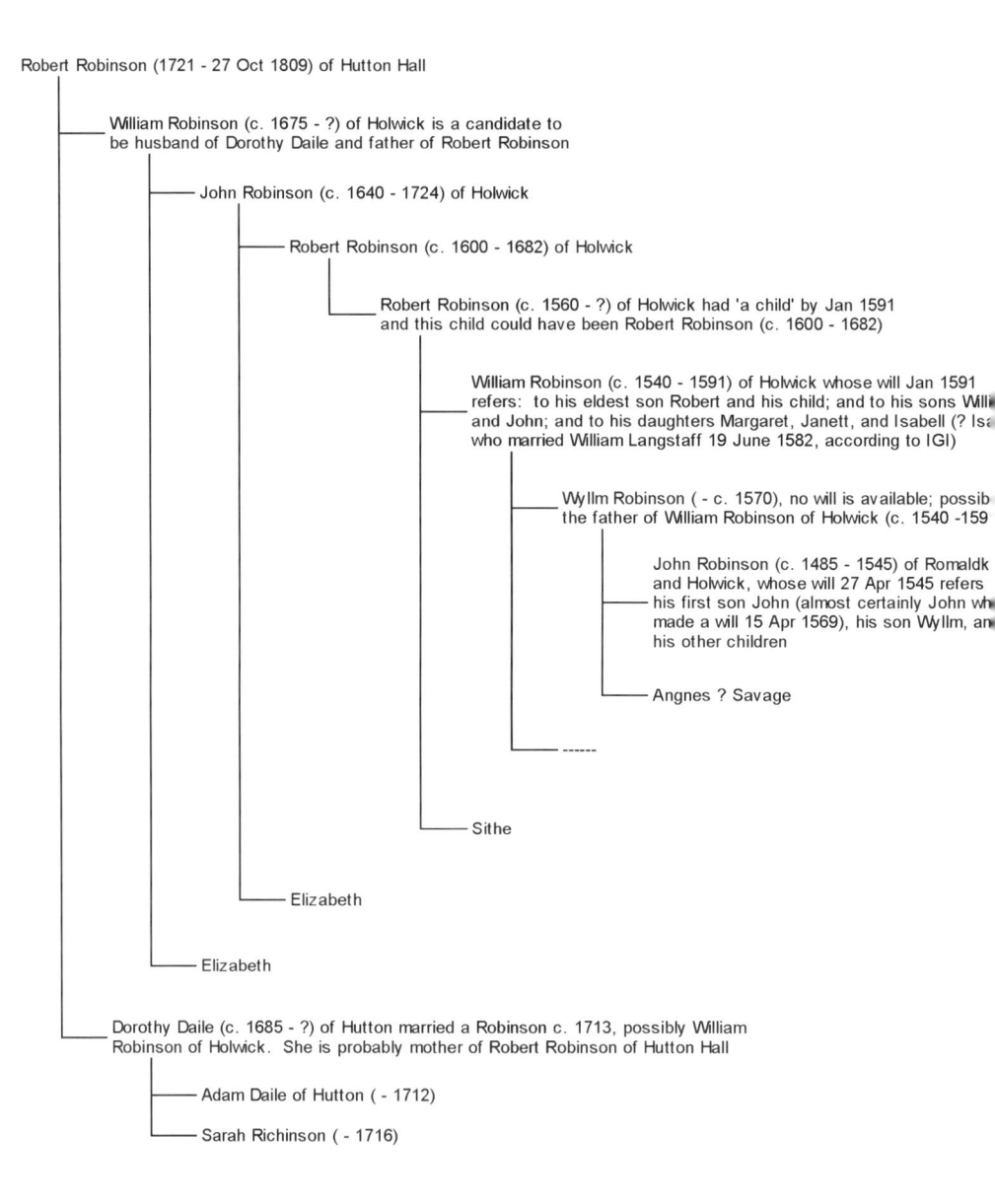

Robert Robinson (1721 - 27 Oct 1809) of Hutton Hall
- William Robinson (c. 1675 - ?) of Holwick is a candidate to be husband of Dorothy Daile and father of Robert Robinson
  - John Robinson (c. 1640 - 1724) of Holwick
    - Robert Robinson (c. 1600 - 1682) of Holwick
      - Robert Robinson (c. 1560 - ?) of Holwick had 'a child' by Jan 1591 and this child could have been Robert Robinson (c. 1600 - 1682)
        - William Robinson (c. 1540 - 1591) of Holwick whose will Jan 1591 refers: to his eldest son Robert and his child; and to his sons Willi and John; and to his daughters Margaret, Janett, and Isabell (? Isa who married William Langstaff 19 June 1582, according to IGI)
          - Wyllm Robinson (- c. 1570), no will is available; possib the father of William Robinson of Holwick (c. 1540 -159
            - John Robinson (c. 1485 - 1545) of Romaldk and Holwick, whose will 27 Apr 1545 refers his first son John (almost certainly John wh made a will 15 Apr 1569), his son Wyllm, an his other children
            - Angnes ? Savage
          - ------
      - Sithe
    - Elizabeth
  - Elizabeth
- Dorothy Daile (c. 1685 - ?) of Hutton married a Robinson c. 1713, possibly William Robinson of Holwick. She is probably mother of Robert Robinson of Hutton Hall
  - Adam Daile of Hutton (- 1712)
  - Sarah Richinson (- 1716)

NOTES AND REFERENCES

Introduction

1. Terrick V. H. Fitzhugh, The Dictionary of Genealogy Fourth Edition revised by Susan Lumas on behalf of the Society of Genealogists, p. 245.

Chapter 1

1. See T. P. Cooper *With Dickens in Yorkshire,* p. 29. According to Cooper, Dickens visited North Yorkshire when carrying out research for his book 'Nicholas Nickleby'. Late at night on Wednesday 31st January 1838, Dickens and Mr Halbot Browne arrived at the George and New Inn, Greta Bridge, formerly a farmstead called Thorpe Grange. The next day Dickens travelled to Barnard Castle, in a post-chase, and met people at the King's Head. On Friday 2nd February he went to Bowes and after an interview with William Shaw 'he returned to the Unicorn Inn, where he lunched and had a brief inquiring gossip with the landlord, Thomas Rudd, Mrs Ann Rudd his mother, and those in attendance'. He then returned to Barnard Castle and the next day, February 3rd, he went to Darlington. Hutton Hall is approximately: two miles from Greta Bridge; five miles from Barnard Castle; and nine miles from Bowes. Although I cannot find any evidence that Dickens visited Hutton Hall it is quite possible that such a visit went unrecorded or that my great-grandfather, Thomas Robinson, who was aged 56 at the time, visited one of these hostelries to meet Dickens.

2. P. R. Harris, *Douai College Documents 1639-1794,* p. 412.

3. M. D. R. Leys, *Catholics in England 1559-1829:* A Social History, p. 19.

4. At Ushaw, the group of students with whom you entered and, then, with whom you proceeded through the course, year by year, were referred to as your 'school'.

5. This was a unit under the command of Lieutenant-Colonel Vladimir Peniakoff which operated behind enemy lines; Gordon was with them when they invaded Italy. For further information on this unit see: Lieutenant-Colonel Vladimir Peniakoff, DSO, MC, *Popski's Private Army.*

6. 'The Holderness Gazette,' Friday, 9th March 1990, p. 9. The decoration was the BEM, not the OBE as reported in the paper. The medal is in the possession of Daisy's son, R. N. Cardwell, who informed me of this.

Chapter 2

1. James Le Fanu, review of 'Book of the month' in *Journal of the Royal Society of Medicine,* LXXXXIV, No. 1, (2001), pp. 46-7.

2. Norman Cardwell, personal communication.

3. Marriage Certificate.

4. J. Anthony Williams, *Sources for Recusant History (1559-1791) in English Official Archives – Recusant History,* XVI, No. 4. (Catholic Record Society), p. 433; also, compiled from the family bible by Doris Robinson: 'Thomas Robinson of Nuthill married Nov. 18th 1852 to Sarah Wright eldest daughter of Thomas Ford and Mary Anne Ford of Burton Pidsea Holderness. (Married at Drypool Church and Catholic Chapel Hull)', personal communication 1993.

5. Baptism Register of the Parish of Burton Pidsey. (County and Archdeaconry Archive Office, Beverley).

6. Baptism Register of the Parish of Humbleton. (County and Archdeaconry Archive Office, Beverley).

7. Marriage Register of the Parish of Humbleton. (County and Archdeaconry Archive Office, Beverley).

8. Sarah Wright Robinson's memorial card.

9. Mrs Paddy Richardson, personal communication.

10. Her name is spelt 'Sara' on her certificate of baptism but I believe she was usually referred to as 'Sarah' which is the name that I heard as a child and which I shall use throughout this account.

11. Bernard Joseph Culver, 'Genealogical Geriatric and Generic Gambles', 1977, p. 1, personal communication, in my possession; also, Bernard Joseph Culver, 'Prelude to the Genealogy – mainly Culver', 1971, p. 4, personal communication, in my possession.

12. Inscribed on a picture presented to my father commemorating this event, in my possession.

13. Jas Fras Robinson, 1937.

14. Jas Fras Robinson, 1937.

15. The name in the Register of the Church of St Mary and St Joseph, Hedon, is not very clear.

16. Will of Thomas Robinson of Nuthill, 3rd June 1873, the first Codicil, dated 1st May 1877.

17. Mr Richard A. H. Neave, Artist in Medicine and Life Sciences, School of Biological Sciences, University of Manchester, in a communication to me of 30th March, 1995, states: 'I have examined the photographs of Catherine Mary Robinson and the Carmelite nun with great care, and I am of the opinion that they are one and the same person. The reasons for this are as follows': and he lists his observations resulting from his comparative analysis.

NOTES AND REFERENCES

18. Letter in my possession.

19. *List of Tathwell Hall Stud 1890*. The Property of Mr. Richard Botterill, Tathwell Hall, Louth, Lincolnshire. (Louth: Printed by C. Parker, Market-Place). In my possession.

20. Richard and Fanny Botterill's Family Bible and engraving on silver spoons, both in my possession.

21. Letter in my possession. On the envelope, Auntie Beatrice has written 'From Eveline on her honeymoon – Keep'.

22. Dr Martin Craven kindly gave me this quotation from his book *The History of Hedon* (1972), p. 252.

23. A copy of this account, which occurs in the *Stonyhurst War Record*, was kindly given to me by my cousin Arthur's son Richard.

24. Unfortunately the altar was removed during restoration work in the 1980s but the plaque is now in the Presbytery. I am indebted to Martin Craven for this information.

25. A letter in my possession.

26. Marriage Certificate.

27. I am indebted to Dr Jan Rhodes and to Fr Dominic Minskip for information extracted from the *Ushaw Diary*.

28. James Francis Robinson who wrote the letter in 1937.

29. Extracted from my correspondence with Father George Forster in 1994. George Forster wrote a book: 'Priest behind Barbed Wire'. In relation to this, he speculates, 'I wonder, was I in POW camp in Italy or Germany with your cousin Arthur? We were both captured at Tobruk in June 1942'. He also comments: 'I think Colonel Lomax (page 2) was Brigadier T. B. Trappes-Lomax (1895-1962) who compiled a card index of recusant priests'.

30. 'Testimonials in favour of H. Robinson, M.B., C.M.', in my possession.

31. I am indebted to my cousin Norman Cardwell for this information.

32. I am indebted to Martin Craven for this account which is taken from his book, *The History of Hedon*, 1972, pp. 207-209.

33. Taken from my correspondence with my cousin Cecily.

34. I am indebted to my cousin Cecily for telling me that in the Robinson family 'Cecily' is traditionally pronounced 'Sissily'.

35. Obituary of Fr Robert Robinson from the Jesuit periodical for private circulation, Letters and Notices, 1944, communication from The Rev. F. J. Turner, Librarian of Stonyhurst College, 13th October 1990.

36. Personal communication from Fr T. G. Holt, SJ, Department of Historiography and Archives, English Province of the Society of Jesus, 114, Mount St., London, 18th October 1990.

37. Will of Thomas Robinson of Nuthill, 3rd June 1873.

38. Very kindly given to me by Norman Cardwell following the death of his mother, Eveline Mary Cardwell, on 23rd February 1989.

39. Gravestone at Burton Pidsea.

40. Personal communication from Monica Robinson, née Ledwith, 1992.

41 Sean O'Faolain, *King of the Beggars: A Life of Daniel O'Connell*, pp. 235-236.

42. M. D. R. Leys, *Catholicism in England 1559-1829: A Social History*, p. 153.

43. J. Anthony Williams, *Sources for Recusant History (1559-1791) in English Official Archives*, p. 331.

44. Edward Norman, *Roman Catholicism in England from the Elizabethan Settlement to the Second Vatican Council*, p. 58.

45. J. P. Smith, 'The Catholic Register of Nut Hill and Hedon in Holderness, East Riding of Yorkshire'. Transcribed by J. P. Smith. Edited and Historical Notes by James Rae Baterden. Catholic Record Society, Records Series, Vol. XXXV, Miscellanea, p. 328.

46. The family album called 'Parterre' in the possession of David the son of my brother, the late W. G. Robinson.

47. Birth certificate.

48. Alberic Stacpoole, OSB, 'The Return of the Roman Catholics to Oxford' in *New Blackfriars*.

49 Crispin Hollis, *Catholic Oxford*, p. 7.

Chapter 3

1. John Henry Newman, An Essay on the Development of Christian Doctrine, p. 30.

2. A letter kindly given to me by Rt. Rev. Mgr. Canon Edward Wilcock who wrote on 25th January 1993 'Canon Thompson was a canon of Beverley Cathedral Chapter and Treasurer of Beverley Diocese for twenty five years, a post in which I succeeded him in 1950 and occupied for the next thirty five years. The 'Dalton Rent' to which the letter refers was the ground rent on a piece of land at Dalton and the sum of £10-16-4 was still being paid to the diocese up to the time I left'.

3. Douai Bible, II, Tim. 4 : 6. The English College at Douai had to leave Flanders, because of political troubles associated with the revolt

NOTES AND REFERENCES

against Spain, and withdrew to Rheims in 1578. It returned to Douai in 1594. It was this English translation of the Bible that was used by Catholics at that time.

4. Gravestone, Hutton Magna, records information relating to the deaths of Thomas, Sarah, and their children; and the Wycliffe Register, information relating to the baptisms.

5. Rt. Rev. Mgr. Canon Edward Wilcock STL, Prot. Ap. *The Pearson Family and the Recusants of West Gilling,* p. 300.

6. International Genealogical Index.

7. Gravestone at Hutton Magna. My cousin Peter Cardwell who lives in Richmond, very kindly checked this gravestone for me recently. He is the one member of our family who lives in the terrain of our ancestors and, as an historian and archaeologist, he is sensitive to the clues of their former presence. He is my ever willing 'agent in North Yorkshire', and is sometimes assisted by his sister Ann.

8. Death certificate of Thomas.

9. E. S. Worrall, transcriber, *Returns of Papists 1767 Diocese of Chester,* p. 170.

10. Wycliffe Register: 'Lawrence Thompson the son of Lawrence and Ann at the Lane Head, sponsors: James Brown the uncle, supply by Anthony Langstaff; and Dorothy Dale, March 4th 1777, 4 days old'.

11. Will of Robert Dale of Hutton Fields, 15th October 1790, 'my brother-in-law James Brown of Aldbrough'.

12. 'The Crack Team of 1858. The Property of Major T. C. Constable of Burton Constable. From an original picture in his possession'. Norman Cardwell told me that Cuthbert Watson is in this picture and the facial appearance of the elderly upright gentleman to whom I have referred seems to be identical to that of Cuthbert's Watson's portrait. The print is in the possession of Peter Cardwell. I am indebted to Dr Martin Craven for informing me that the gentleman sitting next to the man holding the reins is Sir Thomas Aston Clifford Constable, that one of the two grooms is Wilson Ellerton, and that the grey top hat 'should have had Col. Ferguson-Fawcett underneath, but he failed to turn up!'.

13. I am indebted to Br. Basil Ward, a Marist, of Marcellin Hall, Royal Oak, Auckland, New Zealand, for this information, after he read my article 'Hutton Hall – A Nursery for the Second Spring' in *Catholic Ancestor,* VII, No. 3, (1998). The information is extracted from the Ward Papers, A.T.L., MS 110 – Folder 1, in the Alexander Turnbull Library, Wellington, New Zealand.

14. A letter to me, of 4th October 2002, from Richard Robinson of Louth, Lincolnshire.

15. Wycliffe Register; also wills of: Robert Dale of Hutton Hall, 1736; Adam Dale of Wycliffe Grange, 1772; Robert Dale of Hutton Fields, 1790. Adam Dale was almost certainly the son of Adam Dale of Wycliffe Grange who died 13th March 1776, aged 59, and grandson of Robert Dale of Hutton Hall who died in 1736, aged 58.

16. Wycliffe Register.

17. Will of Cecily Robinson, Spinster, of Newsham Grange, 1860, in which she refers to her brother in law, Lawrence Thompson of South Park and also to her nephews: Rev. Robert Thompson; Rev. John Thompson; and William Thompson of South Park; also the Wycliffe Register.

18. Ushaw College Diary.

19. There is sometimes confusion about the Robinsons of South Park and the Robinsons of Nuthill which were two distinct families – both Catholic – living within a mile of each other; and they intermarried. This John Robinson's great-great-grandfather was John Robinson of Hambleton Hills, North Yorkshire and it seems quite likely that the two families had a common ancestor in the remote past. My chart of the Robinsons of South Park is derived from the information given by Miss Elizabeth Robinson in J. S. Hansom, 'Catholic Registers of St. Mary's Domestic Chapel, Everingham Park, Yorkshire 1771-1884', contributed by Joseph Stanislaus Hansom with historical notes on the chaplaincy and mission by J. Gillow, p. 266-67. I am also indebted to Ursula Randall, a descendant of the South Park Robinsons, for generously sharing with me the results of her own research.

20. J. P. Smith, transcriber, 'The Catholic Register of Nut Hill and Hedon in Holderness, East Riding of Yorkshire', p. 348; also: Fr Coleridge, ed. *The Annals of the Bar Convent,* Appendix, 'An Alphabetical List of Young Ladies educated at St. Mary's Convent, York, from the year 1710 to 1886', p. 409. Personal communication with Sister M. Gregory IBVM who says, 'I believe it was originally written by one of our nuns, Sister Hilda Haigh'.

21. Register of Nut Hill, p. 364.

22. Gravestone, Hutton Magna. That Sarah Robinson of South Park came to stay with Maria seems to be the most likely explanation for her grave in Hutton Magna; she died intestate and the Bond of Administration, 20th June 1857, refers to 'Sarah Robinson late of Lane Head in the Township of Hutton'. My first investigation of the graveyard of St Mary's Church, Hutton Magna, was in the excellent company of my cousins Norman and Sheila Cardwell and their sons Michael and Peter and our sons Shaun and Tim. Sheila acted as the 'recording angel' and her notes have proved invaluable ever since. Matters were later subjected to analysis over a pint in the 'Abbey',

opposite Byland Abbey. This was one of the many memorable days when I have enjoyed the generous hospitality of my cousins.

23. Will of Samuel Robinson of South Park, 24th September 1857.

24. Wycliffe Register.

25. 'Communicated Draft Scheme. No. 4874 Sealed 193. No. U. General Foundation – Elizabeth Langstaff's fund for the education of youths for the ecclesiastical state in connexion with St. Cuthbert's College Ushaw, in the county of Durham'. The document is in my possession.

26. Ushaw College Diary, personal communication with Dr Jan Rhodes and Fr Dominique Minskip, 1991.

27. 'Hutton Hall – History of the House and the Robinson Family', Darlington and Stockton Times, April 28th 1928, p. 4.

28. Census – Parish of Hutton Magna, 9th June 1841.

29. Census – Parish of Hutton Magna, 6th April 1851.

30. Letter dated 22nd July 1937, in relation to the 'Elizabeth Langstaff Fund, Ushaw College. Ref. U1788 Z/20' addressed to 'The Secretary, Board of Education, Whitehall, London, S.W.1.' by Jas Fras Robinson.

31. I am very grateful to Mr and Mrs Hodgson, the owners of Hutton Hall, for kindly showing me round and to Mr and Mrs Cole, who live there, for their hospitality; and I am deeply indebted to Mr and Mrs Hodgson for giving me the benefit of their own research findings and to Miss Cole who carried out much of this work.

32. I was told this by Mr and Mrs Hodson.

33. Jas Fras Robinson, 1937: Francis James Robinson is described as married without issue. He would have been aged about 65 in 1937 and might have had children after that time; but it seems unlikely because his brother, Thomas, a bachelor, would probably have mentioned them in his will of 26th July 1946.

34. Birth Certificate of Thomas Robinson of Newsham Grange, born 13th September 1868; Mother 'Elizabeth Robinson formally Hunt'.

35. J. S. Hansom, 'Catholic Registers of Linton-upon-Ouse, Near York, 1771-1840'. Contributed by Joseph Hansom. Historical notes by Joseph Gillow. CRS Vol. XVII, pp. 430-431.

36. Extracts from: 'Short sketch of the Very Revd Canon Thompson's life' a copy of which was very kindly given to me by Sr. M. Gregory, IBVM, of the Bar Convent, York, where the original is held.

37. A newspaper article headed 'LEEDS'. 'YORK. – FUNERAL OF THE VERY REV. F. THOMPSON. – ' A copy of this article was kindly given to me by Sr. M. Gregory who notes that it was un-named and undated.

38. Will of Cecily Robinson of Newsham Grange, 1860.

39. It seems likely that Ann is identical with the Ann Chambers who was godmother to my grandfather, Thomas Robinson of Nuthill, in 1823, and who was godmother to Elizabeth Thompson's daughter, Ann, in 1812. The IGI gives Thomas Chambers marrying Ann Robinson, Stanwick St. John, 16th May 1791; and also Ralph Chambers marrying Ann Robinson, Kirkby Ravensworth, 16th May 1809. In 1791 Ann would have been aged 20 and in 1809 she would have been 38. Ann had no children baptised at Wycliffe and so perhaps the latter marriage refers to her.

40. Newsham Tithe Appointment, 1840; information kindly given to me in 1992 by the late Merryne Watson.

41. Gravestone, Hutton Magna, for Robert of Rokeby Close. Information taken from a written account of himself when Robert joined the Society of Jesus and kindly supplied by Fr T. G. Holt, SJ.

Chapter 4

1. The Rev. John Daniel, C.A.D.A. & PRÆS., *Ecclesiastical History of the Britons and Saxons*, p. iv.

2. *Victoria History of Yorkshire North Riding* Vol. I, p. 84.

3. Bernard Joseph Culver, 'Genealogical Geriatric and Generic Gambles', p. 1.

4. Bernard Joseph Culver, 'Prelude to the Genealogy – mainly Culver', p. 9.

5. 'Hutton Hall – History of the House and the Robinson Family'.

6. I am indebted to my old school friend Father Frank McManus for his help in clarifying this theology. This tradition of the Church was affirmed at the Council of Trent, Session xiii, in the following words: 'In the first place the holy Synod teaches ... that in the precious (almo)[4] [footnote 4 states "Literally: nourishing"] sacrament of the holy Eucharist, after the consecration of the bread and wine, our Lord Jesus Christ, true God and true man, is truly, really and substantially contained under the species of those sensible things' quoted from *The Teaching of the Catholic Church: A Summary of Catholic Doctrine arranged and edited by Canon George D. Smith, D.D., Ph.D.*, p. 841; see also Herbert McCabe OP, *The Teaching of the Catholic Church: A New Catechism of Christian Doctrine*, pp. 16-17; also Richard Conrad OP, *The Catholic Faith: A Dominican's Vision*, pp. 139-157.

7. Gwynne Lewis, *The French Revolution: Rethinking the Debate*, p. 23.

8. David Milburn, *A History of Ushaw College*, pp. 20-25.

9. The parentage of John Daniel – the case is as follows:

In his will, of 23rd March 1778, Robert Daniel of Euxton House refers to his cousin, Robert Foster of Burton Constable; to his uncle, James Foster of Lancaster; and to Robert Foster's sisters Cecily Robinson, and Elizabeth and Grace 'now residing at Dunkirk in Flanders'. He appoints his sister, Jane Daniel, as executrix. In his will, of 27th November 1769, Thomas Daniel, a Douai priest b. 20th March 1714, refers to his brother William Daniel of Hazlewood, also a Douai priest b. October 1725; he also refers to his sister Jane Daniel. In his will, of 20th July 1777, William Daniel refers to his brother Robert Daniel and his sister Jane Daniel and to his cousin Robert Foster of Burton, Yorks.; he leaves two hundred pounds to 'my Cousin's Robt. Robinson, and Cicily his wife'. Robert Robinson was a cousin only by marriage, it was Cicily, née Foster, who was his blood cousin; she was a niece of William's mother, Helen Daniel, née Foster of Burton, Yorks., the sister of Rev. William Foster alias Charnock and daughter of Robert Foster of Charnock Richard. An entry in the seventh Douai Diary states, in relation to William Daniel, that he was the 'Son of Thomas Daniel and Helen dau. of Robert Foster of Foster Charnock [Charnock Richard], and nephew of the Rev. William Foster als Charnock'. Edwin H. Burton and Edmond Nolan, editors, *The Douay College Diaries – the Seventh Diary 1751-1778,* p. 226n. It is evident that Thomas, Robert, and William Daniel are brothers and that they have a sister Jane Daniel and that they are first cousins of my great-great-grandmother Cecily Robinson.

According to Gillow, John Daniel, born in 1745, and Edward Daniel, born in 1749, both Douai priests, were the sons of Edward Daniel of Durton and Mary, daughter of William Penswick. Mary's brother, Rev. Thomas Penswick of Wycliffe, in his will of 17th March 1791, refers to his nephews Thomas, John, and Edward Daniel. Joseph Gillow, *Bibliographical Dictionary of the English Catholics,* Vol. II, pp. 11-15. Anstruther, although agreeing about Edward, considers that 'there is good evidence' that Gillow is mistaken about John Daniel and refers to Robert Gradwell, who came from Preston, as saying that John was born at Kirkham; and he makes the point that John's will describes him as formerly of Kirkham. Anstruther concludes that John Daniel 'is therefore probably of the family seated at Whittingham, Kirkham and a nephew of Thomas and William' the Douai priests who were brothers of Jane Daniel and of Robert Daniel of Euxton House.

When the students left Douai College for Équerchin, during the French Revolution, two students, one of whom was Robert Gradwell, were too sick to travel and John Daniel stayed behind with them. Robert Gradwell probably knew John Daniel very well. Godfrey Anstruther, OP, *The Seminary Priests* Volume IV: 1716-1800, pp. 80-83; David Milburn, *A History of Ushaw College,* p. 22.

It might be concluded that John Daniel was the son of Robert Daniel, apparently the only other brother of Thomas, William, and Jane. However there are difficulties:

In the Return of Papists for the Diocese of Chester 1767, under Euxton, is listed Robert Daniel, farmer, his wife and seven servants. No children are mentioned but John was aged 22 at the time and had entered the English College at Douai. His brother may also have left home.

A more serious difficulty with this hypothesis is that neither Robert Daniel nor his wife, Mary, mentions any children in their wills. Neither is John mentioned as a nephew in the will of Robert's brother William Daniel nor in that of his sister Jane Daniel. John Daniel, by this time, was a priest and he could well have already received any endowment due to him but this would hardly apply to his brother. Wills of: Robert Daniel of Euxton House, Lancaster, 23rd March 1778; Mary Daniel of Euxton, widow, 9th August 1798; William Daniel at Euxton Hall, 20th July 1777; and Jane Daniel of Euxton, 10th August 1780.

Robert Banister, in a letter to his nephew Henry Rutter, wrote about 'Mr President Daniel', who was in England in 1795, 'Wherefore Mr. Daniel returned immediately to Lancashire and is now, and will stay, with his brother the time-maker at Kirkham' Leo Gooch ed., *The Revival of English Catholicism: the Banister-Rutter Correspondence 1777-1807,* p. 251.

According to G. H. Baillie's *Watchmakers and Clockmakers of the World, 1951,* a Thomas Daniel worked at Kirkham circa 1775 and a watch is known as his work. (Information kindly supplied by my very good friend Dr John Pollitt.) This is surely Thomas the brother of John and Edward Daniel, the nephews of Thomas Penswick. Perhaps John Daniel was identified with Kirkham because his base was at the home of his brother Thomas.

On balance it seems likely that John was the son of Edward and Mary Daniel of Durton and not the son of Robert Daniel of Euxton House.

I am greatly indebted to Sam Watkinson of Euxton House Farm for making available to me his collection of information on the Daniels.

10. P. R. Harris, ed., *Douai College Documents 1639-1794,* pp. 152n, 319, 323, 327, 330, 334. It seems highly likely that the Robert Dale referred to in the Douai College Documents is identical with Robert, son of Robert and Dorothy Dale of Hutton Fields, baptised at Wycliffe Hall 23rd November 1774, and also with Robert Dale of Scorton who made a will on 11th November 1848. The case for this is as follows: 1) Robert Dale entered the English College at Douai in October 1788 in the third class of Rudiments and he left in January 1793 when he was in Syntax. This puts Robert, son of Robert Dale of Hutton Fields, in the right age group, 13 on entry and 18 on leaving. 2) Robert and Dorothy Dale of

Hutton Fields may well have sent their second son, Robert, to the English College at Douai because they had strong Douai connections: Cicily Robinson, who acted as sponsor to their daughters, Ann and Mary, had an uncle, William Foster, two first cousins, Thomas and William Daniel, and her half-brother, James Foster, who were all Douai priests; Antony Langstaff, who acted as sponsor to their daughter, Teresa Ann, had two brothers, Robert and Valentine, who were Douai priests and his sister Elizabeth Langstaff created the charitable trust for educating descendants of James Brown (Robert Dale's grandfather) as ecclesiastical students at Ushaw; moreover, Mr John Postlethwaite who acted as sponsor to their eldest son, Adam, was almost certainly the Douai priest of that name serving in Yorkshire at the time. 3) In his will, 'Robert Dale of Scorton ... Gentleman' makes 'John Middleton of Huttonfields' one of his executors; he refers to 'the children of the said John Middleton by my sister Teresa' — hence the option for John Middleton to live at Hutton Fields if this had been the home of Robert and Teresa; he refers to 'the son and daughters off my sister Margaret' (Robert Dale of Hutton Fields had daughters called Margaret and Teresa); he refers to 'the debts which I owe ... to Joseph Tidyman of Hutton, Schoolmaster'; furthermore, Robert Dale Middleton (who, with his wife Teresa, daughter of Henry Robinson of Sproatley Grange, were godparents to my uncle, Harry Robinson, 27th October 1865) was probably a son of 'John Middleton of Huttonfields', and, in addition to his name Robert, he would have been given his mother's maiden name, Dale; a practice which was quite common at that time.

This Robert Dale of Scorton, scholar of Douai, son of Robert Dale of Hutton Fields and his wife Dorothy Brown, was a first cousin, doubly related, of my great-grandmother, Sarah Brown, wife of Thomas Robinson of Hutton Hall.

11. William Martin Hunnybun, 'Registers of the English Poor Clares at Gravelines, Including Those Who Founded Filiations at Aire, Dunkirk and Rouen, 1608-1837' contributed by William Martin Hunnybun, M.A., annotated by Joseph Gillow, in *Catholic Record Society: Miscellanea IX*, p. 25.

12. *The Names of all the Professed Religious: As also the Anniversary [sic] Days of their Confessors, Pensioners, Boarders and Servants* (Dunkirk, 1652). A copy of the relevant entries was very kindly given to me by Sr. Mary Carmel OSC, the Abbess of St Clare's Abbey, Carmel Road North, Darlington, Co. Durham. In her note of 27th August 1994, Sr. Mary Carmel says: 'I do hope M. "Agnes Joseph" is Elizabeth. Anyway they are the only Fosters in the Book'. This identity is confirmed by an entry in: Joseph S. Hansom, 'Laity's Directory Obituaries, 1773-1839' contributed by Joseph S. Hansom in *Catholic Record Society: Obituaries*. Publications of the Catholic Record Society Vol. XII, p. 83, where the following entries appear: '1802. Feb. 2. Sister Grace Maria Foster O.S.C., aged 74,

religious 54, at Churchill Wood. [Feb.] 14. Rev. Mother Abbess Elizabeth Foster O.S.C., at Churchill Wood'.

13. Dom Basil Whelan, O.S.B., M.A., *Historic Convents of To-day: the Story of the English Cloisters in France and Flanders in Penal Times,* pp. 161, 178, 179, 180, 181, 184, 185.

14. Anstruther, *The Seminary Priests Volume IV: 1716-1800,* p. 173.

15. Milburn, *A History of Ushaw College,* p. 33.

16. Milburn, *A History of Ushaw College,* pp. 59-60.

17. Milburn, *A History of Ushaw College,* pp. 89-90.

18. Milburn, *A History of Ushaw College,* pp. 26-27. See also Edward Norman, *Roman Catholicism in England from the Elizabethan Settlement to the Second Vatican Council,* pp. 55-56.

19. Monsignor Edward Wilcock, in a letter to me of 25th January 1993, refers to Peter Pearson as 'the brother of my g.g.grandfather'.

20. North Riding Quarter Sessions 1715-1818: Those Taking Oaths of Supremacy and Allegiance. Information kindly given to me by Mgr. Edward Wilcock.

21. Milburn, *A History of Ushaw College,* p. 28.

22. Milburn, *A History of Ushaw College,* pp. 53-54.

23. David Mathew, *Catholicism in England 1535-1935: Portrait of a Minority: Its Culture and Tradition,* pp. 164-165.

24. Milburn, *A History of Ushaw College,* p. 110.

25. I am indebted to Mrs P. M. Pattinson of Preston for research confirming that Cecily was a sister of Rev. James Foster and not a cousin as previously thought.

26. Will of James Foster of Thurnham, Clerk, 18th December 1821.

27. Anstruther, *The Seminary Priests Volume IV: 1716-1800,* p. 81.

28. Anstruther, *The Seminary Priests Volume IV: 1716-1800,* p. 105.

29. Martin Haile and Edwin Bonney, *Life and Letters of John Lingard 1771-1851,* pp. 247, 364.

Chapter 5

1. Bernard of Chartres, twelfth century, quoted by Edward P. Echlin in 'Salvation of Soil' in *New Blackfriars: A Monthly Review Edited by the English Dominicans,* Vol. 82, No. 960, (Oxford: The Priory of The Holy Spirit, St. Giles, February 2001), p. 89.

2. Wycliffe Register.

NOTES AND REFERENCES

3. For this information I am indebted to Richard Curry of Houghton-le-Spring, a descendant of Richard Robinson of Pecknall House, Romaldkirk, who died in 1790. The murdered man may have been William, baptised at Wycliffe 30th November 1764, the son of Richard Robinson's brother, William, whose father, James Robinson of Saddle Bow, in his will of 27th July 1753, left 'Hungary Close' to his eldest son Ralph; the family evidently possessed land in that area; or he may have been William Robinson, a farmer of Holwick, on whose probate document Jane, wife of John Tinkler, his sister and only next of kin, acted as Administratrix 4th June 1794 (the former William had nine brothers and sisters and his sister Jane was the wife of Thomas Rain).

4. G. M. Trevelyan, *Illustrated English Social History,* Vol. III, p. 82.

5. An article about Rokeby Hall ©1986 Executors of R. A. Morritt Deceased, pp. 4-6; also *The Victoria History of Yorkshire – North Riding* Vol. I, p. 112. There is a family tradition that the Robinson family split in the 16th century to give the Protestant and Parliamentarian branch which went to Rokeby and our Catholic and Royalist branch which went to Hutton Hall; this tradition remains to be proved.

6. Beverley Archives, Acc. Book. Hutton, Wycliffe etc. DDCC (20) Box 20 A, Box 23. Also: Worrall, *Returns of Papists, 1767: Diocese of Chester,* p. 171.

7. J. C. Atkinson, *Quarter Sessions Records.* North Riding Record Society, Vol. III, Registration of Papist's Estates, p. 130.

8. Wills and Probate documents consulted: Robert Robinson of Hutton Hall, 11th February 1805; Richard Robinson of Pecknall House, Romaldkirk, 19th September 1790; James Robinson of Saddle Bow, 27th July 1753; Robert Dale of Hutton Fields, 15th October 1790; Ralph Robinson of Hutton Fields, 5th May 1787; Matthew Robinson formerly of Hutton Fields who died in Jamaica, 6th January 1795.

9. My correspondence with the late Merryne Watson of Hare Close, Newsham, member of the Tees Greta Section of the Yorkshire Vernacular Buildings Study Group, in 1992-93.

10. 'Pedigree of Tunstall, of Thurland Castle, Co. Lanc., and Wycliffe, Co. York' in *The Chronicle of the English Augustinian Cannonesses Regular of the Lateran, at St. Monica's in Louvain 1625-1644.* Vol II; I am indebted to Dr David Connell, Curator, Burton Constable, for this reference.

11. Anstruther, *The Seminary Priests Volume IV: 1716-1800,* pp. 171-172; also, Father David Quinlan, The Father Postgate Story 1599-1973, pp. 30-33.

12. Anstruther, *The Seminary Priests: Volume III: 1660-1715,* p. 234.

13. Leo Gooch, *Paid at Sundry Times: Yorkshire Clergy Finances in the Eighteenth Century,* p. 36; also Beverley Archives, Acc. Book. Hutton,

Wycliffe etc. DDCC (20) Box 20 A, Box 23. I am deeply indebted to my cousin Michael Cardwell for helping me in my investigations into the Beverley Archives where the keen perception of a Classical scholar and Lawyer enriched our findings enormously.

14. Cuthbert Tunstall who took his mother's name, Constable, on inheriting the Burton Constable estate, went to Douai and he was there in 1704. Cuthbert was a first cousin once removed of Peter Brian Tunstall who took the oath at Douai 15th August 1689 and remained there until 1715, so that the cousins would have been there together. Hugh Tootell alias Charles Dodd, the Church Historian, who went to Douai 23rd July 1688, was contemporary with Peter Brian Tunstall. Cuthbert Tunstall/Constable paid for the publication of Dodd's History which was published between 1737 and 1742. Hugh Tootell was related to Robert Foster of Charnock Richard which, perhaps, provided the original introduction of Fosters into the Tunstall and Constable estates. Cuthbert Tunstall/Constable's elder son, William Constable, who inherited Burton Constable in 1747, was at Douai in first year Philosophy in 1738 and was probably taught by Robert and Cecily Foster's uncle, William Foster, who stayed on at Douai after his ordination in 1730 and taught there until 1736. William Foster's nephew, Thomas Daniel, who was at Douai from 1730 until 1740 was contemporary with William Constable. Cuthbert Tunstall/Constable's younger son Marmaduke Constable, who reverted back to Tunstall when he inherited the Wycliffe Estate in 1760, was in Syntax in 1758 and would probably have been taught by Thomas' brother William Daniel who, after ordination in 1750, taught humanities until 1758. See: P. R. Harris, ed. *Douai College Documents* 1639-1794, pp. 81, 120, 214; also Anstruther, *The Seminary Priests Volume IV: 1716-1800*, pp. 81-83; and Anstruther, *The Seminary Priests Volume III: 1660-1715*, pp. 230, 231, 234.

15. Mr Sam Watkinson of Euxton House Farm, Euxton, very kindly gave me access to his research in which the following extract appears: '11th September 1725 – Deed involving James Foster of Charnock Richard, tanner, Elizabeth, his wife, Cecily Heskin, Robert Holden of Legram, Edmund Parkinson of Thornley, William Hawkshead, Robert Parkinson, Lawrence Holme, re lands in Euxton. Ref. LRO QDD 1715-58 11 Roll Geo II p 97 (2 page 97's). (Checked in detail and refers to – it is the marriage settlement when John [James] Foster married Elizabeth. 1st part: James Foster of Charnock Richard, tanner, Elizabeth, his wife, only child of Robert Holden of Legram; 2nd part: Cicely Heskin, widow of John Heskin late of Heskin, sole daughter & heir of William Foster, late of Heskin; 3rd part: Robert Holden of Legram; 4th part: Edmund Parkinson of Thornley, William Hawkshead of Chorley; 5th part: Robert Parkinson of Blindhurst within Bleasdale, Lawrence Holme of Charnock R. Refers to land in Euxton (named fields),

NOTES AND REFERENCES

including Gleadhill [belonged to Robert Foster], formerly leased to William Dandy of Croston by William ffoster, father of sd. James Foster [elsewhere 'by the said William Foster and Robert Foster, father of the said James Foster', (William's daughter was 'sole daughter and heir of Wm. Foster of Heskin')]. Also land in Charnock Richard to 10 acres'. Sam very kindly showed me round Euxton House where he is doing wonderful restorative work and where he is carrying out excavations into its origins. Sam had discovered that the house was unoccupied and neglected, and had possibly been destroyed by fire, when James Foster took it over.

16. International Genealogical Index.

17. Anstruther, *The Seminary Priests Volume IV: 1716-1800*, p. 208; also: Edward Wilcock, *The Pearson Family and the Recusants of West Gilling*, pp. 80, 296; also will of Thomas Penswick, 17th March 1791.

18. This strongly suggests a family relationship between Robinsons and Dales in this generation (in the next generation such a relationship did happen); though not one of uncles, aunts, or grandparents, which, when it occurs, is usually specified by Fr Penswick. Adam Dale was the son of Robert Dale of Hutton Hall, 1672-1736, and Robert had four sisters: Elizabeth; Dorothy; Ann; and Sarah. When their father, 'Adam Daile of Hutton,' made his will, 20th October 1712, he stated: 'I also give to my daughter Elizabeth Robinson five shillings having given at and sined her marriage all I promised or agreed to'. The other daughters are still 'Daile'. When Sarah, the wife of Adam Daile, made her will, 10th November 1716, the following entry appears: 'Item I do give and devise unto my daughter Dorothy Robinson the sum of twentie pounds. Item unto her son Adam Robinson the sum of five pounds. Item unto my daughter Elizabeth Robinson the sum of Twentie pounds. Item unto her son Adam Robinson the sum of five pounds. ... Item I give to my granson Adam Daile twentie pounds'. Her daughter Ann is still referred to as 'Daile' and Sarah is not mentioned. Hence, Elizabeth Daile married a Robinson probably about 1711 and Dorothy married a Robinson between October 1712 and November 1716 and between these dates they each had a son Adam. Either of these Adams could have been Robert Robinson's brother, Adam, who, according to his gravestone, was born in 1715. The evidence suggests that either Elizabeth or Dorothy was the mother of Robert Robinson; and, perhaps, his first-born child, Dorothy, was named after her grandmother. It is then understandable that Adam Dale of Wycliffe Grange, as Robert Robinson's first cousin, was chosen to be her godfather.

19. Anstruther, *The Seminary Priests Volume IV: 1716-1800*, pp. 81-83; also wills of William Daniel of Euxton Hall, 20th July 1777 and Robert Daniel of Euxton House 23rd March 1778; also: Dominic Minskip, *A*

History of St. Wilfrid's Mission, York (1742 to the Present), p. 80; also: Gooch Paid at Sundry Times, p. 8.

20. J. C. H. Aveling, *Catholic Recusancy in the City of York: 1558-1791*, p. 154.

21. P. R. Harris, *Douai College Documents 1639-1794*, pp. 197-214.

22. Leo Gooch, *The Revival of English Catholicism: The Banister-Rutter Correspondence 1777-1807*, pp. 213, 251.

23. Harris, *Douai College Documents 1639-1794*, p. 212.

24. Gooch, *Paid at Sundry Times*, p. 26.

25. Byrne and Smith, 'The Catholic Registers of Thurnham, Lancashire. 1785-1838,' p. 184.

26. Anstruther, *The Seminary Priests Volume IV: 1716-1800*, pp. 81-83. I am much indebted to my friend Kevin Hodgers for pointing out this reference to me over a pint in the 'White Hart' in Wytham; this enabled my research to take a quantum leap forward!

27. Gooch, *Paid at Sundry Times*, p. 24.

28. J. A. Hilton, *Catholic Lancashire: From Reformation to Renewal 1559-199*, p. 65.

29. I am indebted to Father Bernard Shuttleworth for showing myself and Father Frank McManus around Thurnham Church and for producing James Foster's portrait which, up to that time, I had sought in vain, and for allowing me to photograph it.

30. John R. Robinson, 'Charnock Richard to Cornamucklagh: a Bridge Across the Sea', Catholic Ancestor, VII, No. 1, (1998), pp. 27-31.

31. Godfrey Anstruther *The Seminary Priests: a Dictionary of the Secular Clergy of England and Wales 1558-1850. Vol. IV. 1716-1800*, pp. 59-61.

Chapter 6

1. Michael Howard, 'Optimism is not Enough', Peace and the Peace Movements (3), *The Tablet*, 9th January 1983.

2. Uncle Thomas had told me that two branches of our family went to Ireland, one of them Catholic and the other Protestant. Jimmy Robinson of North Kildare (the husband of my wife's sister Monica) and I wondered whether, perhaps, he came from the Catholic branch. Jimmy's subsequent research – which led to his book *The Robinsons of North Kildare: 300 Years of Family History (1997)* – failed to show a family relationship; and we had to be satisfied with this link of friendship which I discovered.

3. David Milburn, *A History of Ushaw College*, p. 8.

NOTES AND REFERENCES

4. Edwin H. Burton, and Edmond Nolan, eds. *The Douay College Diaries: The Seventh Diary 1715-1778 Preceded by a Summary of Events 1691-1715*, p. 226n; the will of Rev. William Daniel of Euxton Hall, Euxton, Lancs., 20th July 1777; Anstruther, *The Seminary Priests Volume IV: 1716-1800*, pp. 81-83 and 208.

5. Rev. P. Byrne, and J. P. Smith, 'The Catholic Registers of Thurnham, Lancashire. 1785-1838' in *Lancashire Registers*, pp. 178-179; also *The Victoria History of the County of Lancashire*, Vol. VI, p. 205.

6. J. E. Smith, 'The Catholic Registers of SS. Mary & James, Scorton, Garstang, Lancashire. 1774-1835' in *Lancashire Registers III*, pp. 224-225.

7. Byrne, and Smith, 'Catholic Registers of Thurnham,' pp. 179 and 225; Richard Marius, *Thomas More a Biography*, pp. 505-511; Anstruther, *The Seminary Priests Volume IV: 1716-1800*, p. 105.

8. Richard Richardson's will, 1730, Document 9, Records of St Gregory's College, Seville, quoted by James Robinson in *The Robinsons of North Kildare: 300 Years of Family History*, p. 19-20.

9. Michael Trappes-Lomax, *Bishop Challoner. A Biographical Study Derived from Dr. Edwin Burton's 'The Life and Times of Bishop Challoner'* pp. 40 and 272.

Chapter 7

1. M. A. Tierney, *Dodd's Church History of England from the Commencement of the Sixteenth Century to the Revolution in 1688, with Notes, Additions, and a Continuation* by The Rev. M. A. Tierney, F.S.A. Vol. I, p. 1. Dodd's Church History was first published in three volumes between 1737 and 1742 and, according to Joseph Gillow, one of the two people who paid for it was Cuthbert Tunstall. Cuthbert adopted his mother's maiden name, Constable, on inheriting Burton Constable estate. He received part of his education at the English College at Douai after which he graduated with the degree of Doctor of Medicine at the University of Montpellier. Cuthbert was the father of Marmaduke Cuthbert Constable who was also at Douai. Marmaduke was a Fellow of the Royal Society and a Fellow of the Society of Antiquaries of London; he changed his name back to Tunstall on inheriting the Wycliffe estate. Michael J. Boyd, ' "The Catholic Maecenas of his Age": Cuthbert Constable (c. 1680-1747) of Burton Constable' in *Burton Constable Hall: The Eighteenth and Nineteenth centuries* (East Yorkshire Local History Society, 1998); also M. J. Boyd and L. Jessop, 'A "truly amiable gentleman": new light on the life and work of Marmaduke Tunstall (1743-1790) of Wycliffe, North Yorkshire' (Archives of Natural History (1998) 25 (2): 221-236.

2. Churchwardens Presentations, information kindly supplied by the late Monsignor Edward Wilcock.

3. Anstruther, *The Seminary Priests Volume III: 1660-1715,* pp. 205-207.

4. Relevant wills consulted: Christopher Tootell of Clayton, gent., 16th August 1623; William Tootell de Whittle le Woods, yeoman, 13th November 1698. The case that Margaret Tootell was a daughter of William Tootell of Euxton and his wife, an unnamed daughter of John Foster, and that she was a niece of Hugh Tootell, alias Charles Dodd, who was William's brother, is as follows: The reference 'Robert Foster, of Charnock Richard, co. Lanc., tanner, [Margaret's uncle] a relative of the Rev. Hugh Tootell, *alias* Charles Dodd' occurs in J. P. Smith, ed., *Lancashire Registers II. The Fylde II.* Catholic Record Society Vol. XVI, p. 517. Hugh Tootell, alias Charles Dodd, who was born in 1671, was believed to have been a native of Euxton. He was a nephew of Christopher Tootell, alias Blacklow, pastor of Fernyhalgh for about thirty years. Christopher was a son of Hugh and Margaret Tootell of Lower Healey, he was baptised on the last day of October 1662. *Victoria History of Lancs,* p. 18; Dom F.O. Blundell, O.S.B. *Old Catholic Lancashire* Vol. II, p. 99; and Anstruther, *The Seminary Priests Volume III: 1660-1715,* p. 230. Hugh's uncle, Christopher, was only nine years his senior and so Hugh was presumably the son of a brother who was about ten years older than Christopher, say born about 1652. Possible candidates for Hugh's parents are William Tootell of Whittle le Woods and his wife Marjerey. In his will of 13th November 1691, which was proved 25th November 1698, William refers to his children John, Hugh, William, and Ann. Blundell states 'The following are some of the autographs found in class-books still at Fernyhalgh: ...John Tootell, his booke, 1667 (a near relative of the Rev. Hugh Tootell alias Charles Dodd, the Church historian, who was born at Durton, close to the school, in 1672, and probably studied his rudiments there);' Dom F. O. Blundell, O.S.B. *Old Catholic Lancashire* Vol. I, p. 184. But Blundell, in Vol. II, p. 99 states: 'Gillow says he [Hugh Tootell] was born in 1671, probably at Euxton, but his uncle Rev. Christopher Tootell was a member of the Lower Healey family and was born at that place'. A Hugh Tootell and a William Tootell appear under Euxton in Bishop Leyburn's Confirmation Register of 1687. Hugh Tootell, alias Charles Dodd, entered the English College at Douai 23rd July 1688. J. A. Hilton, A. J. Mitchinson, Barbara Murray and Peggy Wells, editors, *Bishop Leyburn's Confirmation Register of 1687,* pp. 155 and 150. The 'John Tootell, Yeo, mother & brother [? Hugh]' under Whittle may be identical with the John Tootell whose autograph appears in the class-book at Fernyhalgh in 1667. Allan Joseph Mitchinson, ed. *The Return of the Papists for the Diocese of Chester, 1705.* Edited with an Introduction by Allan Joseph Mitchinson, p. 22. Also of interest is 'Wm Tootell, Yeo, 2 child & 1 servt' under Uxton. This William could be the brother of John and Hugh. He may also have been the Tootell who married a daughter of John Foster of Charnock Richard

NOTES AND REFERENCES

and who had a daughter Margaret Tootell. This hypothesis, that William Tootell of Whittle le Woods was the father of Hugh Tootell, alias Charles Dodd, and of a brother of his, William Tootell of Euxton, who married a daughter of John Foster and who had a daughter Margaret, appears to receive some confirmation from the following entries in the International Genealogical Index: A Hugh Tootell of Chorley has a son, Christopher, who was christened on 31st October 1662, ie. Rev. Christopher Tootell, the uncle of Hugh Tootell alias Charles Dodd. The previous children of Hugh Tootell of Chorley to be christened were: Oliver, 1st October 1661; Dorothy, 29th September 1660; Ann, 29th September 1659; Marg. 14th November 1657; George, 11th March, 1655; and John 28th September 1653; these would all appear to be siblings of Christopher; but the eldest, John, would only have been aged 18 when Hugh was born and was probably not his father. The following children then appear: John, 25th September 1653; Geo., 17th November 1650; and Ricus. 4th October 1646; it seems quite likely that their father is a different Hugh Tootell of Chorley, unless Geo. died and the name was repeated and John, a twin, died and the name was repeated. Then these children appear: Willus., 28th April 1639; James, 21st April 1635; and Richard 26th April 1632. If all these children were of the same family Richard may have died and the name may have been repeated in Ricus. It would have been unusual for one mother to have had thirteen children in the 17th century and, judging by the spacing of the births the youngest seven indicate more fertile parents which would have been unlikely as they grew older. A possible explanation is that Christopher's father married twice and that the eldest three children are the product of the first marriage. Willus. would have been aged 35 in 1671 and may well have been William of Whittle le Woods the father of Hugh born in that year. The International Genealogical Index also gives these christenings: Margaret, 5th February 1693; Ann, 4th June 1695; and William, 28th November 1697; the children of a William Tootell of Chorley. This William could well have been identical with: 1) the William Tootell who, with two of his children, appears under Euxton; 2) the husband of John Foster's daughter; 3) the brother of Hugh Tootell, alias Charles Dodd. If Margaret were christened in 1693 she would have been aged 12 in 1705, and 16 when John Foster made his will.

5. Dom F. O. Blundell, O.S.B., *Old Catholic Lancashire* Vol. I, pp. 181-186; also Joseph Gillow, Bibliographical Dictionary, p. 13.

6. J. E. Smith, 'The Catholic Registers of SS. Mary & James, Scorton, Garstang, Lancashire. 1774-1835'. Contributed by Joseph Edward Smith. Historical Notes by Joseph Gillow. *Lancashire Registers III,* p. 224.

7. Anstruther, *The Seminary Priests Volume III: 1660-1715,* pp. 19-20.

8. Dom Adam Hamilton, O.S.B., edited with notes and additions, *The*

Chronicle of the English Augustinian Canonesses Regular of the Lateran, at St Monica's in Louvain, a continuation 1625 to 1644, p. 205.

9. The Chetham Society, *Remains Historical & Literary connected with the Palatine Counties of Lancaster and Chester.* Published by the Chetham Society, Vol. V, pp. 162, 187, 225; also Leo Gooch, *The Desperate Faction? The Jacobites of North East-England 1688-1745* p. 62. Gooch identifies William Tunstall with the husband of Mary Radcliffe, Derwentwater's great-aunt, but he would have been aged 102 in 1715! I am indebted to Michael J. Boyd, of the Burton Constable Foundation, for introducing me to George Townshend Fox's 'Synopsis of the Newcastle Museum', 1827, in which Marmaduke Tunstall of Wycliffe (1743-1790) refers to his distant relation who was said to be 'the first good shooter flying' Michael Boyd goes on to say: 'There is, interestingly, an (?) early eighteenth century portrait at Burton Constable Hall which is identified in inventories as being that of "William Tunstall, the first to shoot flying". If, as seems likely, this gentleman is the "distant relation" referred to by Marmaduke Tunstall, then we have the name WilliamTunstall linked by the achievement of shooting flying) to a date of death around 1730. This, somewhat mysterious, person is certainly a more plausible candidate for a Jacobite quartermaster general "of advanced years" in 1715 than the well-recorded William Tunstall (1613-1667) suggested by Dr Gooch'. No William of this period appears in the Tunstall Pedigree; but among the children of William Tunstall and his wife Mary, there is mention of 'Others' among whom William may well have featured. It is likely that a son should be named after his father. If he were born in about 1643 he would have been 72 in 1715 and 87 when he died. He would have had good reason to join forces with James Radcliffe, who would have been his first cousin once removed, because family loyalties were strong among the Radcliffes and their friends.

10. Rev. P. Byrne, and J. P. Smith, 'The Catholic Registers of Thurnham, Lancashire. 1785-1838' Contributed by Rev. P. Byrne and J. P. Smith. Historical Notes by Joseph Gillow. *Lancashire Registers III,* p. 182.

11. Thomas Babington Macaulay, 'A Jacobite's Epitaph' in *The Oxford Book Of English Verse 1250-1918* Chosen and Edited by Sir Arthur Quiller-Couch, p. 784. Again, I am indebted to Michael J. Boyd for drawing my attention to this poem which tends to support our hypothesis about the identity of the William Tunstall who was involved in the 1715 Rebellion. Through my dear friend Lucia Boldrini, in fact at her wedding, I was fortunate enough to be introduced to Michael Caesar, Professor of Italian and Head of the Department of Italian Studies at Birmingham University. He was kind enough to make extensive inquiries for me among Italian scholars about this poem. The original title was 'Epitaph on a Jacobite' and it was composed in,

possibly significantly, 1845. Lavernia as a place does not appear to exist. Professor Caesar thought Macaulay might have had La Verna in mind. However, Professor Geoffrey Robertson-Mellor, who wrote to him, did not think so but rather that Macaulay used the name because he liked the Italian sound of it. Professor Robertson-Mellor said 'What is quite certain is that it is concerned with the '15' and not the '45'. He also said that the Jacobite centre had become Italy before the '45' hence the placing of the epitaph in Italy. Although there is no certainty who is the subject of the poem, the fact that it referred to the '15', in which William Tunstall was the Jacobite Paymaster and Quartermaster-General, and the reference to Scargill and the river Tees, which runs by Wycliffe Hall, are very suggestive to me that the poem refers to him. In a subsequent letter to me, dated 10th April 2003, Professor Robertson-Mellor states 'My guess about Macaulay's Jacobite is that he is not to be identified with William Tunstall, but that he may well have been one of the models who inspired him'.

12. I suggest that the Daile/Dale branch of our family married into the Tunstalls; the case is as follows:

My father's sister, Aunt Agnes, told me that our family lived at Hutton Hall for 300 years. I have found no evidence that Robinsons occupied Hutton Hall before Robert Robinson my great-great-grandfather went there in 1760. Robert's great-grandson Thomas Robinson of Newsham Grange gave up Hutton Hall in 1928; the family had been resident for 168 years. Robert Dale, my great-times-four-grandfather took up the tenancy of Hutton Hall in 1715, this adds a further 45 years, so that, through the Dales, we would have been there for 213 years; but there are still 87 years outstanding. Mary, the wife of Robert Dale of Hutton Hall and mother of Adam Dale of Girlington and later of Wycliffe Grange, died 27th December 1777 at the age of 92; her identity may provide an explanation for Robert Dale's tenancy of Hutton Hall and for the oral tradition that our family lived there for three hundred years. The case is as follows:

William Liddell of Wycliffe, gentleman, in his will of 9th May 1742, refers to 'my dear cousin Marmaduke Tunstall [1672-1760] of Wycliffe, esq. [executor]' and also to 'my cousin Adam Dale of Girlington [executor]'. He refers to Adam Dale 'my cousin' twice. William Liddell's father, Henry Liddell, was married to Mary Tunstall, sister of Francis Tunstall (1637-1713, of Hutton Villars, Scargill and Wycliffe) the father of Marmaduke, Lord of Wycliffe. Francis was the eldest son of William Tunstall of Scargill Castle, Lord of the Manor of Hutton Magna, indicted for recusancy at York Assizes in March 1666, and his wife Mary daughter of Sir Edward Radcliffe of Dilston. See: Edward Wilcock, *The Pearson Family and the Recusants of West Gilling*, pp. 270-271; also 'Pedigree of Tunstall, of Thurland Castle, Co. Lanc., and Wycliffe, Co. York'. There is no reason to suppose that William Liddell was using the term cousin loosely in referring to Adam Dale. There are four possible explanations:

1) William Liddell's wife was also a Mary Dale; and if Robert Dale's father, Adam Daile of Hutton, had a brother who was this Mary Dale's father, Adam Dale would have been a first cousin once removed of William Liddell's wife and, hence, William might have referred to Adam as his cousin. 2) The father or mother of Robert Dale's wife, Mary, may have been a Liddell. 3) Adam Dale's wife, Sarah, may have been a Tunstall and a second cousin of William Liddell who may then have referred to Adam Dale as his cousin. 4) The father or mother Robert Dale's wife, Mary, may have been a Tunstall; and this seems to be the most likely explanation.

Adam Dale and his wife Sarah are both buried in the parish church of Wycliffe which came under the patronage of the Tunstalls, though, as Catholics, they did not attend the services there. Such a privilege for Adam and his wife, both Catholics, is strongly suggestive that one of them was related to the Tunstalls.

William Liddell's uncle, Thomas Tunstall, who was aged 25 in August 1665, the second son of William Tunstall, and probably identical with the Mr Tunstall referred to in the Hearth Tax list of 1673 for Barningham (13 hearths), and with the 'Mr Tunstall of Barningham' who, apparently, did not refuse to take the Oath of Allegiance in February 1689, though he was a recusant, could well have been Mary Dale's father; he would have been 45 when she was born. See: Hugh Aveling, *Northern Catholics: The Catholic Recusants of the North Riding of Yorkshire 1558-1790,* p. 329. Adam and Sarah Dale's third son, Thomas, may have been named after him. This would have paved the way for Robert Dale's entry to Hutton Hall in 1715 and for Adam Dale's entry to Wycliffe Grange. See: Beverley Archives, DDCC 2 16 Acc. Book. Hutton, Wycliffe etc. '1715 Received of Robert Daile £55-10 in full of his last March rent'. Alternatively, Mary Dale may have been a daughter of one of the 'Others' among Francis and Thomas Tunstall's brothers and sisters on the Tunstall Pedigree, perhaps a daughter of William Tunstall 'the first good shooter flying', who, I suggest, was one of the 'Others'. This would fit the story told to me by my old uncle Thomas Robinson (1861-1951) of Nuthill, on the Burton Constable estate, that our ancestors were involved in the Jacobite Rebellions.

Nicholas Girlington sold the Manor of Hutton Magna to Francis Tunstall, the great-grandfather of Francis Tunstall (1637-1713) above, in 1614, according to the Victoria History of Yorkshire; and his son Marmaduke Tunstall of Scargill married Katherine, daughter and heiress of William Wycliffe, of Wycliffe, in 1606. Hugh Aveling, referring to the incidence of recusancy at Hutton Magna, gives the following figures:

NOTES AND REFERENCES

1611 – 10 rects. (Tunstalls); 1614 – Mrs. Tunstall; 1655 – William Tunstall; 1666-1669 – 5 Papists (Tunstall). See: Aveling, *Northern Catholics,* pp. 437-438. If Adam Dale's grandmother or grandfather were a Tunstall, this would account for more than the 87 missing years and accords with 'upwards of 300 years' in: '...the fine 16th century building, Hutton Hall, formerly the manor house of Hutton Magna and now a farm house, is to add another chapter to its history by reason of the fact that it is to change hands after being held by the same family upwards of 300 years. The present occupier Mr Thomas Robinson'. See: 'Tudor House to Change Hands after 300 years. Hutton Hall – The Home of the Robinson Family. A Story in Stone'. *Darlington and Stockton Times* April 28th 1928, p. 4.

The Rev. Francis Hodgson, a Douai priest, who was born in the diocese of York in about 1650, 'was himself an itinerant missioner who from his arrival in England in 1677 travelled the Yorkshire and Durham districts. He was staying with the Tunstalls at Hutton Hall when he died on 24th March [24th May according to Anstruther] 1726'. See: Anstruther, *The Seminary Priests, Vol. III: 1660-1715,* pp. 103-104; also Edward Wilcock, *The Pearson Family and the Recusants of West Gilling,* p. 290. Robert and Mary Dale were at Hutton Hall at that time; but if Mary were a Tunstall this statement would be correct. 'Ffrancis Hodgeshon' is one of the witnesses to the will of Robert Dale's mother, Sarah Daile of Hutton Long Villers [Hutton Magna], on 10th November 1716; it is tempting to think that this was the Rev. Francis Hodgson.

13. Anstruther, *The Seminary Priests Volume III: 1660-1715,* pp. 228-230.

14. Anstruther, *The Seminary Priests Volume III: 1660-1715,* pp. 103-104.

15. Father David Quinlan, *The Father Postgate Story 1599-1973,* pp. 11-22.

Chapter 8

1. Christopher Hill, *The Century of Revolution 1603-1714,* p. 268.

2. Norman Gardner, *Lancashire Quarter Sessions Records: Register of Recusants 1679* edited with an introduction by Norman Gardner, pp. 52-53.

3. Norman Gardner, *Lancashire Quarter Sessions Records: Register of Recusants 1679,* p. 1.

4. M. D. R. Leys, *Catholics in England 1559-1829: A Social History,* pp. 97-98.

5. Lancashire Record Office, References QSP 493/18 and QSP 493/1. I am indebted to Jean Stuart of Lower House Farm, Charnock Richard (an old Foster residence), for drawing my attention to these references.

6. J. A. Hilton, A. J. Mitchinson, Barbara Murray and Peggy Wells, eds.,

Bishop Leyburn's Confirmation Register of 1687, pp. 148, 151, 153, 160, 162.

7. IGI.

8. *Victoria History of Lancashire, Vol. VI,* p. 208 n. 5.

9. Anonymous, *Saint Edmund Arrowsmith: a Contemporary Account. With a forward by The Bishop of Salford,* p. 11.

10. Will of Robert Ffoster of Charnock Richard, June 1613; also the International Genealogical Index; also the will of Richard Parker of Charnock Richard, 2nd July 1623, where debts owing to him are from: 'James Charnock the elder, James wiffe Foster'; also the Pedigree of Charnock of Charnock and Astley, a copy of which was kindly given to me by Rose Boyd of Astley Hall; also G. A. Birtill, O.B.E., J.P., *Astley Hall Chorley,* pp. 5-7.

11. G. A. Birtill, *Astley Hall Chorley,* p. 5; also *Victoria History of Lancashire,* Vol. VI, p. 207.

12. C. V. Wedgwood, *The King's War 1641-1647,* pp. 296, 322.

13. J. R. Robinson, 'Charnock Richard to Cornamucklagh: a Bridge Across the Sea' in *Catholic Ancestor,* VII, No. 1, (1998), pp. 27-31.

14. *Victoria History of Lancashire,* Vol. VI, p. 380; I am indebted to George L. Bolton, president of Leyland Historical Society for drawing my attention to this reference.

15. Norman Gardner, *Lancashire Quarter Sessions Records: Register of Recusants 1679,* p. 59; also Tom C. Smith, F.R.Hist.S., *History of the Parish of Chipping,* pp. 30-32.

16. John Weld, D.L., J.P., of Leagram, *A History of Leagram: The Park and the Manor,* pp. 53-62; also Smith, *History of the Parish of Chipping,* Stanley chart opposite p. 45; also the will of John Holden of Laythgrim, Yeoman, 11th June 1694; also Irena Preston, 'Mary Shireburn – 8th Duchess of Norfolk' in *Longer Sen a Miscellany,* pp. 13-15, and 'Tenants of Her Grace the Dowager Duchess of Norfolk taken from a Fieldbook surveyed by Joseph Dickinson Anno 1733' in the same, p. 12.

I am deeply indebted to Andrew Snape for so generously giving me the benefit of his extensive research into the Holden family of Chaigley of which he is a member through his great-great-grandmother Alice Turner (née Holden), of Preston, who was born at Chaigley in 1821 and baptised at Stonyhurst. Her father, Thomas, farmed for many years at Townley House Farm, Leagram. Main sources for
the genealogy of this family are: *Victoria County History of Lancashire* Vol. VII, pp. 15-16; and W. A. Abram in the *Preston Guardian,* 1874, 'Sketches in Local History No. XIX: The Holdens of Chaigley'. Contemporary with John, the eldest son of Richard and Eleanor Holden of Chaigley Hall, was a John Holden of "Chippin Laund" (adjoining Leagram Hall)

who made his will on 10th January 1631/2. Andrew Snape, in establishing the relationship between the 'Chipping Laund' and Chaigley branches of the family, quotes Smith, *History of the Parish of Chipping*, p. 196, who, after quoting an extract from the will of 'Mrs Sherburne,' states: 'John Holden of "Chippin Laund" gent. …made his will, Jan. 10, 1631-2. Gives … to his son, John … [and] to his cousin John Holden of Chageley…'. The sister of this John Holden of Chipping Laund, Ann Holden, later Shirburne, has been stated (John Weld, D.L., J.P., of Leagram, *A History of Leagram: The Park and the Manor*), to be the daughter of Thomas Holden of Greengore. This Thomas appears to be identical with Thomas, a younger son of Richard Holden of Chaigley Hall and Jane Parker whose eldest son was Richard Holden of Chaigley Hall, the father of 'John Holden of Chageley'. John Holden of Chipping Laund's son was John Holden of Townleys, Leagram, whose eldest son, by his wife Elizabeth, was Robert Holden of Leagram. Robert's only child, Elizabeth, married James Foster of Euxton House; James and Elizabeth were the parents of Cecily Robinson of Hutton Hall.

17. Smith, *History of the Parish of Chipping*, p. 155.

18. Anstruther, *The Seminary Priests: Vol. II, 1603-1659*, pp. 158-159. See also: *Gillow, Bibliographical Dictionary, Vol. IV*, pp. 330-341.

19. *Victoria History of Lancashire, Vol. VI*, p. 208; also Anstruther, *The Seminary Priests: Vol. II, 1603-1659*, pp. 76-77. One cannot be certain, but it seems quite likely that the William Crichlow, recusant, and the William Crichlow who witnessed the will of James Foster, were identical with the priest. Again, I am greatly indebted to George L. Bolton for information on the Crichlow/Foster connection.

20. *Victoria History of Lancashire, Vol. VI*, pp. 429-430.

21. Anonymous, *Saint Edmund Arrowsmith: a Contemporary Account. With a forward by The Bishop of Salford*, pp. 11-16.

Chapter 9

1. John Guy, 'Why Starkey is wrong about Elizabeth', *The Sunday Times*, November 11, 2001, News Review, p. 5.7.

2. In a letter to me of 18th January 1991, Norman Cardwell stated, 'I have heard that the family claim relationship to the Wrights of Ploughland from the "Boss" [Uncle Thomas], Mary Agnes [Aunt Agnes] and my Mother [my cousin Daisy]'. Norman adds, 'The tradition seemed to me to be fairly strong, such stories generally gather weight with telling and the "Boss" would see to that!'. So far I have been unable to establish the connection between Robert Wright of Fitling and the Wrights of Ploughland Hall; but there does not seem to be any reason

to doubt the truth of this tradition which Uncle Thomas and Aunt Agnes would have received from their mother, or even from their grandmother Mary Ann Wright who died on 13th July 1883 when Thomas was aged 22 and Agnes was 14. This relationship to the Wrights of Ploughland Hall also probably explains my father's telling me that he thought we were related to Guy Fawkes! The statement would have been only symbolic of the truth but would have had more meaning for a small boy than a reference to the Wrights of Ploughland Hall.

3. Anstruther, *The Seminary Priests: Vol. II, 1603-1659*, pp. 249-250.

4. Father David Quinlan, *The Father Postgate Story 1599-1973*, p. 3.

5. 'Table of Descent of Wright Family, of Ploughland, Welwick'

6. Mary Oliver, I.B.V.M., *Mary Ward 1585-1645*, pp. 12-13.

7. Alan Haynes, *The Gunpowder Plot*, pp. 46-47.

8 Philip Caraman, *Henry Garnet 1555-1606 and the Gunpowder Plot*, pp. 400, 417.

9. Oliver, *Mary Ward*, pp. 38, 41.

10. Mark Nicholls, *Investigating Gunpowder plot*, pp. 3-77.

11. W. A. Newman Dorland, A.M., M.D., F.A.C.S., *The American Illustrated Medical Dictionary*, p. 1402. Strangury is defined as 'Slow and painful discharge of urine: due to spasm of the urethra and bladder'.

12. E. I. Watkin, *Roman Catholicism in England from the Reformation to 1950*, pp. 63-64.

13. J. C. Atkinson, ed., *Quarter Sessions Records,* North Riding Record Society, Vol. III, 5th October 1624. Barningham lies three miles southwest of Hutton Magna. The Catholic Robinsons in Hutton Magna and neighbouring villages, in the early seventeenth century, were highly likely to have been related to our family but insufficient evidence has come to light, so far, to specify the relationships. This is Francis Tunstall who sold Thurland Castle in Lancashire and came into Yorkshire; Scargill, which had come into the Tunstall family through the marriage of his grandfather, Sir Marmaduke Tunstall, Knt., to Alice, co-heiress of Sir Robert Scargill of Scargill, lies about two and half miles to the west of Barningham. Hence, this was probably an early example of the involvement of our family with the Tunstalls. Perhaps this William Robinson, who appears to have been living in the household of Francis Tunstall, was farming for him and perhaps his descendants continued in this role at Hutton Hall; this would provide the simplest explanation for the oral tradition that we lived at Hutton Hall for 300 years.

14. Peter Roebuck, *Yorkshire Baronets 1640-1760 Families, Estates, and Fortunes*, p. 155.

15. Foster, Joseph, ed. *The Visitation of Yorkshire, made in the Years 1584/5, by Robert Glover, Somerset Herald; to which is added: The subsequent Visitation made in 1612, by Richard St. George, Norray King of Arms, with Several Additional Pedigrees, including 'The Arms Taken out of Churches and Houses at Yorkshire Visitation, 1584/5", "Sir William Fayrfax' Book of Arms", and other Heraldic Lists, with Copious Indices, 1875,* pp. 198, 283, 506.

16. Mary Catherine Elizabeth Chambers of the Institute of the Blessed Virgin, *The Life of Mary Ward (1585-1645)* edited by Henry James Coleridge of the Society of Jesus, Vol. I, pp. 7-8.

17 Anstruther, *The Seminary Priests: Vol. 1, 1558-1603,* pp. 181-182.

18. Oliver, *Mary Ward,* p. 51.

19. Joseph Grisar S.J., 'Mary Ward 1585-1645,' p. 8.

20. Margaret Mary Littlehales, I.B.V.M., *Mary Ward (1585-1645) A Woman for All Seasons: Foundress of the Institute of the Blessed Virgin,* p. 25. See also Henriette Peters translated by Helen Butterworth, *Mary Ward: A World in Contemplation,* p. 587.

21. Littlehales, *Mary Ward (1585-1645) A Woman for All Seasons,* p. 27.

22. Grisar, 'Mary Ward 1585-1645,' p. 6.

23. J. R. Robinson, 'Hutton Hall: A Nursery for the "Second Spring"' in *Catholic Ancestor VII,* No. 3, (1998), pp. 112-120.

24. Sister M. Gregory, IBVM, 'Canon John Thompson, 1814-1884', a personal gift from Sister M. Gregory, of the Bar Convent, who has shown me the greatest kindness and help in my research. She continues 'The esteem and affection of the nuns can be measured by the quite astonishing suffrages offered for him, and by the pride of place allotted to him in death, for he lies buried in the very centre of the convent cemetery, surrounded by those who were "all very dear to him"'.

25. Littlehales, *Mary Ward (1585-1645) A Woman for All Seasons,* p. 31

Chapter 10

1. Evelyn Waugh, *Edmund Campion,* pp. 205-206. The title of this article is based on Rev. William Foster alias Charnock (c. 1707-1754) son of my great-times-four-grandparents, Robert Foster and Elizabeth Parker of Charnock Richard. See Edwin H. Burton and Edmond Nolan, eds., *The Douay College Diaries: The Seventh Diary 1715-1778 Preceded by a Summary of Events 1691-1715,* p. 226n.

2. *Victoria History of Lancashire,* Vol. VI, p. 207.

3. Philip Caraman, S.J., *A Study in Friendship: Saint Robert Southwell and Henry Garnet,* pp. 14 and 80; see also Alan Gordon Smith, *The Babington*

Plot, pp. 232-233 and 243-249.

4. In his will of June 1613, Robert Foster refers to his son-in-law James Charnock. The International Genealogical Index refers to the marriage, on 22nd January 1592, under Standish, of Margaret Foster and James Charnock; and I am indebted to George L. Bolton, President of Leyland Historical Society, for the information that 'The actual Standish register as printed in LPRS vol. 43 shows a marriage on 22 January 1592/3 between James Charnocke and Margaret Forster'. The will of Richard Parker of Charnock Richard, 2nd July 1623, refers, among the debts owing to him, to 'James Charnock the elder' followed by 'James' wife Foster'. Hence, it is concluded that Robert Foster of Charnock Richard had a daughter, Margaret, who married James Charnock, second son of Thomas Charnock of Charnock and his wife Mary, daughter of Richard Rathall, whose sixth son was John Charnock. I am indebted to Sam Watkinson for the following information: in 1562, James Foster tenanted Greenehurst; in 1586, William Chorley leased Greenehurst to Robert Foster and Jenett his wife and, in 1618, to James Foster and Cecily his wife; and, in 1623, William Chorley and Richard Chorley leased Greenehurst to Cicely Foster (widow) and Jenet her daughter and to Edward Houghton, Jenet's husband. Ref LCRS A15 33 containing 1662 survey of Chorley estates. I am greatly indebted to Rosemary Boyd of Astley Hall for information on the Charnock family and on Charnock Richard.

5. E. I. Watkin, *Roman Catholicism in England from the Reformation to 1950,* pp. 45-46; see also A. G. Dickens, *The English Reformation,* p. 366. The 'bloody question' was: 'If the Pope and the King of Spain landed in England, for whom would you fight?'.

6. Gillow, *Bibliographical Dictionary,* Vol. I, pp. 474-477.

7. John Bossy, *The English Catholic Community 1570-1850,* pp. 14-20; also Arnold Pritchard, *Catholic Loyalism in Elizabethan England,* pp. 187-191 and 205-206.

8. Caraman, *A Study in Friendship,* pp. 18-19.

9. Maurice Nassan S.J., *Saint Robert Southwell Poet and Martyr,* p. 5.

10. Caraman, *A Study in Friendship,* pp. 89-93.

11. Alison Plowden, *Danger to Elizabeth: The Catholics under Elizabeth I,* p. 17.

12. Carolly Erickson, *Bloody Mary: The Life of Mary Tudor,* pp. 450-454, and 462.

13. G. E. Phillips, *The Extinction of the Ancient Hierarchy,* p. 76.

14. Phillips, *The Extinction of the Ancient Hierarchy,* p. 428.

15. Sir Marmaduke Tunstall, grandson of Thomas and Alice Tunstall of Thurland Castle, married Alice, daughter and of co-heiress of Sir Robert Scargill of Scargill, North Yorkshire; their grandson, Francis Tunstall,

bought the Manor of Hutton Magna from Nicholas Girlington in 1614, according to the Victoria History of Yorkshire; and his son, Marmaduke Tunstall, married Katherine, daughter and heiress of William Wycliffe of Wycliffe. See also John R. Robinson, 'Of Roses White and Red: The Robinsons and Dales and a network of 18th century secular priests in Lancashire and Yorkshire' in *Catholic Ancestor*, VIII, No. 1, (2000), pp. 13-24.

16. David Starkey, *Elizabeth: Apprenticeship*, p. 301.

17. Phillips, *The Extinction of the Ancient Hierarchy*, p. 187.

18. Phillips, *The Extinction of the Ancient Hierarchy*, p. 337.

19. Dickens, *The English Reformation*, p. 361.

20. Plowden, *Danger to Elizabeth: The Catholics under Elizabeth I*, p. 51.

21. Christopher Haigh, *Elizabeth I*, pp. 37-39.

22. Frank Singleton, *Hoghton Tower*, pp. 6 and 22.

23. Graeme Bryson, *Shakespeare in Lancashire also Shakespeare and the Gunpowder Plot*, p. 8.

24. *Victoria History of Lancashire*, Vol. VI, p. 205.

25. Anstruther, *The Seminary Priests: Vol. I, 1558-1603*, pp. 190, 387-388, 90-91; also Joseph Gillow, *Bibliographical Dictionary*, Vol. V, p. 595; also Park Honan, *Shakespeare: A Life*, pp. 63.

26. George L. Bolton, 'Early Influences on Peter Worden 1' (a copy of which paper was very kindly given to me by the author), pp. 2-4.

27. Philip Michael Worthington, *The Worthington Families of Medieval England*, pp. 143-145.

28. Bryson, *Shakespeare in Lancashire* also *Shakespeare and the Gunpowder Plot*, pp. 36-39.

29. Park Honan, *Shakespeare: A Life*, pp. 61-62.

30. Plowden, *Danger to Elizabeth*, p. 186.

31. Anstruther, *The Seminary Priests: Vol. I, 1558-1603*, p. 387.

32. Weld, *A History of Leagram: The Park and the Manor*, pp. 53-62. See also, Smith, *History of the Parish of Chipping*, p. 196; John Holden of Chipping Laund (adjoining Leagram Hall), who made his will 10th January 1631/2, had a son, John, and a cousin, John Holden of "Chageley". See also, J. E. Bamber, 'The Secret Treasure of Chaigley' in *Recusant History*, XVII, No. 4, (1985), pp. 307-329.

33. Anstruther, *The Seminary Priests: Vol. I, 1558-1603*, pp. 101-102 and 130.

34. Anstruther, *The Seminary Priests: Vol. II, 1603-1659*, pp. 76-77.

I am much indebted to George Bolton who very kindly drew my

attention to the Tootell/Crichlow relationship; and he makes the suggestion that, 'applying the usual Catholic convention about religious names,...' these priests' '...maternal grandmother, wife of Oliver Tootell, could have been born Elizabeth Foster'. William Crichlow witnessed the will of Robert Foster's son James Foster on 3rd June 1622. If, as seems likely, this was William Crichlow the priest, it would have been five years before he went abroad to the VEC. The other witnesses were James Foster's son in law, James Parker, his brother-in-law, Thomas Waring, and James Parker's father, Richard Parker; it seems likely that William Crichlow was also related and, if his grandmother Elizabeth had been a sister of Robert Foster, William would have been a first cousin once removed of James Foster. He was probably the same William who appears in the *Victoria History of Lancashire,* Vol. VI, p. 208: 'Jane Foster, widow, [she was probably a widow of one of the sons of James Foster's brother, John Foster], William Crichlow and Elizabeth Parker [James Foster's daughter], as recusants, asked to be allowed to compound for their estates in 1653-4'. There seems to have been a close relationship, probably a blood relationship, between William Crichlow and the Fosters.

Chapter 11

1. Charles Sturge, M.A., Ph.D. (Lond.), *Cuthbert Tunstal: Churchman, Scholar, Statesman, Administrator,* p. 346. I am heavily indebted to this book which I hope I have not misrepresented. Cuthbert Tunstall signs his name 'Tunstal' and Sturge uses this spelling but here, for consistency, the more usual spelling 'Tunstall' will be used throughout.

2. The genealogy of the Holden family of Chaigley Hall is based on: the *Victoria County History of Lancashire,* Vol. VII, pp. 15-16; on W. A. Abram 'The Holdens of Chaigley' in the *Preston Guardian,* 3rd October 1874, p. 7; and on information kindly given to me by Andrew W. Snape who is descended from this family (see Chapter VIII, n. 16).

3. J. J. Scarisbrick, *Henry VIII,* p. 12.

4. Scarisbrick, *Henry VIII,* p. 13.

5. *Victoria History of Lancashire,* Vol. VII, p. 15. John Holden is variously referred to as Holden, Hoden, Howden and Howdon; but here he will be called John Holden.

6. Alfred B. Emden, *A Survey of Dominicans in England,* based on the ordination lists in Episcopal Registers (1268 to 1538), and having been compared with Father Gumley O.P.'s own large biographical collections concerning the Dominicans of the English Province, p. 370.

7. A. B. Emden, *A Biographical Register of the University of Oxford AD 1501- 1540,* p. 301; also Joseph Foster, *Alumni Oxonienses 1510-1714* Vol. II, p. 728: 'Holden, John (Howden); B.D. 1508, D.D. 1 July 1510,

NOTES AND REFERENCES

incorporated at Cambridge 1514; perhaps rector of Cricklade St. Mary, Wilts., 1510. See Foster's Index Eccl'. Tom Ramsden-Binks, Curator of the Cricklade Museum, very kindly helped me with my early investigation of John Holden; and Father Richard Barton and the Friends of St Mary's encouraged me by inviting me to contribute a piece on John Holden to their newsletter.

8. Scarisbrick, *Henry VIII*, pp. 37 and 29.

9. I am indebted to Andrew Snape for the information that Mary, the daughter of John Holden of Chaigley Hall and his wife Isabella Worthington, married Thomas Brockholes of Claughton; and that Thomas and Mary's granddaughter Katherine Brockholes, the daughter of their son John, married Charles Howard of Greystoke, the 10th Duke of Norfolk; and that the 10th Duke and Katherine were the parents of Charles Howard the 11th Duke; see also John Martin Robinson, *The Dukes of Norfolk: A Quincentennial History*, pp. 166-184, and also the Genealogical Table, p. 240.

10. Sturge, *Cuthbert Tunstal*, pp. 3-22.

11. Sturge, *Cuthbert Tunstal*, p. 36; also 'Pedigree of Tunstall, of Thurland Castle, Co. Lanc., and Wycliffe, Co. York' in *The Chronicle of the English Augustinian Cannonesses Regular of the Lateran, at St. Monica's in Louvain 1625-1644* Vol II, very kindly copied for me by Dr David Connell, curator, Burton Constable.

12. Sturge, *Cuthbert Tunstal*, p. 62.

13. G. R. Elton, *Reformation Europe 1517-1559*, pp. 50-51.

14. Richard Rex, *The Theology of John Fisher*, pp. 27-28.

15. Sturge, *Cuthbert Tunstal*, p. 71.

16. Alfred B. Emden, *A Survey of Dominicans*, p. 370. Information about John Holden is followed by the reference: 'Reg. Tunstall, Lond., ordination lists, fo. 1.'.

17. Scarisbrick, *Henry VIII*, p. 236.

18. Richard Rex, *Henry VIII and the English Reformation*, pp. 26-30 and 173-174.

19. Sturge, *Cuthbert Tunstal*, p. 190.

20. A. W. Moore, M.A., Trinity College, Cambridge, *Diocesan Histories: Sodor and Man*, pp. 95-96.

21. Sturge, *Cuthbert Tunstal*, pp. 194 and 183.

22. Diarmaid MacCulloch, *Thomas Cranmer: A Life*, p. 97.

23. Sturge, *Cuthbert Tunstal*, pp. 195-196.

24. Scarisbrick, *Henry VIII*, p. 331.

25. Sturge, *Cuthbert Tunstal*, pp. 185 and 197; also Scarisbrick, *Henry VIII*, p. 330.

26. Sturge, *Cuthbert Tunstal*, p. 198.

27. Sturge, *Cuthbert Tunstal*, p. 24.

28. Sturge, *Cuthbert Tunstal*, p. 52.

29. Susan Brigden, *New Worlds, Lost Worlds: The Rule of the Tudors 1485-1603*, p. 120.

30. Scarisbrick, *Henry VIII*, p. 327.

31. Rex, *Henry VIII and the English Reformation*, p. 36.

32. John Guy, *The Tudors: A Very Short Introduction*, p. 30.

33. Sturge, *Cuthbert Tunstal*, p. 210-211.

34. Thomas Dunham Whitaker, *An History of the Original Parish of Whalley and Honor of Clitheroe* 4th edition revised by J. G. Nichols and P. A. Lyons, Vol. I, p. 103. Whitaker states, 'It is in the highest degree probable that this abbot was younger son of Adam Holden of Holden, and Alice his wife, daughter of William Holland of Heaton'. But, in footnote 2, on page 104, one of the editors of Whitaker adds, 'John Holden of Chageley had a second son Ralph, who is referred to in the Townley Pedigree as living 12th Edw. IV. [1472/3]; and, though he is not mentioned as Monk or Abbot of Whalley, I think it most likely (on account of the vicinity of Chageley to Whalley) that he was the person'. For the Pilgrimage of Grace and the dissolution of Whalley Abbey see, Geoffrey Ainsworth Williams, *Locus Benedictus: The Story of Whalley Abbey*, pp. 78-108. For prevailing attitudes to the Church in England at this time see: Eamon Duffy, *The Stripping of the Altars Traditional Religion in England c. 1400 – c. 1580*.

35. *Letters and Papers Foreign and Domestic of the reign of Henry VIII*, preserved in the Public Record Office, the British Museum and elsewhere in England. Arranged and catalogued by James Gairdner, Vol. XIII, pt. 1, p. 1180.

36. *Victoria History of London*, Vol. I, p. 500, n. 60; also E. B. Fryde, D. E. Greenway, S. Porter, and I. Roy, Handbook of British Chronology, p. 273.

37. *Victoria History of London*, Vol. I, p. 501.

38. Moore, *Diocesan Histories: Sodor and Man*, p. 97.

39. Rex, *Henry VIII and the English Reformation*, pp. 123, 103, and 132.

40. Rex, *Henry VIII and the English Reformation*, p. 68.

41. Guy, *The Tudors: A Very Short Introduction*, op. cit. p. 32.

42. Sturge, *Cuthbert Tunstal*, pp. 222-223.

43. W. Maziere Brady, *The Episcopal Succession in England Scotland and*

NOTES AND REFERENCES

Ireland A.D. 1400 to 1875, Vol. I, pp. 107-109.

44. Sturge, *Cuthbert Tunstal,* pp. 279-280.

45. Sturge, *Cuthbert Tunstal,* p. 286.

46. Sturge, *Cuthbert Tunstal,* pp. 286-287.

47. Sturge, *Cuthbert Tunstal,* p. 293.

48. Sturge, *Cuthbert Tunstal,* p. 306.

49. Sturge, *Cuthbert Tunstal,* pp. 307-308.

50. Sturge, *Cuthbert Tunstal,* pp. 322.

51. Sturge, *Cuthbert Tunstal,* pp. 322-323.

52. Sturge, *Cuthbert Tunstal,* p. 324.

53. Sturge, *Cuthbert Tunstal,* pp. 328-329.

54. Sturge, *Cuthbert Tunstal,* p. 330.

Appendix

1. Conrad Pepler, OP, *New Blackfriars,* January 1985, p. 16.

2. See Chapter V, n. 18.

3. E. S. Worrall, *Returns of Papists, 1767: Diocese of Chester,* transcribed under the direction of E. S. Worrall, pp. 165-172.

4. Letter of 20th December 1993 from C. Boddington, Senior Archivist, County Hall, Beverley.

5. Private communication from Rt. Rev. Mgr. Canon Edward Wilcock, 25th January 1993.

6. J. C. Atkinson, *Quarter Sessions Records,* North Riding Record Society, Vol. III, 'Registration of Papists Estates', pp. 130-131.

7. Hutton Fields is just over half a mile south-east of Hutton Magna village.

8. Private communication from Fr Dominique Minskip, 1994.

9. My correspondence with the late Merryne Watson of Hare Chose, Newsham, member of the Tees Greta Section of the Yorkshire Vernacular Buildings Study Group, in 1992-93.

10. Huddleston and Boumphrey, *An Armorial for Westmorland and Lonsdale,* pp. 251-252.

11. J. C. Atkinson, ed., Richmond Quarter Sessions: 5th October 1624 also 16th January 1627, North Riding Record Society, Volumes I, II, III, IV, 1884-1886, Vol. III.

12. Mgr. Edward Wilcock, personal communication, 23rd March 1995.

Mgr. Wilcock states 'Apart from the Surtees Series the chief sources from which my information has been taken are: N. Riding Record Society. Quarter Session Records. 8 Volumes; Churchwardens Presentations and courts of correction minutes in Leeds Reference Library; Acts of the York High Commission – notes; Act Books of Yorks. Archiepiscopal Visitation – notes – originals in the Borthwick Institute'.

13. Rt. Rev. Mgr. Canon Edward Wilcock, S.T.L., Prot. AP., *The Pearson Family and the Recusants of West Gilling*, p. 333. In a personal communication of 23rd March 1995 Mgr. Wilcock states 'My reference to early 16th century Robinson recusants was one of several mistakes as, of course, the term "recusant" does not occur until the latter part of the century'.

14. Merryne Watson.

15. Thomas Woodcock, Somerset Herald, correspondence of 18th December 1991 – Pedigree of Leonard Robynson; Robynson of Kirkby-Ravensworth, Richmond 19th Aug. 1665.

16. Bernard Joseph Culver, 'Genealogical Geriatric and Generic Gambles', 1977, p. 1; also 'Prelude to the Genealogy – mainly Culver', 1971, p. 4. Personal communications, in my possession.

17. Wills consulted: Ralph Robinson of Hutton Fields, 5/5/1787; Richard Robinson of Pecknall House, Romaldkirk, 19/9/1790; John Robinson of Saddle Bow, Romaldkirk, 14/3/1785; James Robinson of Saddle Bow, Romaldkirk, 27/7/1753; Richard Robinson of Parkend in Crostwhaite, 20/2/1713; John Robinson of Houlwick, Romaldkirk, 7/4/1724; Robert Robinson of Holwick, 1682; William Robinson of Sadle Bow, Romaldkirk, 1693; William Robinson of Holwicke, January 1591; John Robinson of Romaldkirk, 15/4/1569; John Robinson of Romaldkirk and Holdwick, 27/4/1545; John Robinson of Culgaith, 10/9/1625; probate documents of Matthew Robinson of Hutton Fields who died in Jamaica, 12/1/1795.

18. Thomas Woodcock, Somerset Herald, correspondence of 18th December 1991 – Pedigree of Christopher Robinson of Rappahannak, Middlesex County, Virginia; College of Arms, N 27, 59; also Ms 4 D14, 36-37.

19. See Chapter VII, n. 12.

SELECTED BIBLIOGRAPHY

Primary sources

Abram, W. A. 'Sketches in Local History No. XIX: The Holdens of Chaigley' in the *Preston Guardian,* 1874.

Anonymous, *Saint Edmund Arrowsmith: a Contemporary Account. With a forward by The Bishop of Salford.* London: Published by the Office of the Vice-Postulation, 114, Mount Street, London, W. 1, 1960, Fourth Impression.

Atkinson, Rev. J. C., ed., *Quarter Sessions Records* North Riding Record Society, Vols. I, II, III, and IV. London: Printed for the Society, 1884-1886.

Baptism Register of the Parish of Burton Pidsey. (County and Archdeaconry Archive Office, Beverley.)

Baptism Register of the Parish of Humbleton. (County and Archdeaconry Archive Office, Beverley.)

Beverley Archives, Acc. Book. Hutton, Wycliffe etc. DDCC (20) Box 20 A, Box 23.

Brady, W. Maziere. *The Episcopal Succession in England Scotland and Ireland A.D. 1400 to 1875* Vol. I, II, III. Rome: Tipografia Della Pace, 1876-77.

Burton, Edwin H., D.D., F.R.Hist.S., Canon of Westminster Cathedral, Sometime President of St. Edmund's College, Old Hall, Herts., and Nolan, Edmond, M.A., Hon. D.Litt., Canon of Westminster Cathedral, Sometime Master of St. Edmund's House, Cambridge, eds. *The Douay College Diaries: The Seventh Diary 1715-1778 Preceded by a Summary of Events 1691-1715.* London: Catholic Record Society, 1928.

Byrne, Rev. P. and Smith, J. P. 'The Catholic Registers of Thurnham, Lancashire. 1785-1838' Contributed by Rev. P. Byrne and J. P. Smith. Historical Notes by Joseph Gillow. *Lancashire Registers III.* Catholic Record Society, Records Series, Vol. XX.

Census – Parish of Hutton Magna, 372, Ho. 107, 1246, 9th June 1841. Public Record Office.

Census – Parish of Hutton Magna, 543, Ho. 107, 2387, 6th April 1851. Public Record Office.

Charnock. *Pedigree of Charnock of Charnock and Astley.* (From Flower, St.

George, the Parish Registers, &c.).

Chetham Society. *Remains Historical & Literary connected with the Palatine Counties of Lancaster and Chester.* Published by the Chetham Society. Printed for the Chetham Society, 1845. Vol. V.

Dickinson, Joseph. 'Tenants of Her Grace the Dowager Duchess of Norfolk taken from a Fieldbook surveyed by Joseph Dickinson Anno 1733' in *Longer Sen a Miscellany.* Chipping Local History Society, December 1999.

Douai Bible. The New Testament of Our Lord Jesus Christ: Translated from the Latin Vulgate, diligently compared with the original Greek and first published by the English College at Rheims, A.D. 1582. London: Burns Oates & Washbourne Ltd.

Douai: *The Douay College Diaries – the Seventh Diary 1751-1778.* London: Privately printed for the society [the Catholic Record Society] by Titus Wilson & Son, Kendal.

Dunkirk: *The Names of all the Professed Religious: As also the Annivesary [sic] Days of their Confessors, Pensioners, Boarders and Servants.* Dunkirk, 1652.

Emden, A. B. *A Biographical Register of the University of Oxford AD 1501-1540.* Oxford: Clarendon Press, 1974.

Emden, Alfred B. *A Survey of Dominicans in England,* based on the ordination lists in Episcopal Registers (1268 to 1538), and having been compared with Father Gumley O.P.'s own large biographical collections concerning the Dominicans of the English Province. Rome: S. Sabina, Instituto Storico Domenicano,1967.

Estcourt, Very Rev. Edgar E., M.A., F.S.A.; and Payne, John Orlebar, M.A., eds. *The English Catholic Nonjurors of 1715: Being a Summary of the Register of Their Estates with Genealogical and Other Notes and an Appendix of Unpublished Documents in the Public Record Office.* London: Burns & Oates, 1885.

Foster, Joseph. *Alumni Oxonienses* 1510-1714. Vol. II. Oxford: Parker & Co., 1891.

Foster, Joseph, ed. *The Visitation of Yorkshire, made in the Years 1584/5, by Robert Glover, Somerset Herald; to which is added: The subsequent Visitation made in 1612, by Richard St. George, Norray King of Arms, with Several Additional Pedigrees, including 'The Arms Taken out of Churches and Houses at Yorkshire Visitation, 1584/5,' 'Sir William Fayrfax' Book of Arms,'* and other Heraldic Lists, with Copious Indices. Privately printed for the editor, Joseph Foster, 21, Boundary Road, St. John's Wood, London, N.W. 1875.

Gardner, Norman. *Lancashire Quarter Sessions Records:* Register of

Recusants 1679. Edited with an introduction by Norman Gardner. Wigan: North West Catholic History Society, 1998.

Gooch, Leo., ed. *The Revival of English Catholicism: The Banister-Rutter Correspondence 1777-1807*. Wigan: North West Catholic History Society, 1995.

Hamilton, Dom Adam, O.S.B., edited with notes and additions, *The Chronicle of the English Augustinian Canonesses Regular of the Lateran, at St Monica's in Louvain, a continuation 1625 to 1644*. Vol. II. Edinburgh & London: Sands & Co. 1905.

Hansom, J. S. 'Catholic Registers of Linton-upon-Ouse, Near York, 1771-1840.' Contributed by Joseph Hansom. Historical notes by Joseph Gillow. Catholic Record Society, Records Series, Vol. XVII, Miscellanea.

'Catholic Registers of St. Mary's Domestic Chapel, Everingham Park, Yorkshire 1771-1884'. Contributed by Joseph Stanislaus Hansom with historical notes on the chaplaincy and mission by J. Gillow. Catholic Record Society, Records Series, Vol. VII, Miscellanea, 1909.

'The Catholic Register of the Rev. Monx Hervey alias John Rivett alias John Moxon: Oxfordshire 1729-30, London 1730-34, Yorkshire 1734-47, Montgomeryshire 1747-52, and London 1753-56'. Contributed by Joseph Stanislaus Hansom. *Catholic Record Society: Miscellanea IX*. London: printed privately for the Society at the Mercat Press Edinburgh, 1914.

'"Laity's Directory" Obituaries, 1773-1839'. Contributed by Joseph S. Hansom. *Catholic Record Society: Obituaries*. Publications of the Catholic Record Society Vol. XII. London: privately printed for the Society by Strowger and Son, Wigan, 1913.

Harris, P. R., ed. *Douai College Documents 1639-1794*. CRS Publications, Records Series, Vol. LXIII, 1972.

Hilton, J. A.; Mitchinson, A. J.; Murray, Barbara; and Wells, Peggy; editors. *Bishop Leyburn's Confirmation Register of 1687*. Wigan: North West Catholic History Society, 1997.

Hunnybun, William Martin. 'Registers of the English Poor Clares at Gravelines, Including Those Who Founded Filiations at Aire, Dunkirk and Rouen, 1608-1837'. Contributed by William Martin Hunnybun, M.A., annotated by Joseph Gillow. *Catholic Record Society: Miscellanea IX*. London: printed privately for the Society at the Mercat Press Edinburgh, 1914.

Lancashire Record Office, References QSP 493/18 and QSP 493/1.

Lancashire Record Office, Reference LCRS A15 33 containing 1662 survey of Chorley estates.

Langstaff, Elizabeth, 'Communicated Draft Scheme. No. 4874 Sealed 193. No. U. General Foundation – Elizabeth Langstaff's fund for the education of youths for the ecclesiastical state in connexion [sic] with St. Cuthbert's College Ushaw, in the county of Durham'.

Letters and Papers Foreign and Domestic of the reign of Henry VIII, preserved in the Public Record Office, the British Museum and elsewhere in England. Arranged and catalogued by James Gairdner, Vol. XIII, pt. 1. London: Her Majesty's Stationary Office, 1892.

Langstaff. T*he Langstaffs of Teesdale and Weardale: materials for a history of a yeoman family gathered together by George Blundell Longstaff, M.A., M.D., Oxon., F.S.A.* London: printed and published by Mitchell Hughes and Clarke, at the Wardour Press, in the County of London, Anno Dom. 1923.

Marriage Register of the Parish of Humbleton. (County and Archdeaconry Archive Office, Beverley.)

Mitchinson, Allan Joseph, ed. *The Return of the Papists for the Diocese of Chester, 1705.* Edited with an Introduction by Allan Joseph Mitchinson. Wigan: North West Catholic History Society, 1986.

Radcliffe. *Pedigree of Radcliffe, of Dilston and Derwentwater.* Compiled by: R. D. Radcliffe, M.A., Ch.Ch., Oxford, F.S.A., a Vice-President of the Historic Society of Lancashire and Cheshire. Old Swan, Liverpool. 24th February 1906.

Smith, J. E. 'The Catholic Registers of SS. Mary & James, Scorton, Garstang, Lancashire. 1774-1835'. Contributed by Joseph Edward Smith. Historical Notes by Joseph Gillow. *Lancashire Registers III.* Catholic Record Society, Records Series, Vol. XX.

Smith, J. P., ed., *Lancashire Registers II. The Fylde II.* Catholic Record Society Vol. XVI. London: Privately printed for the Society by J. Whitehead & Son, Leeds, 1914.

Smith, J. P. *'The Catholic Register of Nut Hill and Hedon in Holderness, East Riding of Yorkshire'.* Transcribed by J. P. Smith. Edited and Historical Notes by James Rae Baterden. Catholic Record Society, Records Series, Vol. XXXV, Miscellanea. London: Privately printed for the Society by Titus Wilson and Son, Kendal, 1936.

Trappes-Lomax, Richard. 'Archbishop Blackburn's Visitation Returns of the Diocese of York, 1735'. Contributed by Richard Trappes-Lomax. London: Catholic Record Society, Records Series, Vol. XXXII, Miscellanea, 1932.

SELECTED BIBLIOGRAPHY

Tunstall Pedigree. 'Pedigree of Tunstall, of Thurland Castle, Co. Lanc., and Wycliffe, Co. York' in *The Chronicle of the English Augustinian Cannonesses Regular of the Lateran, at St. Monica's in Louvain 1625-1644*. Vol. II. Edinburgh & London, 1906.

Ushaw College Diary. Durham: Ushaw College.

Ware, Samuel Hibbert. *Lancashire Memorials of the Rebellion, 1715.* Chetham Society Vol. V, 1865.

Wills: Botterill, Richard of Tathwell Hall, Louth, 22nd August 1908.
Daile, Adam of Hutton, 20th October 1712.
Daile, Sarah, the wife of Adam Daile, 10th November 1716
Dale, Adam of Wycliffe Grange, 11th March 1772.
Dale, Robert of Hutton Fields, 15th October 1790.
Dale, Robert of Hutton Hall, 7th October 1736.
Dale, Robert of Scorton, 11th November 1848.
Daniel, Jane of Euxton, 10th August 1780.
Daniel, Mary of Euxton, widow, 9th August 1798.
Daniel, Robert of Euxton House, Lancaster, 23rd March 1778.
Daniel, Thomas, 27th November 1769.
Daniel, William, 20th July 1777.
Ffoster, Robert of Charnock Richard, June 1613.
Foster, James of Charnock Richard, Husbandman, 3rd June 1622.
Foster, James of Thurnham, Clerk, 18th December 1821.
Foster, Jane of Charnock Richard, spinster, 25th August 1694.
Foster, John of Charnock Richard, Tanner, Inventory, May 1622.
Foster, John of Charnock Richard, Tanner, 28th July 1709.
Foster, Robert of Burton Constable, Yorks., 9th Dec. 1788.
Foster, Robert of Charnock Richard, Tanner, Administration, 26th July 1720.
Holden, John of 'Chippin Laund', 10th January 1631/2.
Holden, John of Laythgrim, Yeoman, 11th June 1694.
Langstaff, Marmaduke 'commonly called and known by the name of Wilson' of Appleton in Widderns, Co. Lanc., Clerke, 18th June 1798.
Leonard, John of Ryhill in Holderness, 11th January 1890.
Liddell, Thomas, Rev., of Egleston, Durham, Gentleman, 3rd August 1718.
Liddell, William of Wycliffe, and late of Brignall, 9th May 1742.
Parker, Richard of Charnock Richard, 2nd July 1623.
Penswick, Rev. Thomas of Wycliffe, 17th March 1791.
Robinson, Cecily of Newsham Grange, Spinster, 13th March 1860.
Robinson, James of Saddle Bow, 27th July 1753.

Robinson, John of Culgaith, 10th September 1625.
Robinson, John of Houlwick, Romaldkirk, 7th April 1724.
Robinson, John of Romaldkirk and Holdwick, 27th April 1545.
Robinson, John of Romaldkirk, 15th April 1569.
Robinson, Matthew, formerly of Hutton Fields, who died in Jamaica, 6th January 1795.
Robinson, Ralph of Hutton Fields, 5th May 1787.
Robinson, Richard of Parkend in Crostwhaite, 20th February 1713.
Robinson, Richard of Pecknall House, Romaldkirk, 19th September 1790.
Robinson, Robert of Holwick, 1682.
Robinson, Robert of Hutton Hall, 11th February 1805.
Robinson, Samuel of South Park, 24th September 1857.
Robinson, Thomas of Newsham Grange, 26th July 1946.
Robinson, Thomas of Nuthill, 3rd June 1873, the first Codicil, dated 1st May 1877.
Robinson, William of Holwicke, January 1591.
Robinson, William, a farmer of Holwick, on whose probate document Jane, wife of John Tinkler, his sister and only next of kin, acted as Administratrix 4th June 1794.
Robinson, William of Hutton Hall, 5th November 1884.
Robinson, William of Sadle Bow, Romaldkirk, 1693.
Tootell, Christopher of Clayton, gent., 16th August 1623.
Tootell, William de Whittle le Woods, yeoman, 13th November 1698.

Worrall, E. S. *Returns of Papists, 1767: Diocese of Chester.* Transcribed under the direction of E. S. Worrall. Catholic Record Society, Occasional Publications No.1, 1980.

Wycliffe: *Roman Catholic Registers of Wycliffe, Yorkshire, Christenings 1763-1809,* based on the note books of Rev. Thomas Penswick on loan to the Society of Genealogists, London, by the Catholic Record Society, typed and indexed by E. J. Erith, May 1989; also microfilm of the above Records, Public Record Office, Rolls Room, Non-Parochial Registers RG4 and RG6, p. 97, 416-4466. Microfilm.

SELECTED BIBLIOGRAPHY

Secondary Sources

Abram, W. A. 'The Holdens of Chaigley' in the *Preston Guardian*, 3rd October 1874, p. 7.

Anstruther, Godfrey, O.P. *The Seminary Priests: a Dictionary of the Secular Clergy of England and Wales 1558-1850*. Vol. 1. Elizabethan 1558-1603. St. Edmund's College, Ware; Ushaw College Durham, 1968.

The Seminary Priests: a Dictionary of the Secular Clergy of England and Wales 1558-1850. Vol. II. Early Stuarts 1603-1659. Great Wakering: Mayhew-McCrimmon, 1975.

The Seminary Priests: a Dictionary of the Secular Clergy of England and Wales 1558-1850. Vol. III. 1660-1715. Great Wakering: Mayhew-McCrimmon, 1976.

The Seminary Priests: a Dictionary of the Secular Clergy of England and Wales 1558-1850. Vol. IV. 1716-1800. Great Wakering: Mayhew-McCrimmon, 1977.

Aveling, Dom Hugh, Ampleforth Abbey. Post Reformation Catholicism in East Yorkshire 1558-1790. East Yorkshire Local History Society, E. Y. Local History Series No. 11, 1960.

Northern Catholics: The Catholic Recusants of the North Riding of Yorkshire 1558-1790. London: Geoffrey Chapman, 1966.

Aveling, J. C. H. *Catholic Recusancy in the City of York: 1558-1791*. C.R.S. 1970.

Baillie, G. H. *Watchmakers and Clockmakers of the World, 1951*.

Bamber, J. E. 'The Secret Treasure of Chaigley' in *Recusant History*. Vol. XVII, No. 4, October 1985, pp. 307-329.

Birtill, G. A., O.B.E., J.P. *Astley Hall Chorley*. Chorley: Nelson Brothers Printers.

Blundell, Dom F. O., O.S.B. *Old Catholic Lancashire*. Vol. I. London: Burns Oates & Washbourne Ltd., 1925.

Old Catholic Lancashire. Vol. II. London: Burns Oates & Washbourne Ltd., 1938.

Bolton, George L. 'Early Influences on Peter Worden 1.'

Bossy, John. *The English Catholic Community 1570-1850*. London: Darton, Longman and Todd, 1975.

Boyd, Michael J. ' "The Catholic Maecenas of his Age": Cuthbert Constable (c. 1680-1747) of Burton Constable' in *Burton*

Constable Hall: The Eighteenth and Nineteenth centuries. East Yorkshire Local History Society, 1998.

Boyd, M.J. and Jessop, L. 'A "truly amiable gentleman": new light on the life and work of Marmaduke Tunstall (1743-1790) of Wycliffe, North Yorkshire'. Archives of Natural History (1998) **25** (2): 221-236.

Brigden, Susan. *New Worlds, Lost Worlds: The Rule of the Tudors 1485-1603.* London: Penguin Books, 2001.

Bryson, Graeme. *Shakespeare in Lancashire also Shakespeare and the Gunpowder Plot.* Liverpool: Sunwards Publishing, Second edition 1998.

Caraman, Philip, S.J. *A Study in Friendship: Saint Robert Southwell and Henry Garnet.* Anand: X. Diaz del Rio, S.J., Gujarat Sahitya Prakash, P.B. 70, Anand, Gujarat, 388 001, India, 1991.

Caraman, Philip. *Henry Garnet 1555-1606 and the Gunpowder Plot.* London: Longmans, 1964.

Chambers, Mary Catherine Elizabeth of the Institute of the Blessed Virgin. *The Life of Mary Ward (1585-1645)* edited by Henry James Coleridge of the Society of Jesus. London: Burns and Oates, 1882, Vol. I and II.

Coleridge, Henry James, of the Society of Jesus, ed. *St. Mary's Convent, Micklegate Bar York [1686-1887].* London: Burns and Oates, Ltd., 1887. Appendix, 'An Alphabetical List of Young Ladies educated at St. Mary's Convent, York, from the year 1710 to 1886', p. 409.

Cooper, T. P. *With Dickens in Yorkshire.* London: Ben Johnson & Co. Ltd., 92, Fleet St. EC4, First Edition, 1923.

Conrad, Richard, OP *The Catholic Faith: A Dominican's Vision.* London: Geoffrey Chapman, 1994.

Culver, Bernard Joseph. 'Prelude to the Genealogy – mainly Culver.' A personal communication in my possession, 1971.

'Genealogical Geriatric and Generic Gambles'. Personal communication in my possession, 1971.

Darlington and Stockton Times, April 28th 1928, p. 4. 'Hutton Hall. History of the House and the Robinson Family'.

Daniel, Rev. John, C.A.D.A. & PRÆS. *Ecclesiastical History of the Britons and Saxons.* London: printed by Dove, St. John's Square, for Joseph Booker, New Bond Street, 1815.

Dickens, A. G. *The English Reformation.* London: BT Batsford Ltd., Second Edition 1989.

SELECTED BIBLIOGRAPHY

Dorland, W. A. Newman, A. M., M.D., F.A.C.S., *The American Illustrated Medical Dictionary*. 21st ed.; Philadelphia and London: W. B. Saunders Company, 1947.

Duffy, Eamon, *The Stripping of the Altars: Traditional Religion in England c. 1400 – c. 1580*. New Haven and London: Yale University Press, 1992.

Elton, G. R. *Reformation Europe 1517-1559*. London: Fontana Press, 1985.

Erickson, Carolly. *Bloody Mary: The Life of Mary Tudor*. London: Robson Books Ltd., 1995.

Fitzhugh, Terrick V. H. *The Dictionary of Genealogy* Fourth Edition revised by Susan Lumas on behalf of the Society of Genealogists. London: A & C Black, 1994.

Foster, Stewart, O.S.M. *Cardinal William Allen 1532-1594*. London: Catholic Truth Society, 1993.

Fryde, E. B.; Greenway, D. E.; Porter, S.; and Roy, I.; *Handbook of British Chronology*. London: Offices of the Royal Historical Society, University College, Gower Street, 1986.

Gillow, Joseph. *A Literary and Biographical History, or Bibliographical Dictionary of the English Catholics from the Breach with Rome, in 1534, to the Present Time*. 5 Vols. Bristol: Thoemmes Press 1999, reprinted from the 1885-1902 edition.

Gooch, Leo. *The Desperate Faction? The Jacobites of North-East England 1685-1745*. Hull: the University of Hull Press, 1995.

Gooch, Leo. *Paid at Sundry Times: Yorkshire Clergy Finances in the Eighteenth Century*. York: Ampleforth Abbey Archives, St. Laurence Papers X, 1997.

Grisar, Joseph, S.J. 'Mary Ward 1585-1645.' Reprinted from *The Month*. London: 31, Farm Street.

Guy, John. *The Tudors: A Very Short Introduction*. Oxford: University Press, 2000.

Haigh, Christopher. *The Last Days of the Lancashire Monasteries and the Pilgrimage of Grace*. Manchester: printed for the Chetham Society, 1969.

Elizabeth I. London: Longman, 1988.

Haile, Martin and Bonney, Edwin. *Life and Letters of John Lingard 1771-1851*. London: Herbert and Daniel, 21 Maddox Street.

Hardman, Sister Ann, S.N.D. English Carmelites in Penal Times. London: Burns Oates and Washbourne Ltd. 1936.

Haynes, Alan. *The Gunpowder Plot*. Stroud: Alan Sutton Publishing Limited, 1994.

Hill, Christopher. *The Century of Revolution 1603-1714*. London: Routledge, 1980.

Hilton, J. A. *Catholic Lancashire: From Reformation to Renewal 1559-199*. Chichester: Philimore & Co. Ltd., 1994.

Hollis, Crispin. *Catholic Oxford*. London: Catholic Truth Society.

Honan, Park. *Shakespeare: A Life*. Oxford: Oxford University Press, 1988.

Howard, Michael. 'Optimism is not Enough'. Peace and the Peace Movements (3). *The Tablet,* 9th January 1983.

Hughes, Philip. *Rome and the Counter-Reformation in England*. London: Burns Oates and Washbourne Ltd., 1942.

Le Fanu, James. Review of 'Book of the month' in *Journal of the Royal Society of Medicine*. Vol. LXXXXIV, No. 1, 2001, pp. 46-7.

Leys, M. D. R. Catholics in England 1559-1829: *A Social History*. London: The Catholic Book Club, 121 Charing Cross Road, W.C.2.

Lewis, Gwynne. *The French Revolution: Rethinking the Debate*. London and New York: Routledge, 1993.

Littlehales, Margaret Mary, I.B.V.M. *Mary Ward (1585-1645) A Woman for All Seasons: Foundress of the Institute of the Blessed Virgin Mary*. London: Catholic Truth Society, 1974.

Macaulay, Thomas Babington. 'A Jacobite's Epitaph' in *The Oxford Book Of English Verse 1250-1918*. Chosen and Edited by Sir Arthur Quiller-Couch. Oxford: the Clarendon Press, New Edition 1939, 1973 Reprint.

McCabe, Herbert, OP *The Teaching of the Catholic Church: A New Catechism of Christian Doctrine*. London: Catholic Truth Society, Publishers to the Holy See, 1985.

MacCulloch, Diarmaid. *Thomas Cranmer: A Life*. New Haven & London: Yale University Press, 1996.

Marius, Richard. *Thomas More*. London: Collins, Fount Paperbacks, 1986.

Mathew, David, Litt.D., M.A., F.S.A. *Catholicism in England 1535-1935: Portrait of a Minority: Its Culture and Tradition*. London: Special Edition for the Catholic Book Club, 121 Charing Cross Road, 1938.

Milburn, David, Licencié en Sciences Historiques (Louvain), Senior History Master, Ushaw College, Durham. *A History of Ushaw*

SELECTED BIBLIOGRAPHY

College: a Study of the Origin, Foundation and Development of an English Catholic Seminary with an Epilogue 1908-1962. Durham: the Ushaw Bookshop, Ushaw College, 1964.

Minskip, Dominic, B.A. (For Canon Moynagh). *A History of St. Wilfrid's Mission, York (1742 to the Present)*. York: 1989.

Moore, A. W., M.A., Trinity College, Cambridge. *Diocesan Histories: Sodor and Man*. London: Society for promoting Christian knowledge, 1893.

Nassan, Maurice, S.J. *Saint Robert Southwell Poet and Martyr*. London: Catholic Truth Society.

Newman, John Henry. *An Essay on the Development of Christian Doctrine*. London: Sheed and Ward, 1960.

Nicholls, Mark. *Investigating Gunpowder plot*. Manchester: Manchester University Press, 1991.

Norman, Edward. *Roman Catholicism in England from the Elizabethan Settlement to the Second Vatican Council*. Oxford: Oxford University Press, 1986.

O'Faolain, Sean. *King of the Beggars: A Life of Daniel O'Connell*. Dublin: Poolbeg Press, 1980.

Oliver, Mary, I.B.V.M. *Mary Ward 1585-1645*. London: Sheed and Ward, 1960.

Peacock, Edward, F.S.A. *A List of the Roman Catholics in the County of York in 1604*. London: John Camden Hotten, 74 & 75, Piccadilly, 1872.

Peniakoff, Lieutenant-Colonel Vladimir, D.S.O., M.C., Popski's Private Army. Oxford: Oxford University Press, 1991.

Pepler, Conrad O.P. In *New Blackfriars: a Monthly Review Edited by the English Dominicans*. Oxford: The Priory of The Holy Spirit, St. Giles, January 1985, p. 16.

Peters, Henriette. *Mary Ward: A World in Contemplation*. Translated by Helen Butterworth. Leominster: Gracewing, 1994.

Phillips, G. E. *The Extinction of the Ancient Hierarchy*. London and Edinburgh: Sands & Company, 1905.

Plowden, Alison. *Danger to Elizabeth: The Catholics under Elizabeth I*. London: Macmillan London Ltd., 1973.

Preston, Irena. 'Mary Shireburn – 8th Duchess of Norfolk' in *Longer Sen a Miscellany*. Chipping Local History Society, December 1999.

Pritchard, Arnold. *Catholic Loyalism in Elizabethan England*. London: Scolar

Press, 1979.

Quinlan, Father David. *The Father Postgate Story 1599-1973*. Alcester and Dublin: C. Goodliffe Neale

Rex, Richard. *Henry VIII and the English Reformation*. London: Macmillan Press, 1993.

The Theology of John Fisher. Cambridge: Cambridge University Press, 1991.

Robinson, James. *The Robinsons of North Kildare: 300 Years of Family History*. Dublin: McRobin Publications 1997.

Robinson, John Martin. *The Dukes of Norfolk: A Quincentennial History*. Oxford: Oxford University Press, 1982.

Robinson, J. R. "Charnock Richard to Cornamucklagh: a Bridge Across the Sea". *Catholic Ancestor*. Journal of the Catholic Family History Society, Vol. VII, No. 1, February 1998, pp. 27-31.

'Hutton Hall: A Nursery for the "Second Spring" '. *Catholic Ancestor*. Vol. VII, No. 3, November 1998, pp. 112-120.

'Of Roses White and Red: The Robinsons and Dales and a network of 18th century secular priests in Lancashire and Yorkshire'. *Catholic Ancestor*. Vol. VIII, No. 1, February 2000, pp. 13-24.

Roebuck, Peter. *Yorkshire Baronets 1640-1760 Families, Estates, and Fortunes*. Oxford: published for the University of Hull by the Oxford University Press, 1980.

Rokeby: An article about Rokeby Hall ©1986. Executors of R. A. Morritt Deceased, pp. 4-6

Scarisbrick, J. J. *Henry VIII*. New Haven and London: Yale University Press, 1997.

Singleton, Frank. *Hoghton Tower*. Hoghton Tower Preservation Trust, 1999.

Smith, Alan Gordon. *The Babington Plot*. London: Macmillan & Co. Ltd., 1936.

Smith, George D., *The Teaching of the Catholic Church: A Summary of Catholic Doctrine arranged and edited by Canon George D. Smith, D.D., Ph.D*. London: Burns Oates & Washbourne, Publishers to the Holy See, second edition, 1952.

Smith, Tom C., F.R.Hist.S. *History of the Parish of Chipping*. Preston: C. W. Whitehead, 125, Fishergate, 1894.

Starkey, David. *Elizabeth: Apprenticeship*. London: Chatto & Windus, 2000.

SELECTED BIBLIOGRAPHY

Sturge, Charles, M.A., Ph.D. (Lond.). *Cuthbert Tunstal: Churchman, Scholar, Statesman, Administrator.* London: Longmans Green and Co., 1938.

Tierney, M. A., *Dodd's Church History of England from the Commencement of the Sixteenth Century to the Revolution in 1688, with Notes, Additions, and a Continuation by The Rev. M. A. Tierney, F.S.A.* Vol. I. London: Published by Charles Dolman, No. 61, New Bond Street, 1839.

Trappes-Lomax, Michael. *Bishop Challoner. A Biographical Study Derived from Dr. Edwin Burton's 'The Life and Times of Bishop Challoner'.* London: Longmans, Green and Co., 1936.

Trevelyan, G. M. *Illustrated English Social History Vol. III.* London: Readers Union Longmans, Green and Co. 1958.

Victoria History of the County of Lancashire. W. Farrer and J. Brownbill. 8 Vols. London: 1906-1914.

Victoria History of London. Vol. I.

Victoria History of Yorkshire – North Riding. Vol. I.

Watkin, E. I. Roman *Catholicism in England from the Reformation to 1950.* London: Oxford University Press, 1957.

Waugh, Evelyn. *Edmund Campion.* London: Longmans, Green and Co., 1935.

Wedgwood, C. V. *The King's War 1641-1647.* London: Penguin Group, 1983.

Weld, John, D.L., J.P., of Leagram. *A History of Leagram: The Park and the Manor.* Manchester: printed for the Chetham Society, 1913.

Whelan, Dom Basil, O.S.B., M.A. *Historic Convents of To-day: the Story of the English Cloisters in France and Flanders in Penal Times.* London: Burns Oats and Washbourne Ltd., 1936.

Whitaker, Thomas Dunham. *An History of the Original Parish of Whalley and Honor of Clitheroe.* 4th edition revised by J. G. Nichols and P. A. Lyons, Vol. I. London, 1872.

Wilcock, Rt. Rev. Mgr. Canon Edward Wilcock, S.T.L., Prot. AP. *The Pearson Family and the Recusants of West Gilling.* Leeds: Published privately 1993.

Williams, Geoffrey Ainsworth. Locus Benedictus: *The Story of Whalley Abbey.* Whalley: Whalley Abbey Fellowship, 1995.

Williams, J. Anthony. *Sources for Recusant History (1559-1791) in English Official Archives – Recusant History,* Vol. XVI, No. 4. Catholic Record Society.

Worthington, Philip Michael. *The Worthington Families of Medieval England.* Phillimore, 1985.

INDEX

Ackworth Grange, Pontefract, 64
Act against the Pope's Authority of 1536, 135
Act of Annates, in March 1532, 132
Act of Restraint of Appeals, 1533, 133
Act of Settlement of 1701, 96
Act of Succession of March 1534, 133
Act of Supremacy of 1534, 134
Act of Supremacy of 1559, 120
Act of Uniformity of 1559, 13, 52, 120
Acts of 28 & 29 Elizabeth I, 13
Acts of 3 & 4 James I, 13
Aiskew, Bedale, 64
Aldbrough, 58, 62, 64, 83
Allen, Cardinal William, 19, 77, 119, 122, 123
Allen, Gabriel of Rossall, 124
Allen, Gabriel, his daughter married Thomas Worthington son of Richard, 124
Alnwick Castle, 112
Alsop, Ethel Jane, 63
American War of Independence, 77
Amounderness, 105
Ampleforth, 17, 22, 23, 34, 50
Ampleforth Journal, 17
Andertons of Euxton Hall, 88, 102
Anger, 115
Anglican Establishment, 120, 122, 128
Anne, Queen, 94, 96
Anti-Catholic Acts of 1571 and 1581, 123
Appellants, 119
Appleby, 154
Arden, Edward, 125
Arden, Mary, 125
Arras College, Paris, 105
Arrowsmith, Saint Edmund, 105, 106, 107
Arthur, Prince, 129

Ascot, 32
Ascot Bloodstock, 21
Ashton Hall, 88
Astley Hall, 103, 118
Atkinson, Joseph, 147
Atkinson, Mary, 148
Atkinson, William, 21
Aynho, 43

Babington Plot, 118, 119
Babington, Anthony, 118
Ballymurray, 52
Banister, Rev. Robert, 78, 88
Bar Convent, 60, 65, 66, 77, 115
Barberi, Father Dominic, 51
Barlow OSB, St Ambrose, 96
Barnard Castle, 23, 63, 144
Barnborough Hall, 92
Barningham, 160
Bassett, Major Chan, 27
Bastille, storming of, 73
Bates, Thomas, 113
Battle of the Boyne, 1690, 100
Beaumont College, 27
Bedingfield, Frances, 115
Bell, George of East Middleton, 145
Bell, J. President of the Royal College of Surgeons, Edinburgh, 44
Bell, Joseph, 68
Belmont, 48
Benedictine nuns at Dunkirk, 75
Benedictines, 34, 48, 75
Beverley, 45, 151,
Bewsher, Fred, 42
Bewsher, Helen, 42
Biesen, Doctor van den, 17
Bill of attainder, 136
Bilsborrow, Father, 15
Binbrook, 25
Bishop of Durham, Cuthbert Tunstall translated to Durham, 132
Bishop of London, Cuthbert Tunstall is appointed, 131
Bishop of Sodor and Man, John Holden OP is appointed, 131
Bishop Thornton, 64
Black Friars Convent in York, 129
Black Friars in London, 131, 136
Blainscough Hall, 124
Blenkin, Christopher, 51
Blenkin, Jane, 51
Boldren, Helen, 148
Boleyn, Queen Ann, 112, 133
Book of Common Prayer, 120
Booth, Edward alias Barlow, 96
Bossy SJ, Fr, 49
Botterill, Ada, 21
Botterill, Beatrice, 31, 32, 33, 40, 41, 43
Botterill, Douglas, 39, 40
Botterill, Ethel, 21
Botterill, Eveline, 25, 31, 32, 33, 39
Botterill, Gladys Margaret, 15, 16, 19, 32, 33, 37, 38, 39, 40, 41, 42, 43, 49
Botterill, Helen, 32
Botterill, Hilda, 15, 21, 39, 43
Botterill, Jack, 21
Botterill, Leonard S., 42
Botterill, Percy, 41, 42
Botterill, Richard of Tathwell Hall, 32
Botterill, Richard Oswald Filden, 32, 41
Botterill, Richard, 'Dickie', 38
Botterill, Susan Lilian, 39, 40
Bradley, Olive, an Ursuline nun, 48
Bradley, Philip, 48
Bramhill House, 39, 48
Brasenose College, 124
Bridewell prison, 126
Briggs, John President of Ushaw, 61
Brignall, 147, 154, 155
Brignall, the manor of, 153

INDEX

British Empire Medal, 22
Brough, 156
Brown, Ann second wife of Cuthbert Watson, 57, 58
Brown, Ann wife of Lawrence Thompson, 58, 83
Brown, Dorothy wife of Robert Dale of Hutton Fields, 58, 60, 67, 83, 145, 150
Brown, James, 58, 60, 71, 78, 83, 145
Brown, Richard, 57, 83
Brown, Sarah, 57, 58, 62, 71, 73, 83, 84, 145
Brown's Hotel, 26
Browne, Very Rev. Provost, 66
Buckfield, Cecil, 25
Buckle, Genny, 62
Budé, William, 134
Burstal Garth, 44
Burstwick, 27, 36, 37, 38
Burton Constable, 29, 58, 59, 85, 86, 87, 89, 110, 160
Burton Pidsea, 16, 29, 39, 42, 110,
Burton, a member of Tunstall's household, 134
Butler, Alban author of Lives of the Saints, 95

Calais, 120
Caldwell, 155
Cambridge, 24, 129, 130
Campeggio, Cardinal Lorenzo, 131
Campion SJ, Edmund, 124, 125
Cardwell, Michael, 27
Cardwell, Norman, 33, 34
Cardwell, Richard Norman, 22, 28, 31, 33, 34, 35, 48,
Carleton-juxta-Snaith, 153
Carlton, 22, 34
Carmelite, 31, 68
Carson, Mr Robert, 24
Carter, Katherine, 148
Catesby, Robert, 111, 112, 113, 125

Catherine of Aragon, Queen, 119, 129, 133, 135
Catholic exiles in Louvain, 123
Catholic Reformation, 116
Catholic Relief Act, 1778, 77
Catholic Relief Act, 1791, 78
cattle plague, 45
Cecil, Robert, 113
Cecil, William, 122
Challoner, Dr Richard, 85, 87, 89, 91, 92, 93
Chambers, Ann, 30, 60
Chambers, Ralph, 68, 152
Champney, Maria, 31
Chapel House, 87
Chapuys, Eustace Imperial Ambassador, 136
Charitable Trust called 'Elizabeth Langstaff's fund', 60
Charles I, King, 99, 102, 103, 104
Charles II, King, 96, 98, 99, 101
Charles V, Emperor, 130, 131, 135
Charnock Richard, 86, 91, 94, 95, 96, 102, 103, 118, 123, 124, 126
Charnock, Captain Robert, 103
Charnock, Dorothy wife of Richard Worthington, 124, 126
Charnock, James of Astley Hall, 103, 118, 119, 124
Charnock, James who took the Oath of Supremacy, 101
Charnock, John of Astley Hall, 118
Charnock, Robert of Astley Hall, 103
Charnock, Robert of Old Hall, 119
Cheapside, London, 125
Cheltenham, 15, 21, 32, 33, 43, 49
Cheltenham Ladies

College, 32, 43
Chichester-Constable, Blanche, 58
Chichester-Constable, Lieut. Colonel, 58
Chipping, 104
Chorley, Alexander, 106
Chorley, Mary wife of Ralph Holden, a recusant, 106
Chorley, Robert, 106
Chorley, William of Chorley, 106
Church of England, 16, 29, 41, 48, 52, 101, 134, 157
Church Papist, 102
Churchill, Winston, 22
Clayton, William, 148
Cleasby, 156
Cleveland, 98
Cliff Hall, 91
Clifford, Amy Wife of Cuthbert Tunstall/Constable, 59
Clifford, Charles, 59
Clifford, Mr, 58
Clifford, Thomas Hugh of Tixall, 58
Clitheroe Rural District Council, 50
Clockmakers' Co, 96
Cobb, Hannah, 30
Cohen, Miss, 21
Coldwell, 143
Colet, John, 129
Collier, James of Wycliffe, 145
Confirmations in Lancashire, 102
Congo, 48
Constable Bart., Sir Frederick Augustus Talbot Clifford, 63
Constable, Cecily wife of Francis Tunstall (1637-1713), 59, 85, 110, 160
Constable, John, 113
Constable, John 2nd Viscount Dunbar, 85
Constable, John of Hatfield, 113
Constable, Major T. C., 58
Constable, Marmaduke Cuthbert, 85, 86

211

Constable, Maude heiress of Hatfield, 113
Constable, Sir Robert of Flamborough, 113
Constable, Sir Thomas Aston Clifford, 110
Constable, Sir William, 113
Constables of Burton Constable, 110
Constantine, 132
Convocation at York, 5th May 1534, 133
Convocations of Clergy, Canterbury and York, 132
Conyers, Sir John of Hornby Castle, 130
Coppul, 124
Corbishly, Monsignor Charles, 22
Cornamucklagh, Co. Kildare, 92
Coronation of Ann Boleyn, 133
Cotswolds, 17, 42, 43
Cottam, a poet who celebrated in verse the sportsman Dr Penketh, 104
Cottam, John (preferred to spell his name Cottom), 124, 125
Cottam, Thomas, 124, 125
Cottingham, 39
Council of Nicaea, 132
County Westmeath, 51
Court of Correction, 94
Cradock, Christopher, 63
Cranmer, Thomas Archbishop of Canterbury, 133
Creswell SJ, Father, 111
Crichlow, Oliver alias Foster and John Gerard, 126
Crichlow, Ralph of Clayton-le-Woods, 105, 126
Crichlow, Richard alias Christopher Foster, 126
Crichlow, William alias John Foster, 105, 126
Cromwell, Oliver, 105

Cromwell, Thomas, 132, 135, 136
Crook Hall, 19, 52, 77, 79
Cross, Mr, 21, 23
Crostwhaite, 149
Crostwick, 157
Culgaith, 156, 158
Culver, Captain Bernard Joseph Francis, 27, 30
Culver, Major Herbert, 27
Cumberland, the Duke of, 85
Curtis, Susanna, 38

Daile, Adam of Hutton, 94, 142, 158, 159
Daile, Ann, 158
Daile, Dorothy, 94, 142, 158, 159, 160
Daile, Elizabeth, 94, 144, 160
Dale, Adam (probably Adam son of Robert Dale of Hutton Fields, 152
Dale, Adam of Colburin, 78
Dale, Adam the elder of Wycliffe Grange, 83, 84, 87, 94, 142, 143, 145, 160
Dale, Adam the younger of Wycliffe Grange, 60, 67, 73, 82, 86, 87, 160
Dale, Ann first wife of Cuthbert Watson, 57
Dale, Ann wife of James Brown, 58, 64, 71, 83, 145
Dale, Dorothy wife of Ralph Robinson of Hutton Fields, 83, 145, 146
Dale, Elizabeth sister of Adam Dale the elder of Wycliffe Grange, 143
Dale, Lawrence, 83, 142, 143, 160
Dale, Mary (? Tunstall, ? Liddell), 83, 97, 142, 143, 159, 160
Dale, Mary sister of Adam Dale the elder of Wycliffe Grange, 87, 143
Dale, Mary wife of William Liddell, 84
Dale, Robert of Hutton Fields, 83, 87, 144, 145, 146, 147, 148, 149, 150, 159
Dale, Robert of Hutton Hall, 83, 94, 97, 98, 142, 143, 159, 160
Dale, Robert of Scorton, 73, 76
Dale, Sarah daughter of Adam Dale the elder of Wycliffe Grange, 87, 145
Dale, Sarah wife of Adam Dale the elder of Wycliffe Grange, 64, 87, 160
Dales, 130
Dalton, 56, 148, 149, 150, 151, 159
Dalton fields, 82, 151
Dalton Rent, 151
Dalton, Colonel Thomas, 92, 103, 104
Dalton, Dorothy wife of Edward Riddell of Swinburne Castle, 104
Dalton, John, 91
Dalton, Robert, 91, 92
Dalton, Robert out in the '15', 97, 104
Dalton, Robert son of Colonel Thomas Dalton, 104
Dalton, William, 91
Daltons of Thurnham Hall, 89, 103
Daniel, Edward of Durton, 73, 86
Daniel, Jane, 89
Daniel, Mary wife of Robert Daniel of Euxton House, 89
Daniel, Rev. John, 73, 74, 77, 79, 86, 95
Daniel, Robert of Euxton House, 89
Daniel, Thomas, 87, 88, 89, 92
Daniel, William, 86, 88, 89

INDEX

Daniels of Durton, Alston, Whittingham, and Catteralls, 95
Davy, Arnold, 41
Davy, Margaret, 41
Dayles, Elizabeth of Romaldkirk, 150
Defence of the Seven Sacraments, 131
Defender of the Faith, 131
Dent, Ann wife of John Robinson of Crostwick died in 1569, 156, 157
Dent, Margaret daughter of Richard Robinson of Parkend, 150
Derby, 4th Earl of, 125
Dicconson, Bishop Edward, 85
Dickens, Charles, 16
Dickinson, Francis, 126
Diet of the Empire, 130
Digby, Sir Everard, 113
Dissolution of the monasteries, 135
Divine Right of Kings, 103
Dixon, Isaac, 29
Dixon, J., 30
Dominican, 53
Doncaster races, 26
Douai Martyrs, 19
Douai priests begin to return to England, 123
Douglass, Bishop John, 79
Doullens, 52, 74, 76
Dover, 126
Drypool, 29,
Duckworth, 106
Dudley, John Earl of Warwick, 128, 137
Dunbar, Lady widow of Sir Henry Cunstanle, 110
Dunkirk, 88
Durham, 15, 22, 45, 61, 66, 77, 137

Earl of Mar, 96
Easingwold Turnpike Co., 87
East Carlton Farm, 22
East Middleton, 145

East Yorkshire, 27, 29, 85, 94, 110, 129
Eaton, William, 63
Ecclesiastical Commission of the North, 114
Eddis, Major Lancelot Arthur, 58
Edinburgh University, 22, 25
Edward VI, King, 121, 137
Eeles, John, 62
Eeles, Tom, 25
Egton Bridge, Lythe, 84
Elizabeth I, Queen, 19, 111, 112, 118, 119, 120, 121, 122, 123, 125, 128, 133, 137
Elsternwick, 51
Elston, Elizabeth married in childhood to James Anderton of Euxton, 106
Eltham, 129
Ely, Humphrey, 125
Emmerson, Elizabeth daughter of Richard Robinson of Parkend, 150
England declares war on France, 1793, 75
English Benedictine house at Douai, 74
English Bible, 136
English Catholic Hierarchy, 121, 122, 128
English Catholic troops in the Netherlands, 111
English Civil War, 103, 115
English College at Douai, 18, 52, 73, 76, 79, 85, 86, 87, 91, 95, 98, 99, 104, 110, 119, 123, 124, 126
English College at Lisbon, 84, 95
English College at Seville, 92
English College at St Omer, 52
English Prayer Book of 1549, enforcement of use, 137
Epsom, 32

Erasmus, Desiderius, 129, 134
Essex, Robert Devereux, 2nd Earl of, 112
Euxton, 95, 102
Euxton Hall, 88
Execution of More and Fisher, 134
Eyre, Rev. Thomas, 77, 79

Farington, Alice, 103
Farington, Colonel William of Worden, 103
Fawkes, Guy, 16, 111, 112, 113
Fernyhalgh, 88, 95, 98
Fisher, John, 129, 131, 133, 134
Fisher, Joseph, 30, 52, 61
Fitzhugh, Terrick, 13
Flanagan, Rev. Christopher, 'Flanny', 16, 37, 38
Fleming, Mr, 24
Fletcher, 40
Flodden, Battle of, 130
Ford, James Francis 'Fritz', 26
Ford, Joan Ursula, 18
Ford, Monica, 27
Ford, Captain Philip Wright, 15, 18, 26, 30, 50, 156
Ford, Sarah Wright, 16, 29, 32, 43, 51, 110
Ford, Theresa, 27
Ford, Thomas of Burton Pidsea, 29, 110
Formby, George, 21
Foster DCL, Canon James, 41
Foster, Cecily, 71, 75, 76, 79, 82, 86, 87, 88, 89, 91, 94, 126, 130, 144, 150, 158, 160
Foster, Cecily sister of Robert Foster of Charnock Richard, 102
Foster, Elizabeth, Abbess Agnes Joseph OSC, 75, 76, 86, 88
Foster, Ellen sister of Jane Foster spinster, 102

213

Foster, Ellen wife of John Foster (1640-1710), 95, 101
Foster, Gennett wife of Edward Houghton, 102
Foster, Grace, Sister Grace Maria OSC, 75, 76, 86, 88
Foster, Helen wife of Thomas Daniel of Whittingham, 87, 96
Foster, James of Charnock Richard, will 1622, 105
Foster, James of Euxton House, 86, 88, 89, 104, 126
Foster, Jane spinster, 102
Foster, Jane widow, 105
Foster, John (c. 1640-1710), 94, 95, 101, 102, 103
Foster, John died 1622, 103, 119
Foster, Julia, 41, 43
Foster, Margaret wife of James Charnock, 103, 119, 124
Foster, Rev. James, 79, 80, 88, 89
Foster, Robert of Burton Constable, 85, 89, 160
Foster, Robert of Charnock Richard, 95, 96, 97, 101, 102, 105
Foster, Robert of Greenehurst, 118, 124, 125
Foster, Sarah, 80
Foster, William alias Charnock, 89, 91, 92
Foster, William of Burton, 71
Fotheringay Castle, 119
Francis I, King of France, 131, 135
Franciscan church at Greenwich, 129
French priests fleeing from the Revolution, 78

Garlick, Mr, 99
Garnet SJ, Henry, 111
Garton Manor, 21

Garton-on-the-Wolds, 21
Gatehouse prison, 126
George I, King, 96
George III, King, 77
George VI, King, 22
Gerard of Bryn, Lord, 73
Gerard of Ince, Miles, 105
Gerard SJ, John, 112, 115
Gerard, Alice of Euxton, 102
Gerard, Eleanor, wife of Richard Holden of Chaigley Hall born c. 1565, 105, 126
Gerard, Miles, martyr, 126
Gerard, Thomas, 112
Gibson, Bishop William, 77, 78, 79
Gibson, Mr, 158
Gibson, W. G., 29
Giffard, Bishop Bonaventure alias Joseph Leveson, 91
Gillow, John President of Ushaw, 64
Girlington, 94, 142, 143, 159, 160
Girlington, Nicholas, 130
Glover, Elizabeth, 62
Goldie, Mgr., 66
Gordon DD, Rev. Canon, 66
Gordon Riots, 78, 93
Gordon, Sir John Watson, 59
Grant, John, 113
Grant, John of Norbrook, 112
Gravelines, 119
Gravesend, 137
Gray's Inn, 87
Green Gates, 25, 43
Green, Sarah, 62
Greta Bridge, 22
Grey, Lady Jane, 128
Griffin, Rev. J., 42
Grimston, Ann, 111
Grimston, Thomas of Grimston Garth, 111
Guadalcanal, 92
Gully, John, 34, 79
Gunpowder Plot, 27, 101, 111

Haddon, Walter, 138
Hall, Henry, 62
Halsham, 110
Hancocke, Elizabeth, 129
Hancocke, Richard of Lower Higham, 129
Hapwood, Mrs, 41
Hardwick Hall, 86
Hardwicke Marriage Act, 29
Harrison, Alice, 'Dame Alice', 95
Harrison, Mrs of Burton Pidsea, 158
Haydock, William Rector of Standish, 101
Hayes MRCS, John J., 51
Hazlewood, 61, 88, 89
Hearth Tax Returns of 1673, 155
Hedon, 22, 25, 30, 34, 36, 38, 42, 45, 52, 60, 61, 62
Heighington, 142
Helmsley Quarter Sessions, 155
Henrietta Maria, Queen, wife of Charles I, 99, 102
Henry IV, King of France, 102
Henry VII, King, 131
Henry VIII and Ann secretly married in January 1533, 133
Henry VIII, King, 23, 92, 111, 112, 119, 121, 128, 129, 131, 132, 133, 134, 135, 136, 137
Henry VIII's marriage to Catherine asserted to be invalid, 133
Hervey, Rev. Monox, 84, 85
Hesketh, Sir Thomas of Rufford Old Hall, 125
Hewarth, 115
Hewick in Middlesex County Virginia, 157
Heyes, Emerentia, 'Eamy', 88
Heythrop College, 17, 18
Hodgson, M. E. E., 63
Hodgson, Rev. Francis, 98, 100, 160
Hoghton family of Park

INDEX

Hall, 103
Hoghton, Alexander of Hoghton Tower, 124, 125
Hoghton, John father of William Hoghton who married Elizabeth Dalton, 103
Hoghton, John of Mawdsley, 101
Hoghton, Lieut. Colonel William, 91, 103
Hoghton, Richard of Park Hall, 123, 124
Hoghton, Robert, 91
Hoghton, Thomas of Hoghton Tower, High Sheriff, 123
Hoghton, Thomas son of Thomas Hoghton the High Sheriff, 123
Hoghton, William born 1659 married Elizabeth Dalton, 95, 97, 103
Hoghton/Dalton, John, 91, 97, 104
Hoghtons, of Hoghton Tower, 125
Holbeach, 112, 113, 114
Holborn, London, 125
Holden OP, John, 129, 131, 132, 135, 136
Holden, Abbott Ralph, 135
Holden, Ann of Greengore, 104
Holden, Captain George, 104
Holden, Dr Henry, 104, 105, 110
Holden, Elizabeth daughter of Robert Holden of Leagram, 86, 104, 126
Holden, Elizabeth wife of John of Townleys, 104
Holden, Henry Royalist officer, 104
Holden, John of Chaigley Hall born c. 1425, 130
Holden, John of Chaigley Hall born c. 1495, 128, 129
Holden, John of Chipping Laund, 110
Holden, John of Townleys, 104
Holden, Margaret wife of Richard Holden of Crawshaw, 104
Holden, Ralph of Chaigley Hall born c. 1462, 129
Holden, Ralph, a recusant, 106
Holden, Richard of Chaigley Hall born c. 1535, 104, 128, 138
Holden, Richard of Chaigley Hall born c. 1565, 105
Holden, Richard of Crawshaw, 104
Holden, Robert of Holden, 105, 106, 107
Holden, Robert of Leagram, 86, 104
Holden, Thomas of Chaigley Hall born c. 1456, 129
Holden, Thomas of Greengore in Bailey born c. 1570, 104, 126
Holden/Elston, Robert a 'Papist', 106
Holdens of Chaigley Hall, 104, 107
Holdens of Holden in Haslingden, 105
Holderness, 22, 29, 111
Holderness Agricultural Society, 45
Holderness Hunt, 16, 33, 38
Holmes, head waiter at Brown's Hotel, 26
Holt SJ, T. G., 49
Holwick, 158
Holwick Fell, 82
Holy League, 129, 133
Holy Sacrifice of the Mass, abolishment of under penalty, 120
Home Guard, 34
Hornby, 79, 89
Hornsea, 38
Houghton, Cecily, 102
Houghton, Edward, 102
Houghton, John, 102
Howard, Cardinal Philip, 99
Howard, Charles 11th Duke of Norfolk, 130
Howard, Sir William Viscount Stafford, 98
Howard, Thomas 3rd Duke of Norfolk, 130, 133, 135, 136
Howard, Thomas Earl of Surrey, 130
Huddleston OSB, John, 99
Huguenot, 32
Hull, 22, 25, 29, 36, 44, 45,
Humbleton, 29, 51,
Hunt, Elizabeth, 62
Hutton, 154
Hutton Hall, 26, 27, 29, 49, 56, 57, 58, 59, 61, 62, 63, 67, 71, 72, 75, 82, 83, 84, 87, 91, 94, 98, 100, 104, 126, 130, 142, 143, 144, 149, 150, 151, 157, 159, 160,
Hutton Long Villers, 155
Hutton Longvillers, 155
Hutton Magna, 26, 29, 31, 57, 60, 62, 63, 71, 73, 76, 83, 91, 94, 121, 130, 144, 150, 151, 155, 157, 159
Hutton Rudby, 115
Hyde, Ann first wife of James II, 94, 99

India, 20
Ingelby, Sir John, 113
Ingleby, Francis, 113
Ingleby, Jane, 113
Ingleby, Sir William of Ripley, 113
Ingram, Elizabeth, 'Betty', 22, 36
Inquisition, 115
Institute of the Blessed Virgin Mary, 28
Ireland, 51, 154
Irwin SJ, Frank, 49
Isabella Naylor, 68
Isle of Man and the Reformation, 136
Isle of Wight, 27
Italy, 22, 36,

215

Jackson, Sarah, 148
Jacobite Rebellion of 1715, 89, 91, 96
Jacobite Rebellion of 1745, 92
Jacobite Rebellions, 23, 160
Jacobites, 85, 96, 97, 98
James I, King, 96, 102, 111, 112
James II, King, 94, 96, 98, 99, 102
James IV, King of Scotland, 130
Jersey, 48
Jesuits, 17, 18, 27, 35, 49, 119, 123, 124, 126
Johnson, Anna Maria, 30
Johnson, Carolus, 38
Johnson, Grace wife of William Penswick of Lytham, 73, 86
Johnson, John Richardson, 48
Johnson, Lawrence, 30, 38, 48, 86, 124, 125

Kate Greenaway, 40
Kelke, 106
Kendal, 27, 154, 156
Kennard, Canon Arthur, 53
Kent, 111
Kershaw, Mr Basil, 24
Keyes, Robert, 113
Keyingham, 34
King's Book of 1543, 136
King's Own Yorkshire Light Infantry, 33
Kingston Technical College, 25, 26
Kirby Ravensworth, 149, 150, 151, 159
Kirkby Ravensworth, 152
Kitchen, Bishop of Llandaff, 121
Kitchen, Edward chaplain at Lartington Hall, 73
Knavesmire, 99
Knockdomney, 51
Koch, Robert, 51
Kodak, 20
Kynaston, Charles, 43

Ladbroke Grove, 31
Lady Well, Fernyhalgh, 95, 98
Lamb, Richard, surgeon, 147
Lambeth Palace, 122, 138
Lancashire Jacobites, 92
Lancaster, 79, 88, 89, 103
Lancaster Castle, 106, 124
Lane Head, 31, 58, 60, 83
Langstaff, Anthony, 60, 78, 84, 88
Langstaff, Elizabeth, 44, 61, 88
Langstaff, Margaret wife of Anthony Langstaff, 60, 84
Langstaff, Robert alias Wilson, 88
Langstaff, Robert of East Layton, 84
Langstaff, Valentine alias Marmaduke Wilson, 88
Larkspur (prize puppy), 51
Lartington, 148
Lartington Hall, 73, 84
Lathom House, sieges of, 103
Layton, Frances wife of George Robinson of Cleasby, 156
Leagram Hall, 104
Ledwith, Catherine Josephine, 36, 49, 51
Ledwith, Thomas, 51
Lee SJ, Henry, 114, 115
Lee SJ, Roger, 114
Legatine Court in London, 131
Leicester Abbey, 132
Lelley, 51
Leonard, Elizabeth, 32
Leonard, Fanny of Ryhill Manor, 30, 32, 33
Leonard, John of Ryhill Manor, 32
Leviticus, 131
Leyburn, Bishop John, 95, 99, 102
Leyland, 119
Liddell, Catherine, Bridgettine Nun, 84
Liddell, Henry, 85

Liddell, Mary, Bridgettine Nun, 84
Liddell, Thomas, 84
Liddell, Thomas son of William, 84
Liddell, William of Wycliffe, 84, 85, 130
Linacre, Thomas, 129, 138
Lincoln, 42
Lingard, Doctor John, 19, 66, 76, 77, 79, 80, 89
Linton-upon-Ouse, 64, 87
Little Blake Street, York, 85, 87
Little Ease, 125
Littlebeck, 98
Littlemore, 18, 41, 51
Littlemore Hospital, 18
Littleton, Stephen, 112
London, 26, 137
London University, 34
Lonsdale Cup, 44
Lop Lane, York, 87
Lords of Scargill, Wycliffe and Hutton Magna, 121
Lostock, 102
Lougher, Ann, 103
Louis XII, King of France, 129, 133
Louis XVI, King of France, 74
Louth, 32, 41
Lovell, Tony, 22
Lower Slaughter, 15, 16, 25, 30, 38, 43, 49
Luftwaffe, 22
Luther, Martin, 130, 131
Lutheran princes, 135
Lyford Grange, 125
Lyth, Matthew, 98

Machell, Henry, 158
Madrid, 111
Magdalen Farm, 59
Magdalen House, 22
Maire family, 84, 86
Maire, Ann wife of Francis Maire, 86
Maire, Francis, 86
Maire, John, 87
Maire, Thomas of Lartington and Hardwick, 87

INDEX

Mallory, Ann, 113
Mallory, Jane, 111
Mallory, Sir William of Studley Castle, 111
Malone, Mr Wilfrid, 24
Malthouse, Francis, 148
Malton, 21
Man, Henry, 137
Manfield, 83, 94, 146, 159
Marian priests, 122
Marlborough, John Churchill, Duke of, 94, 96, 100
Marley, near Dunleer, in Co. Louth, Ireland, 83
Martial Law, 135
Marton, 37, 58
Mary I, Queen, 119, 120, 128, 131, 137
Mary, Queen, wife of King George V, 25
Mary, Queen, wife of King William III, 77, 99
Mass, prohibited in penal times, 72
Mathew, David, 78
Mayhew, Doris Mary, 31, 38,
Mayne, Cuthbert, the first of the Douai Martyrs, 123
McGoldrick, Mr 'Tommy', 24
McRobin, Daniel, 92
Meagher, Dr Robert, 45
Meagher, Fr, 45
Measures, Ann, 48
Measures, Robert, 48
Measures, Stanley, 48
Melling, Edward, 98
Messinger, John, 154
Middlesex County, Virginia, 157
Middleton, Robert Dale, 44
Milbank (of Barningham) family, 84
Mitchell, Anthony, 62
Mobreck Hall, 88
Modena, Mary of, second wife of King James II, 96
Monmouthshire, 27
Monteagle, Lord, 111, 112

Moore, Sarah, 60
More and Tunstall's friendship, 134
More, Bridget, 92
More, Sir Thomas, 23, 92, 128, 129, 130, 131, 132, 133, 134
More, Thomas of Barnborough Hall, 92
Morritt Arms, 22
Mortham estate, 153
Mottor [Motler] Very Rev. Canon, 66
Mountjoy, Lord, 120
Munich, 115
Murray, Bridget, 51

Napoleonic Wars, 78
National Farmer's Union, 36
Naylor, Isabella, 50
Netherwood, Euxton, 95
Netley Military Hospital, 42
Neville SJ, Edmund (heir to Earldom of Westmorland, 114
New Zealand, 59
Newbury, first battle of, 92
Newbury, second battle of, 92
Newby, 27
Newcastle, 21
Newman, John Henry, 24, 51, 56
Newsham, 82, 150, 151, 153, 155, 159
Newsham Grange, 23, 62, 63, 67, 68, 151, 152
Newsham House, 84, 152, 153
Newsham Tithe Apportionment, 152
Newsham, Charles, 61
Newsham, Henry, 52
Nicholas Postgate, 84, 98, 110, 113
Nine Articles of Henry VIII, 133
Ninety-five theses, 130
North Africa, 20
North Kildare, 91
North York Moors, 98, 110

North Yorkshire, 23, 26, 121, 156
Northallerton, 78
Northleach, 43
Northumberland, Henry Percy 9th Earl of, 112
Nottingham, 103
Nowell, Alexander, 138
Nowell, Ann, 138
Nun Monkton, 63
Nuthill, 25, 26, 29, 30, 31, 35, 36, 45, 49, 50, 51, 60, 62, 63, 110, 160,

O'Connell, Daniel, 52, 76
Oates, Titus, 98
Oath of Succession taken by Tunstall, 133
Oath of Succession, refused by Fisher and More, 133
Oath of Supremacy, 19, 101, 120, 126, 138
Oaths of Supremacy and of Uniformity, 85, 123
Old Hall Green, 79
Old Palace Yard, Westminster, 113
Old Testament, 132
Oldcorne SJ, Edward, 112
Ollerton Hall, 77
Oriel College, 19
Oscott College, 58
O'Shea, Josephine, 18
Oxford, 17, 18, 19, 27, 31, 33, 52, 53, 119, 124, 125, 129, 130
Oxford and Mortimer, Robert Earl of, 96

Padua, 129, 130
Palatinate of Durham, 137
Palestine Police, 20
Papal primacy, 132
Papists' Estates, 83
Park Hall, 91, 95, 96, 97, 102, 124, 125
Parker, Ann, 102
Parker, Cecily, 102
Parker, Elizabeth sister of Jane Foster spinster, 105

217

Parker, Elizabeth wife of Robert Foster of Charnock Richard, 95, 96, 102, 105
Parker, James nephew of Jane Foster, 102
Parker, Jane relict of Thomas Shirburne, second wife of Richard Holden, 138
Parker, Matthew Archbishop of Carterbury, 138
Parker, Richard brother-in-law of Robert Foster of Charnock Richard, 102
Parker, Robert of Browsholme Hall, 104, 138
Parry, Sir Thomas, 138
Parsons, William, 52
Patchelle, Mrs, 40
Paul SJ, Father, 18
Payne, Mr Bernard, 24
Peacock, Mary, 153
Pearson, Peter, 78
Pendle Forest, 129
Penketh, Dr Charles alias Rivers, 104
Penrith, 156
Penswick, Bishop Thomas, 73, 74
Penswick, John student at Douai, 73
Penswick, Mary, 73, 86
Penswick, Rev. Thomas, 67, 71, 73, 86, 88, 148, 160
Penswick, Thomas, steward, 73
Penswick, William of Lytham, 73, 86
Percy, Thomas, 112, 113
Persons SJ, Robert, 124
Petre, Edward, 79
Philip II, King of Spain, 119, 120
Philip III, King of Spain, 111
Phillippe Esq., Hen., 153
Phillippe, Agnes, 153
Phillippe, James of Barningham, 153
Pilgrimage of Grace, 113, 135

Pinder, Robert, 44
Pinkney, Margaret daughter of James Robinson of Saddle Bow, 149
Ploughland Hall, 27, 29, 111, 114
Plowden, Alison, 125
Plunkett, Oliver Primate of Ireland, 98
Pole, Cardinal Reginald, 137
Poor Clare Convent at Gravelines, 114
Poor Clare Convents at Aire, Dunkirk and Rouen, daughter houses of Gravelines, 75
Poor Clare nuns in Dunkirk, 75
Poor Clares in St Omer, 114
Poor Clares settled at Churchill Wood, 76
Pope Clement VII, 131, 133
Pope John XXIII, 141
Pope Julius II, 129, 131
Pope Leo X, 131
Pope Paul III, 135
Pope Pius V's, Bull Regnans in Excelsis, 123
Pope Urban VIII, 115
Popish Plot of 1678, 98, 99, 101
Popski's Private Army, 20
Porter, Elizabeth, 44
Postgate, Nicholas, 99, 100
Potter, Elizabeth, 157
Potts, Luke, 84, 85
Poulton-le-Fylde, 92, 124
Praemunire, Statute of, 131
Pratt, William, 61
President of the Council of the North, Cuthbert Tunstall became, 132
Preston, 97, 105
Priest's hiding hole, 72
Priesthood, training for at Ushaw, 23
Prince Bishop of Durham, 121

Prince Rupert, 103
Protestant succession, 94
Protestation of Allegiance to Queen Elizabeth, 119
Pullen, John, 112

Quarter Sessions Court at Wigan, 1679, 101
Quicklime (racehorse), 32

Radcliffe Bart., Sir Everard, 53
Radcliffe Infirmary, 27
Radcliffe OP, Timothy, 53
Radcliffe, Edward 2nd Earl of Derwentwater, 96
Radcliffe, James 3rd Earl of Derwentwater, 96, 97
Rawstorne, justice of the peace, 105
Recusancy, fines for, 120, 124
Recusants, 13, 78, 92, 94, 101, 104, 105, 106, 124, 144, 155, 159
Redbarns, 98
Reformation, 27, 91
Reformation Parliament, 132
Relief Act of 1791, 52
Return of Papists for the Diocese of Chester, 1705, 95
Return of Papists for the Diocese of Chester, 1767, 86
Rheims, 126
Richardson, Captain Richard, 92
Richardson, James, 31
Richardson's farm, 159
Richinson, Sarah wife of Adam Daile of Hutton, 100, 142, 158, 159
Richmond, 61, 77, 86, 113, 151
Richmond Quarter Sessions, 154, 155
Riddell of Swinburne Castle, 104

INDEX

Riddell, Ann, 85
Riddell, Sir Thomas of Fenham, 85
Riddell, Thomas out in the '15', 97, 104
Ripley Castle, 64
Rising of the Northern Earls, 1569, 123
River Tees, 66, 156, 157
Robertson, of Struan, 154
Robespierre's Reign of Terror, 74, 75
Robinson, Robert of Rokeby Close, 67
Robinson M. Phil., James, 92
Robinson MP, John, 154
Robinson Richard of Parkend, 156
Robinson SJ, James, 49
Robinson SJ, Jim, 49
Robinson SJ, Robert, 49, 50, 68
Robinson William of Saddle Bow died in 1693, 156
Robinson, 'a child' of Robert son of William Robinson of Holwick died in 1591, 157
Robinson, Adam brother of Robert Robinson of Hutton Hall, 158, 160
Robinson, Agnes, 'Little Agnes', 27, 38
Robinson, Ann daughter of Robert Dale of Hutton Hall, 87
Robinson, Ann daughter of Robert Robinson of Hutton Hall, wife of Ralph Chambers, 64, 68, 71, 150, 152
Robinson, Ann daughter of Robert Robinson of Rokeby Close, 68
Robinson, Ann daughter of William Robinson above Smallways, 149
Robinson, Ann sister of Robert Robinson of Hutton Hall, 158
Robinson, Anthony son of Ralph Robinson of Hutton Fields, 83, 145, 146

Robinson, Arthur, 22, 27, 36, 37, 38, 158
Robinson, Catherine Mary, 26, 31, 68
Robinson, Cecily daughter of Robert Robinson of Rokeby Close, 68
Robinson, Cecily Mary, 30, 51
Robinson, Cecily of Stonely, 48
Robinson, Cecily of Newsham Grange, 30, 64, 67, 71, 87, 150, 152
Robinson, Christopher of Rappahannak, 157
Robinson, Diana, 22
Robinson, Dr Edward, 25, 31, 48
Robinson, Dr Henry, 22, 23, 26, 44, 45, 62
Robinson, Dorothy daughter of Robert Robinson of Hutton Hall, 64, 71, 87, 152, 158
Robinson, Dorothy granddaughter of Ralph Robinson of Manfield, 146
Robinson, Dorothy Mary, 39
Robinson, Dr Richard, Archbishop of Armagh, 83, 154
Robinson, Dr Robert, 63
Robinson, Edith Monica, 44
Robinson, Eleanor daughter of William Robinson above Smallways, 149
Robinson, Elizabeth daughter of Robert Robinson of Rokeby Close, 68
Robinson, Elizabeth wife of John Robinson of Holwick died in 1724, 157, 158, 159
Robinson, Elizabeth wife of Lawrence Thompson of South Park, 58, 60, 64, 71, 83, 87, 152

Robinson, Elizabeth wife of Ralph Robinson of Manfield, 146
Robinson, Elizabeth wife of Robert Robinson of Holwick died in 1682, 157
Robinson, Eveline Mary 'Daisy', 22, 33
Robinson, Eylnor daughter of Robert Robinson of Holwick died in 1682, 157
Robinson, Frances daughter of William Robinson above Smallways, 84, 148
Robinson, Frances wife of John Robinson a gardener, 155
Robinson, Francis James son of William Robinson of Hutton Hall, 63
Robinson, George Francis, 44
Robinson, George of Cleasby, 156
Robinson, George of Holwick, 157, 158
Robinson, George son of Richard Robinson of Pecknall House, 147, 148
Robinson, George son of William Robinson above Smallways, 84, 148, 149, 153
Robinson, Harry Francis Nixon, 22, 23, 45
Robinson, Henry Francis of Burstal Garth, 22, 44
Robinson, James Francis, 22, 25, 38, 43, 44, 61
Robinson, James of Saddle Bow, 149, 150, 156, 157, 158, 159
Robinson, James who died aged 5 years, 57
Robinson, Jane daughter of Richard Robinson of Pecknall House, 147
Robinson, Jane daughter of William Robinson above Smallways, 149

219

Robinson, Jane wife of George son of William Robinson above Smallways, 153
Robinson, Jennet spinster, 155
Robinson, Jennet wife of Thomas Robinson recusant, 155
Robinson, John (1778-1846) of South Park, 60
Robinson, John Bishop of Bristol, 157
Robinson, John grandson of Ralph Robinson of Manfield, 146
Robinson, John of Cleasby, 157
Robinson, John of Crostwick died in 1545, 156, 157, 158
Robinson, John of Crostwick died in 1569, 156, 157
Robinson, John of Culgaith, 158
Robinson, John of Holwick died in 1724, 157, 158, 159
Robinson, John son of James Robinson of Saddle Bow, 149, 150
Robinson, John son of Ralph Robinson of Hutton Fields, 146
Robinson, John son of Richard Robinson of Pecknall House, 147, 148
Robinson, John William, 'Shaun', 49
Robinson, John, a Douai martyr, 19
Robinson, Margaret daughter of Richard Robinson of Pecknall House, 147
Robinson, Margaret wife of William Robinson a yeoman, 155
Robinson, Margaret wife of William Robinson of Saddle Bow, 156
Robinson, Maria of South Park, 31, 60, 152

Robinson, Mary Agnes, 25, 26, 30, 32, 38, 45, 48
Robinson, Mary Ann, 30, 48
Robinson, Mary Ann who died aged 15 years, 57, 61, 152
Robinson, Mary daughter of Richard Robinson of Pecknall House, 147
Robinson, Mary daughter of William Robinson above Smallways, 84, 149
Robinson, Mary Elizabeth daughter of William Robinson of Hutton Hall, 63
Robinson, Mary Helen, 39
Robinson, Mary of Stonely, 48
Robinson, Mary widow, 147, 148, 149, 150
Robinson, Mary wife of William Robinson above Smallways, 84, 144, 148, 149, 153, 154
Robinson, Matthew of Field House, 143, 144, 145, 159, 160
Robinson, Matthew who died in Jamaica, 83, 145, 146
Robinson, Mr Matthew at Ravensworth, 155
Robinson, Mrs at Kirby Hill, 155
Robinson, of 'The White House', 154
Robinson, Old Mary sponsor to George son of William Robinson above Smallways, 148, 149, 150
Robinson, Ralph Citizen and Haberdasher of London, 153, 154
Robinson, Ralph of Hutton Fields, 83, 144, 145, 146, 149, 150, 156, 157, 158, 159
Robinson, Ralph of Manfield, 146, 159
Robinson, Ralph son of

Ralph Robinson of Hutton Fields, 145, 146
Robinson, Richard grandson of Ralph Robinson of Manfield, 146
Robinson, Richard of Crostwick, 156, 157
Robinson, Richard of Louth, 59
Robinson, Richard of Parkend, 149, 150
Robinson, Richard of Pecknall House, 83, 144, 147, 148, 149, 150, 156, 157, 158, 159
Robinson, Richard son of Richard Robinson of Pecknall House, 147
Robinson, Richard son of William Robinson above Smallways, 84, 148
Robinson, Richard sponsor to George son of William Robinson above Smallways, 148, 149
Robinson, Richard, 'Dick', 16, 31, 38,
Robinson, Robart witness to Robert Dale's will, 142
Robinson, Robert eldest son of Thomas Robinson of Hutton Hall, 58, 61
Robinson, Robert grandson of John Robinson of Culgaith, 158
Robinson, Robert grandson of William Robinson above Smallways, 84, 152
Robinson, Robert of Holwick died in 1682, 157
Robinson, Robert of Hutton Hall, 26, 49, 67, 71, 73, 82, 83, 86, 87, 142, 144, 146, 149, 150, 151, 152, 155, 156, 157, 158, 159, 160
Robinson, Robert of

INDEX

Hutton Hall takes modified Oath of Allegiance, 77
Robinson, Robert of Rokeby Close, 68, 71, 82, 87, 151, 152, 158
Robinson, Robert son of William Robinson of Holwick died in 1591, 157
Robinson, Rose daughter of William Robinson above Smallways, 84, 148
Robinson, Ruth wife of Richard Robinson of Pecknall House, 144, 147, 149
Robinson, Samuel of South Park, 60
Robinson, Sarah, 26, 30, 52, 68, 71
Robinson, Sir Thomas, 83
Robinson, Sythe wife of William Robinson of Holwick died in 1591, 157
Robinson, Teresa of Sproatley Grange, 44
Robinson, Thomas Botterill, 22, 35
Robinson, Thomas Ford, 22, 23, 25, 27, 28, 31, 32, 34, 36, 37, 38, 39, 42, 49, 57, 59, 61, 156, 160
Robinson, Thomas Ford, died as an infant, 31
Robinson, Thomas of Hutton Hall, 26, 30, 56, 62, 64, 67, 71, 73, 80, 82, 83, 145, 151, 152
Robinson, Thomas of Newsham Grange, 23, 62, 72
Robinson, Thomas of Nuthill, 16, 25, 26, 29, 43, 45, 50, 51, 59, 61, 62, 68, 110, 115, 152
Robinson, Thomas of Ovington, 50, 68
Robinson, Thomas of Rokeby Hall, 83
Robinson, Thomas of Walworth, 142
Robinson, Thomas recusant, 155
Robinson, Thomas son of John Robinson of Culgaith, 158
Robinson, Thomas son of William Robinson above Smallways, 149
Robinson, Thomas witness to Robert Dale's will, 142
Robinson, Thomas, 'Tommy', 16, 39
Robinson, Timothy Paul, 49
Robinson, Tom brother of Robert Robinson of Hutton Hall, 142, 158
Robinson, William above Smallways, 84, 144, 148, 149, 150, 153, 154, 156, 157, 158, 159
Robinson, William Francis died in infancy, 44
Robinson, William Gordon, 15, 19, 20, 25, 42, 44, 45, 48
Robinson, William Joseph, 15, 16, 18, 25, 38, 51
Robinson, William of Barningham, 155
Robinson, William of Crostwick, 156
Robinson, William of Holwick, 157, 158, 159, 160
Robinson, William of Holwick died in 1591, 157, 158
Robinson, William of Hungry Hall Farm, 82
Robinson, William of Hutton Closes, 154
Robinson, William of Hutton Hall, 30, 43, 56, 59, 61, 62, 63, 68, 151, 152, 158
Robinson, William of Kendal, 154
Robinson, William of Rokeby, 153, 154
Robinson, William of Saddle Bow died in 1693, 158
Robinson, William of White Hall, 154
Robinson, William Robinson son of William Robinson of Holwick died in 1591, 158
Robinson, William son of George Robinson of Newsham, 153
Robinson, William son of Robert Robinson of Holwick died in 1682, 157
Robinson, William son of William Robinson above Smallways, 84, 148
Robinson, William son of William Robinson of Hutton Hall, 63
Robinson, William who bought Rokeby, 83
Robinson, William yeoman, 111, 113, 154
Robinson, Wyllm of Crostwick, 157
Robinsons above Smallways, 153
Robinsons of Hutton Hall, 91, 110, 153
Robinsons of North Kildare, 91
Robynson, Leonard of Kirkby Ravensworth, 155
Rochester, 126
Rockliff, Frances Sarah, 'Fanny', 30
Rockliff, Helen, 39
Rockliff, Henry Aloysius, 30
Rockliff, James Robert, 30
Rockliff, Mary Alice, 'Clytie', 30
Rokeby, 27, 154
Rokeby Hall, 83
Rokeby, Sir Thomas, 83, 153
Rokeby, the manor of, 153
Romaldkirk, 147, 148, 149, 150, 156, 158
Roman Catholic Emancipation Act of 1829, 52

Rome, 115, 131, 132
Rome, Henry VIII's break with, 132
Rookwood, Ambrose, 113
Roper, Charles, 62
Roscoe, William nephew of Cecily Houghton, 102
Rowell, Mary, 62
Royal Air Force, 25
Royal Supremacy, 133, 137
Royalist cavalry, 103
Rudston, Nicholas of Hayton, 111
Rudston, Ursula, 111, 113
Rutter, John, 84, 153
Rutter, Mary, 153
Ryther, Alice, 111
Ryther, Sir William, 111

Sacraments, 135
Sanderson, Rev. Thomas, 77
Savage, Agnes wife of John Robinson of Crostwick died in 1545, 156
Scargill, 85
Scargill, Alice, 130
Scargill, Sir Robert, of Scargill in Yorkshire, 130
Scotland, 158
Scottish Highlands, 77
Sculcoates, 44
Second Vatican Council, 42, 141
Secular priests, 23
Sedgley Park, 64
Serionne, George de, 16, 19
Seymour, Edward Duke of Somerset, 128, 137
Shakespeare, William, locally called Shakeshafte, 125
Shaw, Catherine, 92
Shaw, Rev. Gerard, 92, 93
Shirburne, Jane relict of Thomas Shirburne, 104
Shirburne, Mary Duchess of Norfolk, 104

Shirburne, Richard of Stonyhurst, 104
Simba, 48
Sir Picton (racehorse), 21
Skeffling, 44
Sledmere, 32, 34
Smallways, 84, 149, 153
Smith, Bishop James, 66, 94, 99, 100
Smith, Mr Alfred, 24
Somerset House, 99
Somerville College, 38
Sorbonne, 17, 105
South Park, 31, 60, 67, 68, 152
Southwell SJ, Robert, 118, 119, 120
Southworth, Saint John, 106
Spanish Armada, 119
Spanish Chapel, London, 93
Spanish Netherlands, 123
St Aloysius' Church, 18, 38
St Charles Borromeo, 74
St Cuthbert, 22
St Giles, London, 118
St John, Miss, 33
St Mary and St Joseph, 30, 36
St Mary's Catholic Church at Wycliffe, 57
St Mary's Church, Cricklade, 129
St Mary's Church, Hutton Magna, 23
St Mary's Hall, Oxford, 19, 122
St Michael le Belfry, York, 87
St Patrick's, Leeds, 64
St Paul's Churchyard, 113
St Peter's School in York, 112
St Thomas Becket, 74
St Thomas' shrine at Canterbury, 136
St Thomas' Hospital, 26
St Vedast, 41
St Wilfrid's York, 85, 87
Stacpoole OSB, Alberic, 53
Stanley, Edward 3rd Earl of Derby, 104
Stanley, Lady Ann, 104

Stanley, Sir William, 111
Stanwick, 155
Stapleton, Gregory, 78
Statute of 27 Elizabeth, treason to be ordained overseas, 99
Stephenson, William son-in-law of Richard Robinson of Pecknall House, 147
Stickney, Maria, 31
Stickney, William, 31
Stokesley, John Bishop of London, 134
Stonely, 48
Stonyhurst, 18, 23, 25, 35, 36, 38, 49, 50, 68, 126
Stonyhurst Hunt, 104
Story, Rev. Arthur, 77
Stourton, Catherine, 104
Stourton, Lord, 77
Stourton, Lord Charles, 104
Stow-on-the-Wold, 16
Strange, Lord, 125
Struan, 154
Stuart monarchy, 94
Stuart, Charles Edward, 'Bonnie Prince Charlie', 85
Stuart, Mary, Queen of Scots, 112, 118, 119, 123
Stuart, Prince James Edward, 96, 99, 104
Supreme Head of the English Church, Henry VIII seeks the title, 132
Sutton, Surrey, 25
Swinburn, Fr Joseph, 52
Sykes, Sir Richard, 34
Syon Abbey, 134

Tanhouse Farm, Charnock Richard, 95
Tank Corps, 20
Tate DD, Robert, 15, 52, 61, 62
Tathwell Hall, 21, 32, 39
Ten Articles of July 1536, 135
Territorial Army, 22
Tesimond SJ, Oswald, 111, 112

INDEX

Test Act, 1673, 101
The Robinsons of North Kildare, 92
Thirsk Quarter Sessions, 83, 155
Thompson, Ann, 60, 64, 152
Thompson, Canon John, 60, 64, 66, 67, 111, 115
Thompson, Canon Robert, 56, 60, 63, 64, 67, 68, 151
Thompson, Frances Mary, 68
Thompson, Henry of Newsham, 148
Thompson, Henry, blacksmith, 148
Thompson, Henry, son of a Farmer, 148
Thompson, Lawrence of Lane Head, 58
Thompson, Lawrence of South Park, 60, 67, 83
Thompson, Rev. James, 60, 64
Thompson, Richard, 60
Thompson, Richard grand vicar in Lancashire, 74
Thompson, William, 31, 60, 64, 67, 68, 152
Throckmorton, Mary wife of Edward Arden, 125
Throckmorton, Sir George of Coughton Court, 111, 125, 134
Thurnham Hall, 79, 89, 91, 92, 97, 103, 104
Thurnham mission, 89
Thurnham, Catholic chapel, 89
Tinkler, Alice daughter of James Robinson of Saddle Bow, 149
Tobruk, 22
Todd, Sheila, 34
Tompion, Thomas, 96
Tootell, Christopher, 95, 98
Tootell, Hugh alias Charles Dodd, 95
Tootell, Hugh steward to Marmaduke Tunstall, 64, 83, 87, 160

Tootell, Katherine, 105, 126
Tootell, Margaret granddaughter of John Foster, 95
Tootell, Mrs wife of Hugh Tootell, 87
Tootell, Oliver and Elizabeth of Chorley, 105, 126
Tootell, William, 95
Topcliffe, Richard, 120, 126
Tournai, 92
Tower Hill, 97
Tower of London, 97, 111, 113, 115, 120, 125, 133, 137
Trafford SJ, Robert de, 18, 50
Trappes, Francis, 52
Treasons Act, 1534, 134
Tremouill, Charlotte de la, Countess of Derby, 103
Tresham, Elizabeth, 112
Tresham, Francis, 111, 113, 125
Tudhoe, 77
Tudor, Lady Mary, 96
Tudor, Margaret, 130
Tunstall Esq., Francis of Barningham, 113, 154
Tunstall Knt., Sir Marmaduke of Thurland Castle and Scargill, 130
Tunstall, Christina, Bridgettine Nun, 84
Tunstall, Cuthbert, 66, 121, 122, 129, 130, 131, 132, 133, 134, 135, 136, 137, 138
Tunstall, Francis (1637-1713), 59, 85, 94, 99, 100, 113, 159, 160
Tunstall, Francis of Ovington, 85, 160
Tunstall, Francis of Thurland in Lancashire, 130
Tunstall, Marmaduke (1672-1760), 84, 85, 160
Tunstall, Marmaduke of Scargill and Wycliffe died 1657, 130
Tunstall, Mary sister of Francis Tunstall (1637-1713), 85
Tunstall, Mary, Bridgettine Nun, 84
Tunstall, Peter Bryan, 85, 87
Tunstall, Sir Brian 'The stainless knight', 130
Tunstall, Thomas of Barningham, 159
Tunstall, Thomas of Thurland in Lancashire, 121, 130
Tunstall, Thomas, ? Thomas Tunstall of Barningham, 159, 160
Tunstall, William Jacobite Quartermaster-General, 96, 97, 159
Tunstall, William of Scargill Castle, 160
Tunstall/Constable, Cuthbert, 85
Tunstall/Constable, Marmaduke Cuthbert, 96
Tunstalls of Wycliffe Hall, 84, 110
Tunstalls/Constables of Wycliffe and Burton Constable, 130
Turner SJ, F.J., 49
Tyburn, London, 125

Ugglesbarnby, 110
Ugthorpe, 84, 85
Unicorn, 16, 18
University College, 53
University of Wittenburg, 130
Ushaw, 15, 18, 19, 23, 24, 29, 30, 36, 38, 39, 44, 45, 48, 52, 60, 61, 62, 63, 64, 65, 67, 68, 79, 80, 88,
Usk, 104

Vane, 26, 27, 154
Vaux, Catherine, 111
Vavasour, Sir Walter, 61, 88
Venerable English

College at Rome, 86, 105, 126
Venice, 129
Virginia, 156, 157, 158

Walsh, Sir Richard Sheriff of Worcester, 112
Walshaw, Canon, 66
Ward, Francis, 59
Ward, Joseph of Tixall, 58, 59
Ward, Marmaduke of Mulwith, 113
Ward, Mary, 28, 75, 113, 114, 115
Ward, Miss Jessie, 19
Warham, William Archbishop of Canterbury, 130, 131, 132
Watson, Canon, 66
Watson, Cuthbert, 30, 35, 57, 58, 59, 61
Watson, Merryne, 84, 152, 153, 155
Watson, William, 57
West Layton, 27
Westend, 147
Westminster Hall, 125
Whalley, Cistercian Abbey, dissolution of, 135
Whitby, 85
White, Thomas, 105
Whitmore, Mrs, 25
Wilcock, Monsignor Edward, 151, 155
Wilkins, Mrs, 17
Wilkinson, Monsignor Francis, 15
William III, King, 66, 77, 99, 100
Williamite persecution of Catholics, 100
Wilson, Mary wife of Robert Langstaff, 84
Wilson, Ralph of Manfield, 84
Winter [or Webster], Sarah wife of Robert Wright of Fitling, 29, 110
Wintour, Dorothy, 112
Wintour, Robert, 113, 125

Wintour, Thomas, 111, 113, 125
Wiseman, Tom, 148
Witham, Robert of Cliff Hall, 85, 87, 91, 94
Witham, William, 88
Withams of Cliff Hall, 98
Wolsey, Cardinal Thomas, 130, 131, 132
Woodside, priest's house at Thurnham, 89
Worcester, Battle of, 99
World War I, 16, 22, 33, 35, 39, 42
World War II, 20, 34, 36
Worms, City of, 130
Worthington, Richard of Blainscough Hall, 124, 126
Worthington, Thomas, 124
Worthington, Thomas son of Richard, 124
Wreathall, Ann, 39
Wreathall, Charles Clement, 39
Wreathall, Henry, 39
Wright, Christopher, 28, 111, 112, 113
Wright, Francis, 29
Wright, John, 28, 112, 113
Wright, John Seneschal to Henry VIII, 111, 129
Wright, Martha, 112
Wright, Mary Ann, 29, 110
Wright, Robert, 114
Wright, Robert of Fitling, 29, 110, 129
Wright, Robert of Ploughland Hall, 111
Wright, Sarah Ann, 29
Wright, Ursula, 28, 113
Wrightington, 102
Wrights of Ploughland Hall, 110, 125
Wycliffe, 35, 57, 59, 60, 61, 63, 64, 65, 66, 67, 73, 78, 82, 83, 84, 85, 86, 87, 94, 96, 98, 99, 100, 110, 121, 130, 142, 144, 148, 149, 152, 153, 160
Wycliffe Hall, 160

Wycliffe Parish Church, 160
Wycliffe, Catherine (Katherine) wife of Marmaduke Tunstall of Scargill Castle and Wycliffe, 160
Wycliffe, William, 130

York, 20, 113
York Castle, 114
York gaol, 85, 98
Yorkshire, 21, 22
Yorkshire Brethren's Fund, 87, 88, 143
Young, David, 16

Zon, Rev. T. Van, 66